Frederic Remington

REMINGTON

THE YEARS OF CRITICAL ACCLAIM

REMINGTON: THE YEARS OF CRITICAL ACCLAIM

© Copyright 1998 The Peters Corporation
ISBN 0-935037-89-6

Catalog coordinated by Kellie Keto
Photography coordinated by Dan Morse
Design by Laura McCurdy
Printing by Asiaprint Ltd.
Printed and Bound in Singapore

COVER: Frederic Remington, *The Grass Fire*, 1908 oil on canvas, 27 ⅛ x 40 ⅛ inches (detail)
Courtesy of Amon Carter Museum, Fort Worth, TX (1961.228)

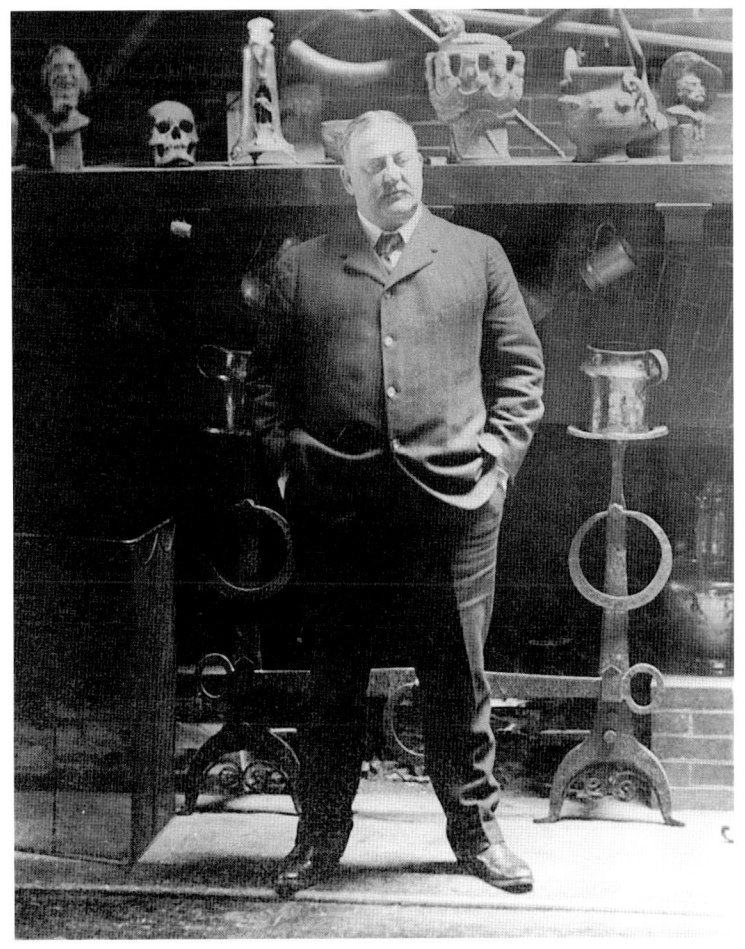

Frederic Remington
(1861-1909)

REMINGTON

THE YEARS OF CRITICAL ACCLAIM

CONTENTS

FOREWORD

Over the course of the twentieth century, the art of Frederic Remington has become inextricably linked in the public consciousness to the American West and the dramatic heyday of the frontier. His striking images of anonymous cavalrymen, cowboys, Indians, and trappers perpetuated both the fact and fantasy of America's westward expansion. Despite the popular appeal of Remington's subjects, his commitment to such American themes ultimately came to overshadow his remarkable stylistic achievements as an artist.

In the last years of his life, Remington strove for academic approval and for recognition in the world of fine arts. His early Darwinian dramas and their clear, dry western light, and tight linear renderings evolved towards a more introspective style typified by atmospheric settings and impressionistic brushwork on canvas, and expressive surface treatments in bronze. The focus of this catalogue is upon Remington's *nocturnes* and bronzes, a body of work that provides a clear view of the artist's mature vision. In the years between 1905 and his death in 1909, the new direction of Remington's art finally earned him the critical recognition he had been seeking. Royal Cortissoz, the freelance art critic, stated in a review of the artist's last one-man show, "the mark of the illustrator disappeared and that of the painter took its place."

The realization of this catalogue would not have been possible without Peter Hassrick and Melissa Webster's recent publication of *Frederic Remington: A Catalogue Raisonné*. Melissa Webster and Peter Hassrick brought their considerable knowledge to the project with essays that provide discerning insights into Remington's late production, including the details of his influences and working methods. To a large extent, the fulfillment of this catalogue relied on the participation of private collectors and public institutions including the Amon Carter Museum, the Frederic Remington Art Museum, the Gilcrease Museum, the Hood Museum of Art, the National Cowboy Hall of Fame, the National Museum of American Art, the Sid Richardson Collection of Western Art, and the Rockwell Museum. The task of marshaling a major catalogue is inevitably shared by members of the Gerald Peters Gallery staff. My thanks to Kellie Keto for establishing the basis of the book and researching and documenting the collection, David Clemmer for editorial direction, and Laura McCurdy and Dan Morse for their sensitivity to the presentation of Remington's work.

Gerald P. Peters III

INTRODUCTION

Although he had long attained popular recognition and financial success as a commercial artist, it was only late in Frederic Remington's career that he transcended the rank of illustrator and began to receive serious consideration in the world of fine arts. *Frederic Remington: The Years of Critical Acclaim* celebrates the artist's mature vision and brings together some of the most significant of his paintings and bronzes from public and private collections throughout the country.

As early as 1887, Remington entered works in major exhibitions with the National Academy of Design and the American Watercolor Society in an effort to gain academic distinction. Above all else, he wanted to be recognized as a fine artist rather than as an illustrator, and it was his sculptural compositions that earned him his initial success.

With the encouragement of his friends Frederick Ruckstull and Augustus Thomas, Remington began work on his first sculptural subject in 1894. Thomas, Remington's neighbor, had offered the use of the back of his house to Ruckstull, a highly successful, academically trained sculptor. Ruckstull was preparing the model for an equestrian monument of General John Hartranft, intended for the Pennsylvania statehouse. Remington was so enthralled by Ruckstull's commission that both Ruckstull and Thomas urged him to try his hand at the medium. According to Michael Shapiro, by 1895, Remington was infatuated with the permanence of bronze sculpture, the palpable properties of clay, and most especially with the opening of a new mode of expression.[1] The emergent sculptor wrote in January 1895 to his friend, the novelist Owen Wister, "My oils will all get old and watery...my watercolors will fade—but I am to endure in bronze."[2]

Remington's bronze compositions, initially created with the sandcast method, broke with sculptural tradition. At the turn of this century, when the process of lost wax casting was introduced into American foundries, he experimented with and exploited the new technology. With the assistance of Roman Bronze Works founder Riccardo Bertelli, Remington evolved into one of he most innovative sculptors of his day. His technical and aesthetic accomplishments defied the structural limitations of bronze . Remington's initial subject in bronze, *Bronco Buster*, 1895, shattered the conception of equestrian sculpture. Rather than reiterate the static poses utilized in traditional equestrian compositions, he captured horse and rider in an asymmetrically balanced pose that would seem impossible to maintain. With tremendous originality in conception and execution, Remington executed twenty-one additional sculptures, moving from the linear realism of his early bronzes to the richly tactile surfaces of his lost-wax pieces.

Remington's sculptural accomplishments did not go unnoticed by the academic establishment. 1905 marked Remington's tenth year as a sculptor, and saw the Corcoran Gallery of Art acquire two bronzes, *The Mountain Man* and *Coming Through the Rye*, for their permanent collection. As further testament to his success, The Metropolitan Museum of Art purchased four bronzes in 1907—*The Mountain Man*, *The Cheyenne*, *Dragoons 1850* and *The Bronco Buster*.

As with his sculpture, Remington's oils progressed from a rather simple, reportorial realism towards evocative impressionism. In 1899, he made his final submission of a painting to the National Academy of Design's annual juried exhibition, hoping, as he had for the last ten years–to finally win approbation. Although the theme of the painting, *Missing*, was more subdued than some of his earlier action scenes, the critics and academicians refused to acknowledge any substantive change in Remington's work, and denied him full recognition in the form of membership. Remington thus turned his back on the country's leading arbiter of taste, refusing to participate ever again in its exhibitions.

However, the Academy's spurning of Remington's talents did ultimately have a beneficial effect on the artist. The rejection forced him to reexamine his aesthetic approach, resulting in a turn away from his strongly narrative, illustrative traditions towards a greater concern with the pictorial effects of light, color, and atmosphere. At the turn of the century, as Remington developed as a colorist and honed his observational skills, an opportunity arose to encourage his expanding vision. In 1903, he accepted an exclusive four-year contract to produce paintings for *Collier's Weekly*. The lucrative contract offered $1,000 dollars for the reproduction rights to each painting, but also gave the artist total freedom to select his own subjects– a minimum of twelve per year.

As Melissa Webster has observed, "It is in Remington's later paintings, particularly his night scenes, that he found both success as a fine artist and a new way of preserving his interpretation of the spirit of the West."[3] In attempting to capture the subtleties of moonlight effects, Remington reduced extraneous detail and the tonal range in his works to imbue his scenes with a new sense of mystery and introspection. "His exploration of nocturnal effects earned him his first official accolades as a painter since the tentative critical approval he had gained in 1889 with *A Dash for the Timber* and some of his early academic efforts."[4] Remington's final one-man show at M. Knoedler & Company in December, 1909, was the most critically acclaimed exhibition of his career. *The Globe* summarized Remington's development as a painter: "Mr. Remington has greatly improved. He handles his pigment with surer brush, in a bigger way and a more logical manner, with greater simplicity than hitherto. His color is purer, more vibrant, more telling, and his figures are more in atmosphere."

In the end, it was perhaps Remington himself who was his harshest critic. It was not until 1908, a year before his death that he finally acknowledged satisfaction in achieving the transformation from illustrator to fine artist: "My show made a great hit this winter...I am no longer an illustrator."[5]

Kellie Keto

[1] Michael Shapiro, *Frederic Remington: The Masterworks*, "Remington: The Sculptor," (New York: Harry N. Abrams, 1988), p. 182
[2] Frederic Remington to Owen Wister [January, 1895], Owen Wister Papers, Library of Congress, Washington, D.C.
[3] *Frederic Remington: The Years of Critical Acclaim*, Melissa Webster, "The Nocturne Paintings of Frederic Remington," Gerald Peters Gallery, Santa Fe, NM, 1997, p. 1
[4] Peter Hassrick, *Frederic Remington: The Masterworks*, "Remington: The Painter," (New York: Narry N. Abrams, 1988), p. 126
[5] Frederic Remington to John Howard [January 27, 1909] Remington Papers, St. Lawrence University Library, Canton, NY

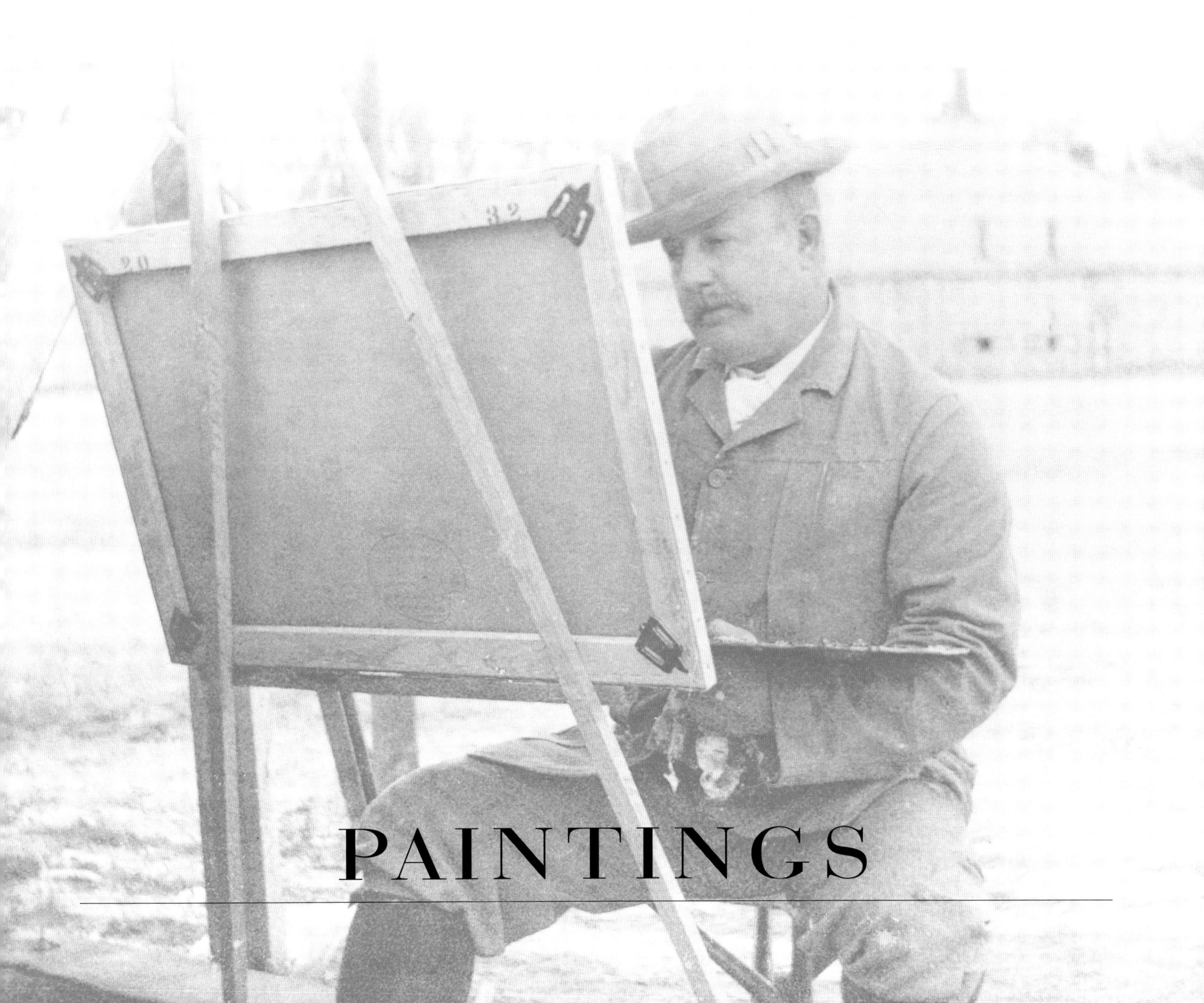

PAINTINGS

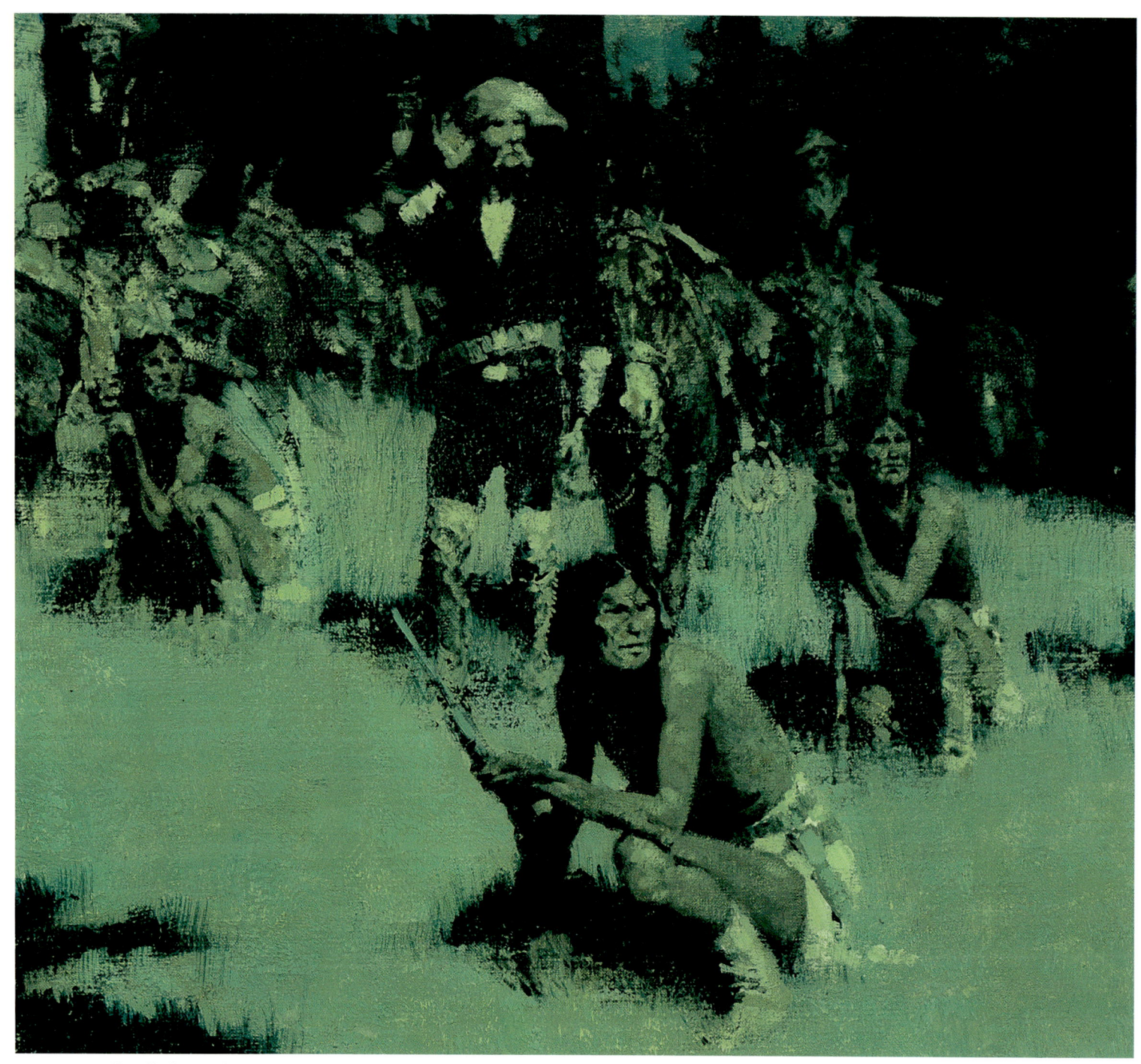

Detail of APACHE SCOUTS LISTENING, 1908. Oil on canvas, 27 x 40 inches (Courtesy: Cindy and Alan Horn, see pg. 69)

Shall never come west again—It is all brick buildings— derby hats and
blue coveralls— it spoils my earlier illusions— and they are my capital.[1]

On his trip to the Southwest in 1900, Frederic Remington (1861-1909), realized that the West that he had been trying to record before it slipped away was already gone. He admitted that his concept of the West was a fantasy, and he recognized the dilemma of wanting to record the West faithfully, accurately, *en plein-air*, when the world that he wanted to paint was no longer extant. On January 15, 1908, Remington made the following entry in his diary:

I sometimes feel that I am trying to do the impossible in my pictures
in not having a chance to work direct but as there are not people such
as I paint its [sic] "studio" or nothing.[2]

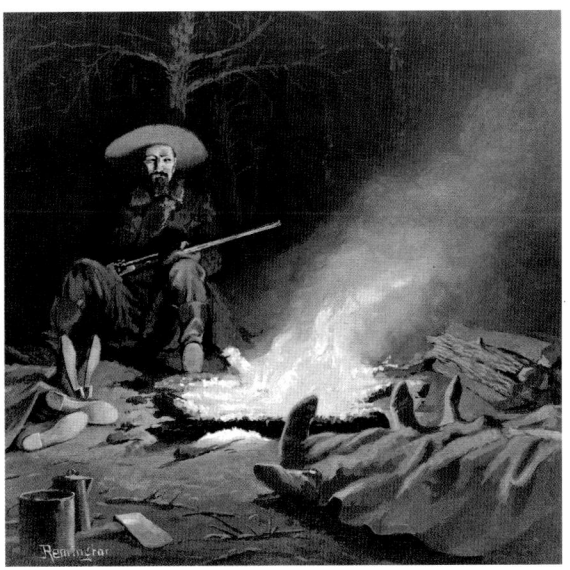

ON GUARD AT NIGHT, *c. 1888, oil on board, 16 x 15 ¼ inches*
(Courtesy of Frederic Remington Art Museum, Ogdensburg, NY)

He went on to state, "These transcript from nature fellows who are so clever cannot compare with the imaginative men in the long run." It is in Remington's later paintings, particularly his night scenes, that he found both success as a fine artist and a new way of preserving his interpretation of the spirit of the West. With a mixture of his observations of nature and endless creativity, Remington sought to capture the intangible image of the West that had been.

The night scenes that Remington painted after 1900 were not a new phenomenon in his work. He had been painting the subject throughout his career and in illustrations dating as early as 1886. These earlier nocturnes, however, were strictly narrative in nature. Remington utilized the night as a setting, a piece of background information employed to assist in describing the scene, much in the same manner as the model of a rifle that a soldier might be holding, the style of boot that he was wearing, or the type of military tent beside which he was sitting. Such is the case in *On Guard at Night*, published in *Century Magazine* in May of 1888. In this painting, Remington was illustrating a scene from a story by Theodore Roosevelt, "Sheriff's Work on a Ranch." Roosevelt describes the sheriff and his men taking turns through the chilly night, keeping watch over their prisoners, shown asleep in the foreground in Remington's painting.

Many of Remington's early nocturnes are interior scenes, depicting a room, tent, or tepee void of any hint of moonlight or night air. One such composition is *Merry Christmas in a Sibley Tepee* (p. 17) published in *Harper's Weekly* (December 5, 1891) as an illustration for Remington's article of the same title about one of his excursions with the army. He was illustrating his experience, celebrating a cavalry Christmas with the troops of the United States Cavalry, giving the viewer a snippet of frontier soldier life and holiday camaraderie. His approach was factual and informative: He documented the interior of a Sibley tent, the structure of a Sibley stove, and the men and their actions in contemporary military uniforms. The artist even included himself in the painting, seated in the left background, facing the viewer with his back to the tent.

On Guard at Night and *Merry Christmas in a Sibley Tepee* are early nocturnes, executed in black and white oils. In neither painting did Remington concern himself with the color of the shadows, or the color that objects and the atmosphere take on in conditions of darkness with artificial illumination. He was intent on creating a specific scenario, the subject of which was dictated to him by text. The absence of daylight is merely another element in the composition, serving to inform the viewer about the time of day the action was taking place.

Historically, night scenes as an artistic subject were by no means unique to Remington. Night scenes had long been used in religious paintings and other genres to identify a particular story or theme. In the 1700s and early 1800s, night settings were often used to impart paintings with an ominous feeling. Throughout the nineteenth century, when the American wilderness was being developed and cities were increasingly industrialized, nature, which had previously been thought of as wild and threatening, came to be looked upon as sacred or inspirational. Artists painted landscapes flooded with moonlight to romanticize scenes. During the last half of the nineteenth century, painters were producing night scenes in an effort to give expression to their personal feelings. By the close of the century, many American mood painters, influenced by Impressionism and photography, were finding night scenes to be a particularly attractive subject.

These painters, now known to us as Tonalists, practiced a distinct style "of intimacy and expressiveness interpreting very specific themes in limited color scales, and employing effects of light to create vague suggestive moods." The Tonalist style reached its greatest popularity between 1880 and 1910.[3] In various of their paintings, these artists tended to envelop their scenes with a single, dominating hue, dissolve hard edges, and to omit detail creating soft, unfocused contours, and simplified forms and sentimentalizing moods.

Remington was one such painter who employed Tonalist techniques with increasing frequency in the first decade of the twentieth century as he explored the possibilities of night light. The Tonalist painters, and those influenced by their ideas, largely rejected objective rendering for subjective response,[4] and Remington parallels their approach in his increasing deviation away from sharply focused illustrative scenes and towards obscure evocative visions.

George Innes and James McNeil Whistler were two artists who were instrumental in developing these American mood or tone paintings. They influenced many of Remington's contemporaries, including the American Impressionists Childe Hassam, John Twachtman, and Thomas Dewing—artists whom Remington deeply admired. The Tonalist approach also pervaded the modern art photography of Alfred Stieglitz, Edward Steichen, and Gertrude Kasebier. Their photographs of the night and twilight were moody scenes, in which objects were intentionally obscured beneath a film of mist. Often chemicals were added during the developing process to give the entire scene one dominating hue of green, blue, or brown.[5]

In his posthumous article "Recollections of Frederic Remington," Augustus Thomas relates that Remington credited the popular mood painter Charles Rollo Peters (1862-1928) with having inspired him to want to paint the night:

Apparently, Remington first encountered the work of Peters in 1989 when Peters had a successful one-man show at the Union League Club in New York City. Between 1899 and 1904 Peters exhibited in New York City several times, providing Remington with numerous opportunities to study his work. Peters and Remington both exhibited in the 1901 Pan-American Exposition in Buffalo, New York, and again in 1904 at the St. Louis Exposition, (where Peters won an honorable mention for his nocturnal painting *When the Gringos Came*). Remington was apparently enchanted with the evanescent moonlight that pervaded Peters's paintings, illuminating adobe buildings or shimmering on the ripples of the ocean.[7]

Peters was born in San Francisco in 1862. He was raised there and, like Remington, was initially encouraged to pursue a career in business. In 1885, at the age of 23—the year that Remington abandoned his goal of making a life for himself in the West and returned to New York to become an artist—Peters, too, quit his job and began to study art. He initially attended the Urban Academy under Jules Tavernier, and then studied at the San Francisco School of Design with Virgil Williams and Chris Jorgensen. Unlike Remington, who decided not to study art in Europe in order to preserve a more authentic American style, Peters continued his art education in Paris. In 1887 he enrolled in the Ecole National des Beaux Arts to study under Jean-Léon Gérôme. Afterward, he attended the Julian Academy, studying under Jules Lefebvre. Peters exhibited a painting at the Paris Salon in 1889—the same year that Remington exhibited *Last Lull in the Fight*, 1888, a painting which won a second class medal at the Paris International Exposition.

Peters returned to San Francisco in 1890 and opened a studio, but remained for only a year. In 1891 he again made the crossing to France, where he lived in Brittany until 1895. He then moved back to California, and during the next decade he became a successful artist in San Francisco and on the Monterey Peninsula. He gained particular notoriety for his nocturnes, which are well represented at the Colton Hall Museum in Monterey. Although Peters did not consistently date his late paintings, he did date his early works painted in France between 1890 and 1895. Several of his paintings made in Brittany already show the subtle, low-keyed gray-blue coloration, painterly brush work, simplified forms, and generalized detail which influenced Remington.

Nine of Peters's nocturnes in the Colton Hall Museum evidence a range from light, clearly defined renderings, to darker, more mysterious and vague subjective abstractions of nature. As with Remington, the lucid and objective pictures exemplify Peters's early style, while the suggestive and evocative ones represent his mature work.

Remington's night scenes, *The Cossack Post* and *The Scout: Friends or Enemies* (pg. 33), date to the early 1900s, and the initial years of his exploration of night light. These paintings reveal why he continued to be dissatisfied with his ability to handle tone and color. In neither work did he capture the moon's subtle lighting. The scenes and their stark

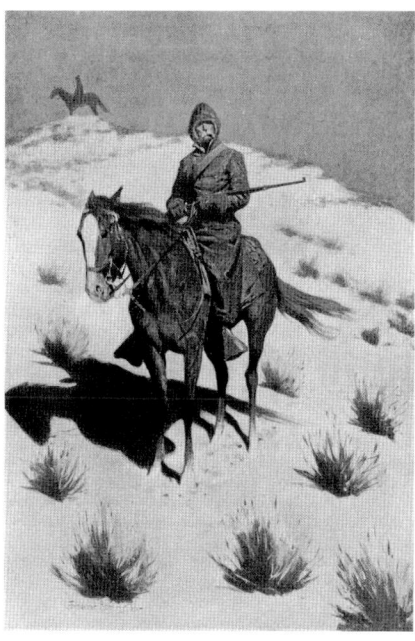

THE COSSACK POST, *c. 1902, oil on canvas. Courtesy: Buffalo Bill Historical Center, Cody, WY.*

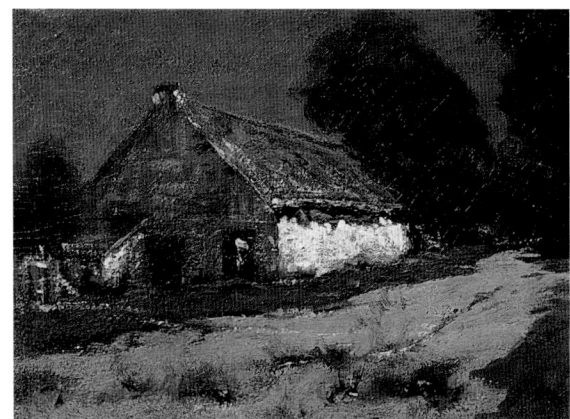

Charles Rollo Peters, DARK BARN, *oil on canvas, 11 x 15 inches.*
(Courtesy: Colton Hall Museum, Monterey, CA.)

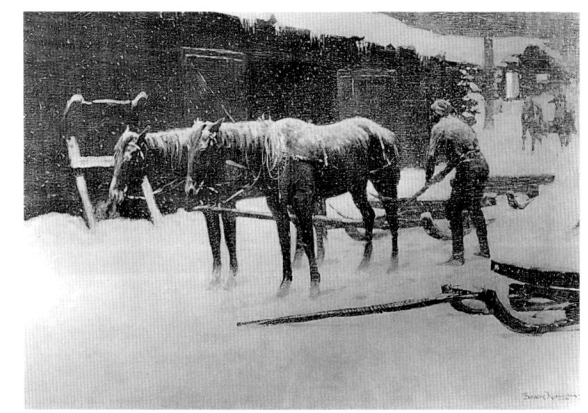

THE END OF THE DAY, *c. 1904, oil on canvas, 26 ½ x 40*
inches (Courtesy of Frederic Remington Art Museum, Ogdensburg, NY)

landscapes are evenly lit with a bright spotlight illumination. In *The Cossack Post*, the snowy ground contrasts sharply with the bundled Cossack, as it does with the Indian in buckskins wrapped in a red blanket astride his black mount in the latter painting. In both paintings the subjects stand out distinctly as clear, crisp shapes in the night air; there is no fusion of backdrop and figure.

While Remington used snow to reflect the moon's rays in his paintings, Peters often employed adobe, as in *Dark Barn*. This painting, although fairly bright, does not have the wide range of colors found in Remington's *The Scout: Friends or Enemies?*. The focal point of Peters's canvas is the white, moon-drenched side of the barn. The rest of the scene is bathed in a grey-green light that, along with the thick brush work, obscures detail and gives a unifying softness to the painting.

Remington's *Indian Scouts in the Moonlight* (pg. 27) and *A Reconnaissance* of 1902 (pg. 29) show a closer affinity to Peters's nocturnes. Major changes are found in brush work and color—elements with which Remington had been struggling for almost a decade. The paint is more fluid, brush strokes are thick and visible, and there is more surface texture as a result. However, Remington still renders details, such as the fringe on the Scout's outstretched arm or each button on the cavalryman's cape, rather than generalizing or unifying them to give an overall impression.

In *Indian Scouts in the Moonlight* and *A Reconnaissance*, the colors are also muted and their tonal range is limited. The moon's light casts a grayish-green or bluish hue over everything, in contrast to the full spectrum of color that sunlight would reveal. There is, however, little tonal definition to be found in either painting. In *Indian Scouts in the Moonlight*, for example, there is none to be found in the wooded background, in the figures' and horses' shadows, or in the dark patches of snow in the foreground. A third of the canvas in *A Reconnaissance* is the pale aqua snow—Remington has kept the color consistent: He has not yet mastered the subtle variation of hues that are hidden in the reflections of moonlight or in night shadows. These observations are equally true for *The Old Stage Coach of the Plains*, which dates to 1901. Although the entire painting is imbued with a rich blue-green tone, the shadows are too dark for the eye to penetrate. In *End of the Day*, painted three years later in 1904, there is no tonal variance in the blue that evenly tints the entire scene.

In Remington's nocturnes of the early 1900s, the thematic content of the work remains the dominant factor. However, in paintings such as *A Reconnaissance* and *Indian Scouts in Moonlight*, there is a pervading sense of vagueness and uncertainty. Both pictures leave the viewer wondering just who is being trailed: Have the scouts found new evidence or are they confused? Are they the pursuers or are they being pursued? Although the subject matter remains a major aspect of these paintings, it is not as explicit as was typically the case in Remington's art. This sense of mystery is an element that became increasingly prevalent as he explored night painting.

In Peters's nocturnes narrative content seems unimportant. In paintings such as *Dark Barn*, *House in Moonlight* or *Dark Street Scene* there is no human drama, nor are the paintings pure landscapes: their dominating subject is architecture.

Peters seems more concerned with light, form, and space than with a specific theme, and his titles serve to reinforce this conclusion.

In Paris, Peters had met the American artists James McNeil Whistler and Alexander Harrison. Both men had encouraged Peters's painting, especially his night scenes. That Peters was strongly influenced by Whistler is clear when comparing various of the painters' works. For example, Peters directly improvised upon Whistler's *Arrangement in Grey and Black No. 1: The Artist's Mother* for his composition, *Woman Knitting*. Like Whistler, his chooses as his subject an older woman seated in profile on a straight-back chair, facing left. Both works are also mainly gray and black, Whistler's more tinged with green, where Peters incorporates shades of white. Peters's work, however, does not possess the sophistication of Whistler's complex patterning of rectangles. He does, though, mimic Whistler's appropriation of the Japanese-style tilting of the floor, creating a foreshortened, shallow space. Peters also uses a floral patterning in the bottom right corner that looks like tapestry but overlaps the skirt, while going behind the chair, which confuses the relationship between the foreground and background further flattening the picture. The flowered tapestry—perhaps a remnant of a previous composition—adds a wonderful splash of color to an otherwise monochromatic work, and recalls the patterned background draperies and decorative effects that Whistler borrowed from Japanese prints.

Elements of Whistler's works are also evident in Peters's nocturnes, such as in *Bay in Moonlight*. This work contains a significant degree of abstraction, and its forms are undefined, much like Whistler's earlier atmospheric mood piece, *Nocturne in Black and Gold: The Falling Rocket*. The focal point of both works (pg. 6) are glittering specks of light. Whistler's painting, however, has a more complex, harmonious, and appealing mixture of blues, black, greens, and browns compared to Peters's limited tonal range. The heavy, vague, and unfocused forms in Peters's *Bay in Moonlight* bear resemblance to the dark seascapes of Albert Pinkham Ryder in their execution and mysticism.

Although Remington appreciated Peters's nocturnes, he did not like the work of Peters's mentor. As with his initial dislike of Impressionism, Remington was strongly critical of Whistler's night scenes, describing one to be "as black as the inside of a jug"[8] and calling others "punk."[9] Remington found Whistler's work contemptible, writing in his diary on July 19, 1908, "Whistler was lacking in the only characteristic which distinguished an artist from a common man—imagination."

Remington's negative reaction to Whistler was not surprising. Although they both painted nocturnes, their art was very different. Whistler's compositions largely devoid of narrative content—were abstract renderings of mood in color and form. Whistler believed that art and music were similar, and he stressed harmony, not subject matter, in his work. Whistler stated:

> *As music is the poetry of sound, so is painting the poetry of sight,*
> *and the subject-matter has nothing to do with harmony of sound*
> *or of color... Art should be independent of all clap-trap—*

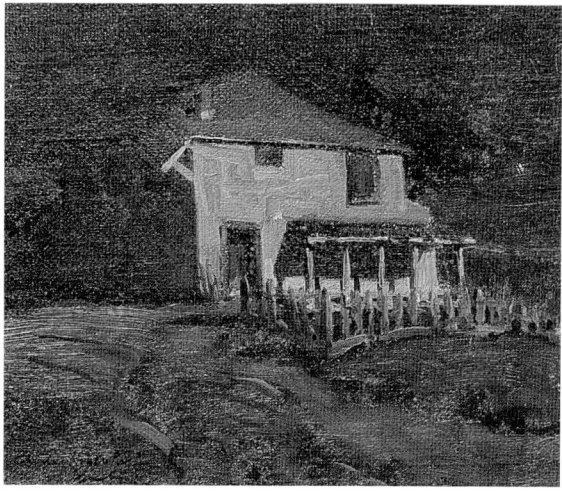

Charles Rollo Peters, HOUSE, IN MOONLIGHT, oil on canvas, 9 x 11 inches. (Courtesy: Colton Hall Museum, Monterey, CA.)

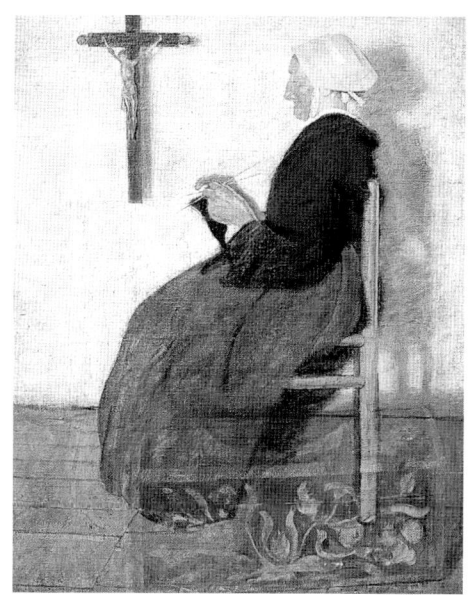

Charles Rollo Peters, WOMAN KNITTING, oil on canvas, 29 x 23 inches. (Courtesy: Colton Hall Museum, Monterey, CA.)

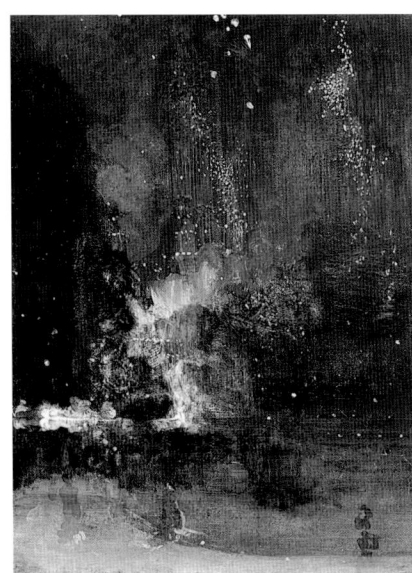

James McNeill Whistler, NOCTURNE IN BLACK AND GOLD, THE FALLING ROCKET, c. 1875, oil on oak panel (Courtesy of Detroit Institute of Arts, gift of Dexter M. Ferry, Jr.)

Whistler's work did, however, possess a balance and control of tone and color for which Remington was striving, and which he found more assimilable in the work of Whistler's follower, Peters. Remington had his own reasons for mastering the painting of moonlight and firelight, apart from the more purely formal properties espoused by Whistler and his contemporary mood and tone painters. Remington was eclectic: he borrowed, adopted, and adapted as he developed his own way of expressing his vision of the West.

In January of 1906, Remington copyrighted a group of approximately fifteen paintings. These works are noteworthy in that they mark a definite stride toward tonalist aesthetics and Remington's mastery of night effects. For the most part, they are quiet, mysterious scenes with lighting effects created by the moon, such as in *A Belated Traveler* (pg. 47); the setting sun, as seen in *Sunset on the Plains* (pg. 7); or by daylight diffused through misty, gray clouds, as exemplified in *Hole in the Day*. The majority are also smaller than the canvases Remington typically produced, ranging in size from 12 x 16 to 23 x 30 inches, as opposed to his more standard 27 x 40 inches. Even though Remington's contract with *Collier's Weekly* to produce monthly illustrations did not end until January 1909, he apparently created the artworks in this group as fine art rather than as illustrations: he exhibited them, but did not submit them to the magazine for reproduction. These paintings, of which six were nocturnes, evidence Remington's continued preoccupation and experimentation with color and form as revealed in varied lighting conditions.

Remington was determined to paint the intricacies of night illumination. He placed special emphasis on nocturnes while at Ingleneuk, where, away from city light, he could stay outdoors late into the summer night to concentrate on mastering the effects of moonlight. On June 25, 1907, he recorded, "We have first moon now. Clear nights and I studied until near 11 o'c last night." The following day he recorded, "Worked on moonlight from my observations of last night." Remington created studies outdoors, but unlike the Impressionists (who typically began and finished their paintings in the open air), he then incorporated his *plein air* observations into his paintings in the studio.

Throughout the years of 1907 and 1908, Remington filled his diaries with notations of his travails in learning to paint the reflections of moonlight and firelight. His entries were short and concise: oftentimes he simply wrote, "Studying moonlight." His reflections concerning his work express his concerns and steadfastness in mastering night lighting. On July 24, 1907, he wrote, "Exastic [sic] about my moonlights." On August 17 of the same summer he noted, "Beautiful moon more than half full... Studying moonlight." That autumn, on October 11, he wrote, "I worked on my *In From the Night Herd* and am going to study a fire light outdoors tonight."

Remington experienced great difficulties in painting night light. On January 19, 1908, he jotted in his diary, "Wonderful moonlight night—tried to distinguish color in some sketches I took out of doors but it is too subtle a light and does not

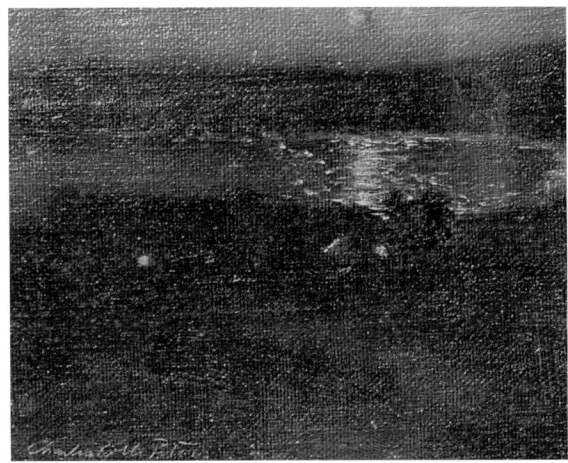

Charles Rollo Peters, BAY IN MOONLIGHT, oil on canvas, 7 ½ x 9 ½ inches. (Courtesy: Cotton Hall Museum, Monterey, CA.)

differentiate." And again in March, still struggling, he wrote on the 17th, "Those moonlight are elusive and require a world of monkeying." A week later, on March 28, he noted, "Worked on my firelight pictures. They are more difficult than I expected. Low tones in the darks are fugitive." Remington's diary notations reveal that he was dealing with many of the same concerns being addressed by contemporary night painters and tonalists, both in the United States and abroad.

Despite the subtlety and elusiveness of night lighting, Remington continued his studies, writing on April 4, 1908, "Worked on 'Grass Fire' and 'Shotgun Hospitality' [.] A new moon and I will soon get a chance to work on the later picture. Firelight and moonlight—very difficult." Finally, that same month, Remington showed more optimism, noting on April 12, "Wonderful moonlight night—studying—it has not yet been painted but I think I am getting nearer all the time." And on June 22 Remington felt that he had triumphed with moonlight. "Painted in studio and I have now discovered for first time how to do the silver sheen of moonlight."

His works between 1905 and 1909 show his steady progress in learning to paint night lighting. By 1906 his paintings evidenced an understanding of nocturnal illumination, and a command of some of the tonal subtlety found in Peters's works. In *The Last March* (pg. 8), 1906, for example, the scene is bathed in a blue-green light, similar to Peters's *House in Moonlight*. The "low tones in the darks" that Remington found so elusive are beginning to emerge in the shadows, and the viewer can distinguish the distant hills from the night sky.

Waiting in Moonlight, 1907 (pg. 53), displays an even greater control over night colors. The tonal range is lower than in *The Last March*, yet Remington successfully differentiates between forms within a narrow spectrum. Like Peters's *The Dark Barn*, the focal point is a white rectangular form. In Remington's painting, however, it is the lower skirt of the woman's dress that reflects most brilliantly the moon's light, as opposed to the side of a building. The skirt is not completely white; it is dappled with a pale green that permeates the entire composition. The figures, veiled in an atmospheric cloak of grey-green as revealed in the moon's sheen, are made anonymous by their own shadows and by brush work that obscures detail.[11]

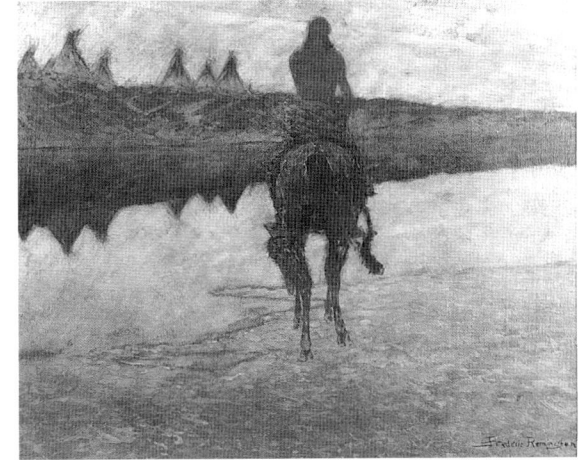

SUNSET ON THE PLAINS, *1905-06, oil on canvas, 20 x 26 inches (Courtesy West Point Museum Collections, United States Military Academy)*

These and other of Remington's moonlight paintings between 1907 and 1909, such as *Trail of the Shod Horse*, 1907, *Fired On*, 1907 (pg. 55), *Moaning of the Bulls*, 1907, and *Apache Scouts Listening*, 1908 (pg. 69), display similarly subtle nuances of related hues and became almost monochromatic (though apparently this was not Remington's intention). When he exhibited his nocturnes at Doll and Richards Gallery in Boston in January of 1909, Remington felt they were not well received. He recorded in his diary on January 13, 1909, "The Boston papers give me hell. I never got such a roasting in my life." On January 11 he wrote of one critic, "He must have liked the frames since he didn't put acid on them." The review he was referring to was by art critic Philip Hale in *The Boston Herald* (January 9, 1909). Of *Apache Scouts Listening* Hale wrote, "'Apache Scouts Listening' is highly interesting, and the attitudes of the Indians crouched to the ground, seem well studied. It is hard to decide whether this picture is meant for a monochrome or for a night effect. It seems that the color note is a trifle greenish." Remington noted in his January 14 diary entry, "They call my moonlights 'monochromes.' No sales. I fear Boston will never enjoy Freddie again." At least two reviews equated the term monochrome with a lack of color, and not with an ability to control tonal values. The critics' deprecating comments, recalled Remington's productions of his black and white days as an illustrator. These criticisms came after Remington had spent years trying to establish himself as a fine artist, and after over a decade working on his color and tonal values—challenges that preoccupied many artists on both sides of the Atlantic throughout the 19th century. Winslow Homer, who had also worked in black and white during his days as an illustrator, remarked:

I have never tried to do anything but get the true relationships of
values; that is the values of dark and light and the values of color.
It is wonderful how much depends upon the relationship of black
and white. Why, do you know, a black and white, if properly balanced,
suggests color.[12]

It was during Remington's years as illustrator that he learned to control and define a range of tonal values within the limited vocabulary of black and white. This experience equipped him with the insight and ability to discriminate between and represent the fugitive tones and hues of night light. It was precisely his tonal sensitivity and ability to reproduce the subtle differences between similar hues as defined by moonlight and firelight that gave him command of the atmospheric effects found in the nocturnes created in the last years of his life. And it was this sense and appearance of mood and atmosphere that became the subject and focal point of his later paintings—his final message about the West. While many contemporary painters utilized monochromatic palettes and softened their forms beneath vaporous veils to create quiet, reflective moments, Remington manipulated his color and brush work to establish and intensify a variety of moods—including some of a uniquely violent nature. In *Taint in the Wind*, 1906 (pg. 51), and *Fired On*, 1907 (pg. 55), Remington's fluid use of paint to create a murky, moonlight setting compounds the sense of panic and mystery as the horses rear at an unseen danger. The frantic and fearful reaction that the invisible foe elicits from the horses and men becomes the painting's subject. The night in *Scare in a Pack Train* (pg. 67) is more obscure: the atmosphere implied by the animals' focus and alerted ears is more foreboding. Remington ordered a special, rougher canvas for this nocturne to heighten his subtle and obscure moonlight effects. On March 9, 1908, he recorded in his diary, "Worked my 'Scare in Pack Train'—color looses readily from the heavy mesh canvas[,] but if one knows how to work it[,] it is a good thing."

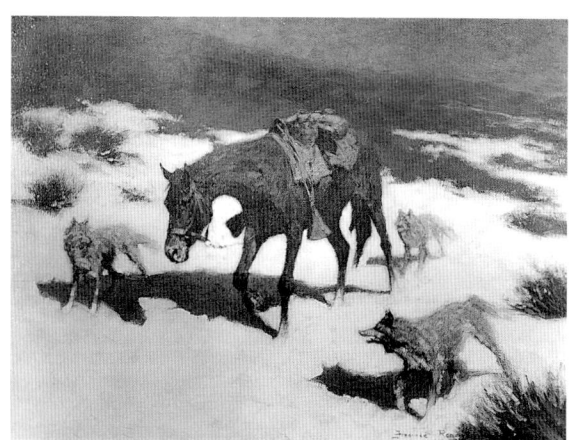

THE LAST MARCH, *1906, oil on canvas, 22 x 30 inches (Courtesy of Frederic Remington Art Museum, Ogdensburg, NY)*

Scare in a Pack Train, *Night Halt of the Cavalry* and *Impression Moonlight* (a landscape study in moonlight) are among Remington's darkest and most caliginous works. The paint is applied in even, visible vertical strokes: forms are unfocused and detail dissolves beneath a vaporous atmosphere. Submerged in rich tones of blue and green, the diffused forms in *Night Halt of the Cavalry* look almost as if they are being viewed under water. Though similar to the night scene in *Scare in a Pack Train*, it is not so generous a light as in *Night Halt* of the Cavalry. The moon seems grudgingly to shine down on the troop, withholding most of its illumination. The center soldier, alarmed by some unseen threat, leans forward and tries to discern something through the darkness. The scene is imbued with a feeling of uneasiness and impending danger.

While Remington studied tonal matters in moonlit scenes, he was exploring similar problems of illumination by firelight. *The Grass Fire* (pg. 61) was painted at the same time as *Scare in a Pack Train* and *Night Halt of the Cavalry*, and it is similarly dark, obscure and sketchy. *Scare in a Pack Train* and *Night Halt of the Cavalry* are the furthest that Remington went in reducing his tonal range in moonlight pictures. *The Grass Fire* uses a different sort of nocturnal illumination, and Remington's handling of light is quite different.

Unlike *Scare in a Pack Train* and *Night Halt of the Cavalry*, the light in *The Grass Fire* is not uniformly diffused, but sporadic and dramatic: It etches the forms sharply. In baroque fashion, a stream of light cuts diagonally through the painting, throwing the foreground and background into utter darkness, except for the tip of the front left corner, where flickers of flame leap up. The fire illuminates the figures from below, in a manner similar to the fashion in which Degas utilizes stage lights in his pictures of the ballet. The result is a theatrical and eerie lighting that highlights and casts unexpected black shadows and distorts the Indians' features, augmenting the picture's drama. The eye is drawn immediately to the bright yellow blaze on the horse's head in the forefront of the composition, lit by the flaming grass. Surrounding this horse are figures of other horses and Indians, whose mottled skins are rendered in shades of orange with black shadows, reflecting the flickering, erratic illumination of fire. Remington also introduces patches of green, red's complimentary color, to further accent the red glowing fire light.

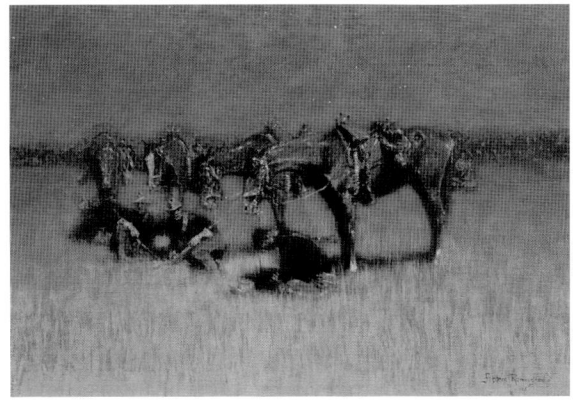

NIGHT HALT OF THE CAVALRY, *1908, oil on canvas, 27 x 40 inches (see color plate pg. 67)*

Like *The Grass Fire*, *The Sundance* (pg. 77) deals with a special Indian subject. *The Grass Fire* depicts an offensive tactic used by the Plains Indians to hold off enemies [13]; the Sundance illustrates a religious ceremony. As with *The Grass Fire*, Remington dramatically juxtaposes light and dark without a softening, modelled chiaroscuro: it is as though the tortured youths are on stage, spotlighted by the fire and surrounded by an audience of their tribesmen. The figures in the background are abbreviated, rendered with suggestive forms. Out of range of the fire's direct light, they are obscured by a smokey green haze. Remington combines subtle tonal variation in the background with the high contrast of the middle and foreground figures, and he repeats the green and red color scheme used in *The Grass Fire*.

This disturbing painting is unique in Remington's oeuvre. Though his goal to inform the public about images and events in the West had always been a motivating force behind his art, at times he found the task overwhelming. For example, during a low ebb, he wrote in his diary on July 14, 1908,

> *I have had a good loaf today and am feeling blue and tired of the whole game of art—almost want to go to Oregon and settle on a fruit ranch and chuck the whole thing. Try in short to reach the public through its belly instead of its brain.*

The Sundance is a piece that Remington painted for himself, and he anticipated public condemnation and lack of understanding of the painting, as evidenced in his diary entry of February 28, 1909:

> *Am starting 'Sun Dance' for the love of Record of Great Themes*
> *but I'll never sell it— it will give everyone the Horrors. It is in my*
> *system and its got to come out.*

Although based on actual events, *The Grass Fire* and *The Sundance* were rendered in a fashion that emphasized dramatic action over factual detail. These paintings were Remington's subjective response to objective episodes, and through 1909 his work continued in this subjective vein.

In four nocturnes painted in 1908 and 1909, Remington depicted quiet, personal moments in the lives of his subjects, rather than spectacular events. *Apache Medicine Song*, 1908 (pg. 65), *The Hunters' Supper*, 1909 (pg. 75), *The Winter Campaign*, 1909 (pg. 79), and *Untitled* (Remington's last painting), 1909 (pg. 83), all have this sense of intimacy. Remington imbued an occurrence as common as an evening around a campfire with ritualistic significance. He allows the viewer a privileged glimpse into a private act. All four paintings combine nuances of color revealed in moonlight with the contrast of bright, spotlighting fire to create magical scenes. *Apache Medicine Song*, the first of the four, depicts a circle of Indians sitting and crouching around a fire, enshrouded in a sea of green moonlight. With great skill and sensitivity, Remington defines his forms within a narrow tonal range: the trees and adobe buildings in the distance, the modeled contours of the Apaches and of the pots in the midground, and the trees' dark shadows in the foreground. In contrast to their monochromatic surroundings, the figures of the Indians within the circle are alight with dabs of orange, yellow, and red from the fire's light. Remington's brush work is thick and painterly, the trees in the background are sketchy, and the Indians' facial features are abbreviated and look as though they were quickly rendered. Their bodies, however, have been subtly modeled to create solid and convincingly three-dimensional forms: they are not dissolved or unfocused in the moon's light, as are the forms in Remington's paintings after his encounters with Impressionism. Gone is the attention to detail that so typified his early work, yet unlike nocturnes such as *Fired On*, *Scare in a Pack Train*, and *Night Halt of the Cavalry*, the renderings in this painting retain palpability: they do not dissolve in a murky atmosphere.

Remington successfully employs these same effects in *Winter Campaign* and *The Hunters' Supper*—night atmosphere does not obscure their imagery. In *Winter Campaign*, men and horses alike hover around the fire to ward off the cold of the night. The winter moon casts a chilly, blue light that reflects brightly off the snow and dully, but clearly, illuminates the solidly delineated horses. The fire's light is crisp and clear as it etches out a small, vibrant circle of pale yellow on the snow, and reflects from the trees and the faces of the soldiers in an orange glow. *The Hunter's Supper*, too, is illuminated by a bright moon. The foreground is empty and the background is dark and sketchy, but the midground figures are clearly illuminated by the moon and by the bright fire. As in *Apache Medicine Song* and *Winter Campaign*, Remington has balanced the fugitive tones of night in the periphery with a limelighted central action—the focal point of the painting. The fire is central in the picture, but the eye follows its light diagonally, to the upper left corner to the tent which, aglow with a yellow light, is a second light source in the painting. The effect is reminiscent of the diagonal baroque lighting that Remington utilized in *The Grass Fire*.

In composition and technique, *Untitled* (Remington's last painting) is a companion piece to *Apache Medicine Song*. As with *Apache Medicine Song*, a group of figures (white men in this instance) sit, crouch, and recline around a central campfire. The scene is surrounded by a blue-green light, similar to the green atmosphere in *Apache Medicine Song*. Light and dark shades of blue-green are modulated to distinguish highlights and shadows and create three-dimensional forms in a convincing space. In the moonlit far distance, a cabin, rather than adobe buildings, emerges from the darkness. Behind the structures in both pictures appears the night sky.

In these four late paintings, Remington has chosen a universal, timeless theme—the camaraderie and closeness shared around an evening fire. The characters are gathered together after a long day of travel, hunting, or wrangling, and relax under the cloak of night, comforted and mesmerized by the glowing fire as they tell stories, sing, smoke, or just dream. There is a unity between the figures that binds them together, which the viewer, though excluded, can enjoy vicariously. Many of the figures' backs are turned to us, obstructing our view of the fire and closing us out of their circle; in *The Winter Campaign*, the string of horses prevents our getting any closer.

In his final exhibition, held in New York City at M. Knoedler and Company in December 1909, Remington showed twenty-three paintings. Several of the night scenes received the critical acclaim that Boston had withheld. The critic for the *New York Times* (December 8, 1909) wrote, "It is in the night scenes... that as mere art lovers we find the most satisfaction." In an unidentified clipping from Remington's 1909 diary for December 11 is a review of the show in which the author singled out three nocturnes—*The Love Call*, *The Luckless Hunter* and *The Winter Campaign*—as ranking "among the best Remington has done." It is interesting to note that after his years of studying and 'monkeying' with moon lighting, Remington had attained a level of adeptness that enabled him to paint *The Love Call* (pg. 81) to his satisfaction in just one sitting, as noted in his diary entry of July 6, 1909.

Remington spent the last decade of his life studying color and form as revealed by light—especially by diffused light, moonlight, and firelight. Remington ably discriminated between hues in an abbreviated tonal range as he depicted objects in moonless nights, or brightly lit by moon or fire. It is through the sophisticated atmospheric effects in these paintings that Remington was able to create a style with which to portray his vision of the West he loved. By 1909, the last year of his life, Remington's command of color and shape enabled him to produce strongly reflective and somber scenes. His final message was one of a resolved, but melancholic, nostalgia for the West that he had spent a lifetime trying to keep alive in his art—an art now tinged with a sense of loss of an era that he realized was gone forever.

Melissa Webster

PLATES

ON GUARD AT NIGHT
c. 1888
oil on board (en grisaille)
16 x 15 ¼ inches
signed ll: *Remington*

PROVENANCE: Mrs. Hugh Hyde; [M. Knoedler & Co., New York, NY]; Robert Purcell estate, NY; Frederic Remington Art Museum, Ogdensburg, NY

ILLUSTRATION: Theodore Roosevelt, "Sheriff's Work on a Ranch," *Century Magazine* (May 1888), p. 48, wood engraving

LITERATURE: Harold McCracken, *Frederic Remington: Artist of the Old West* (Philadelphia: J.B. Lippincott Co., 1947), p. 124; *An Exhibition Honoring Harold McCracken*, Buffalo Bill Historical Center, Cody, WY (1974) ill. p. 63, no. 79; Harold & Peggy Samuels, *The Collected Writings of Frederic Remington* (Garden City, NY: Doubleday & Co., Inc., 1982), p. 92; Peter Hassrick & Melissa Webster, *Frederic Remington: A Catalogue Raisonné*, Buffalo Bill Historical Center, Cody, WY (1996), p. 138, pl. 306

EXHIBITIONS: Buffalo Bill Historical Center, Cody, WY (1974)

Remington painted night scenes throughout his career, including illustration works dating as early as 1886. These earlier nocturnes, however, were strictly narrative in nature. Remington utilized the night as a setting, a piece of background information employed to assist in describing the scene, much in the same manner as the model of a rifle that a soldier might be holding, the style of boot that he was wearing or the type of military tent beside which he was sitting. Such is the case in *On Guard at Night*, published in *Century Magazine* in May of 1888. In this painting, Remington was illustrating a scene from a story by Theodore Roosevelt, "Sheriff's Work on a Ranch." Roosevelt describes the sheriff and his men taking turns through the chilly night, keeping watch over their prisoners, shown here asleep in the foreground. (Webster, "The Nocturne Paintings of Frederic Remington," p. 2)

Photograph courtesy Frederic Remington Art Museum, Ogdensburg, NY

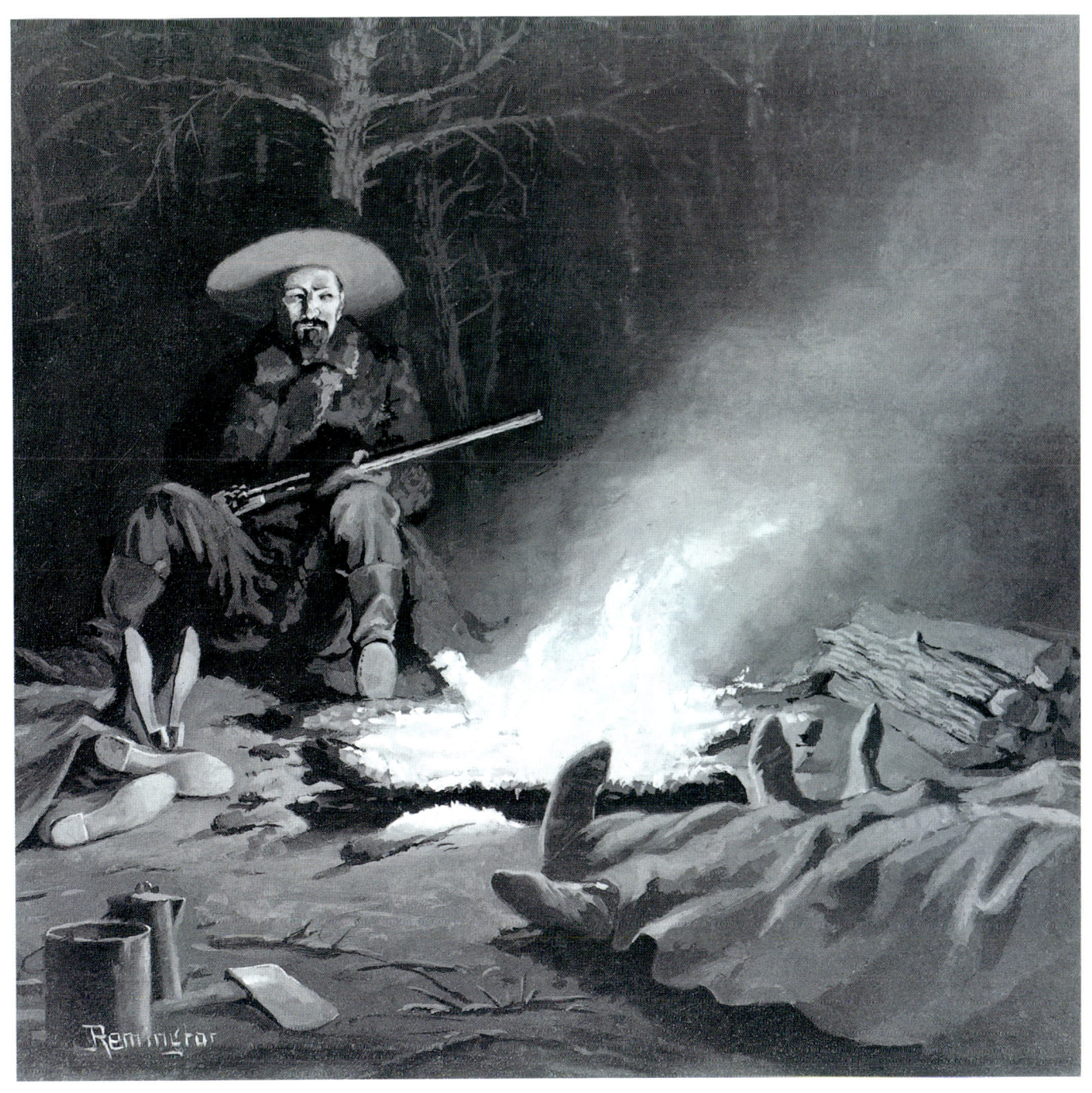

MERRY CHRISTMAS IN A SIBLEY TEPEE

1891

oil on canvas (en grisaille)

21 ½ x 32 ½ inches

signed ll: *Remington-*

ILLUSTRATION: *Harper's Weekly* (December 5, 1891), p. 973, wood engraving

PROVENANCE: "21" Club Collection, New York, NY

LITERATURE: Harold McCracken, *Frederic Remington: Artist of the Old West* (Philadelphia: J.B. Lippincott Co., 1947), p. 137; Harold McCracken, *The Frederic Remington Book: A Pictorial History of the West* (Garden City, NY: Doubleday & Co., Inc., 1966), p. 284, ill. p. 246, no. 348; *Frederic Remington: An Exhibition Honoring Harold McCracken*, Buffalo Bill Historical Center, Cody, WY (1974), ill. p. 40, no. 43; Brian Dippie, "Frederic Remington's Wild West," *American Heritage*, vol. 26, no. 3 (April, 1975), p. 22, ill. p. 78; Harold & Peggy Samuels, *The Collected Writings of Frederic Remington* (Garden City, NY: Doubleday & Co., Inc., 1979), ill. p. 89; George Rockwell, *The History of Ridgefield, Connecticut* (Harrison, NY: Harbor Hill Books, 1979), ill. p. 89; Allen & Marilyn Splete, *Frederic Remington: Selected Letters* (New York: Abbeville Press, Inc., 1988), p. 124; James Ballinger, *Frederic Remington's Southwest*, Phoenix Art Museum, Phoenix, AZ (1992), p. 61, ill. p. 60; Peter Hassrick & Melissa Webster, *Frederic Remington: A Catalogue Raisonné*, Buffalo Bill Historical Center, Cody, WY (1996), p. 394, pl. 1309; Maria Naylor, "Frederic Remington at the 21 Club," *Persimmon Hill*, National Cowboy Hall of Fame (Autumn, 1996), ill. p. 53

EXHIBITIONS: *Frederic Remington: An Exhibition Honoring Harold McCracken*, Buffalo Bill Historical Center, Cody, WY (1974); Military Academy, West Point, NY (1979); Rockwell Museum, Corning, NY (1984)

Many of Remington's early nocturnes are interior scenes, of a room, tent, or tepee void of any hint of moonlight or night air. One such composition is *Merry Christmas in a Sibley Tepee*, published in *Harper's Weekly* (December 5, 1891) as an illustration for Remington's article of the same title about one of his excursions with the army. Although Remington had been experimenting with night scenes as early as 1886, they remained largely narrative throughout the 1890s. He was merely intent on creating a specific scenario, the subject of which was dictated by text. Absence of daylight is employed solely as a compositional element with which to inform the viewer about the time of day during which the action was taking place. (Webster, "The Nocturne Paintings of Frederic Remington," p. 2)

Photograph courtesy "21" Club Collection, New York, NY

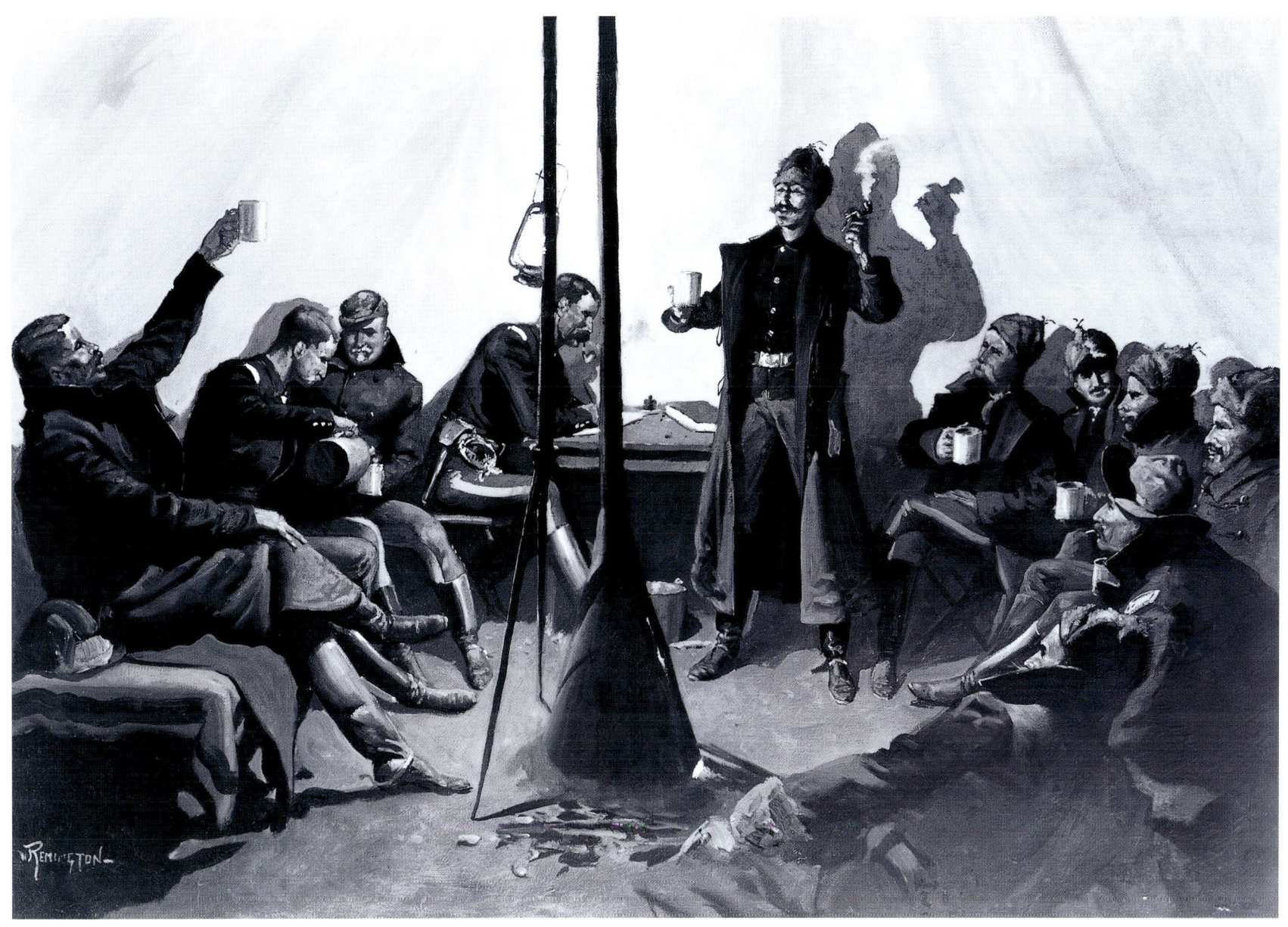

CAVALRYMAN
1887
oil on canvas
26 ¼ x 22 ½ inches
signed lower left: *Frederic Remington '87*

PROVENANCE: Frederick Harvey, Kansas City, MO; Miss Katherine Harvey (daughter); Nelson Atkins Museum, Kansas City, MO (bequest of Katherine Harvey); [Gerald Peters Gallery, Santa Fe, NM]

LITERATURE: Clyde Hollmann, *Five Artists of the Old West* (New York: Hastings House, 1965), p. 81; *How the West Was Won: Frederic Remington and Charles Russell* (New York: Wildenstein & Co., 1968), n.p.; pl. I; Cadet Fine Arts Forum, *Frederic Remington: The Soldier Artist* (1979), ill. p. 56; The Denver Art Museum, *Frederic Remington: The Late Years* (1981), ill. p. 18; James K. Ballinger, *Frederic Remington* (New York: Harry N. Abrams, 1989); The Gerald Peters Gallery, Santa Fe, New Mexico, *Frederic Remington* (1991), ill. p. 38; *American Art Review*, Vol. VIII, No. 3 (1996), ill. p. 135; Peter Hassrick & Melissa Webster *Frederic Remington: A Catalogue Raisonné*, Buffalo Bill Historical Center, Cody, WY (1996), p. 83, pl. 79

EXHIBITIONS: Wildenstein & Co., New York, NY, *How the West Was Won: Frederic Remington and Charles M. Russell* (May 22-June 22, 1968); The U.S. Military Academy, West Point, NY, *Frederic Remington: The Soldier Artist* (May 19-June 6, 1979); The Denver Art Museum, Denver, CO, *Frederic Remington: The Late Years* (July 11-August, 30, 1981); The Gerald Peters Gallery, Santa Fe, NM, *Frederic Remington* (1991)

In 1887, Frederic Remington undertook a trip to Canada on commission from *Harper's Weekly*—an excursion that produced this bold portrait of a Canadian cavalryman. By concentrating on his career as an illustrator, Remington had largely ignored the modern styles then being exhibited in New York. There were, however, two artists whose influences were to have a profound effect on the development of Remington's mature style. The two were French military artists by the names of Jean-Baptiste-Edouard Détaille and Alphonse de Neuville. Remington's equestrian portrait of the Cavalryman is similar in both composition and handling to the works of these European artists, whose work he greatly admired. The composition is held delicately in balance by the use of red, ranging from the subtle tones in the ground cover and horse's coat to the brash red of the cavalryman's jacket. The single figure isolated against a minimal background allowed Remington to focus on the specifics of dress, stance, and physical type (details which conveyed his acute, firsthand observations of the military). The weapon this "Mountie" is carrying is easily identifiable as a Model 1876 Winchester.

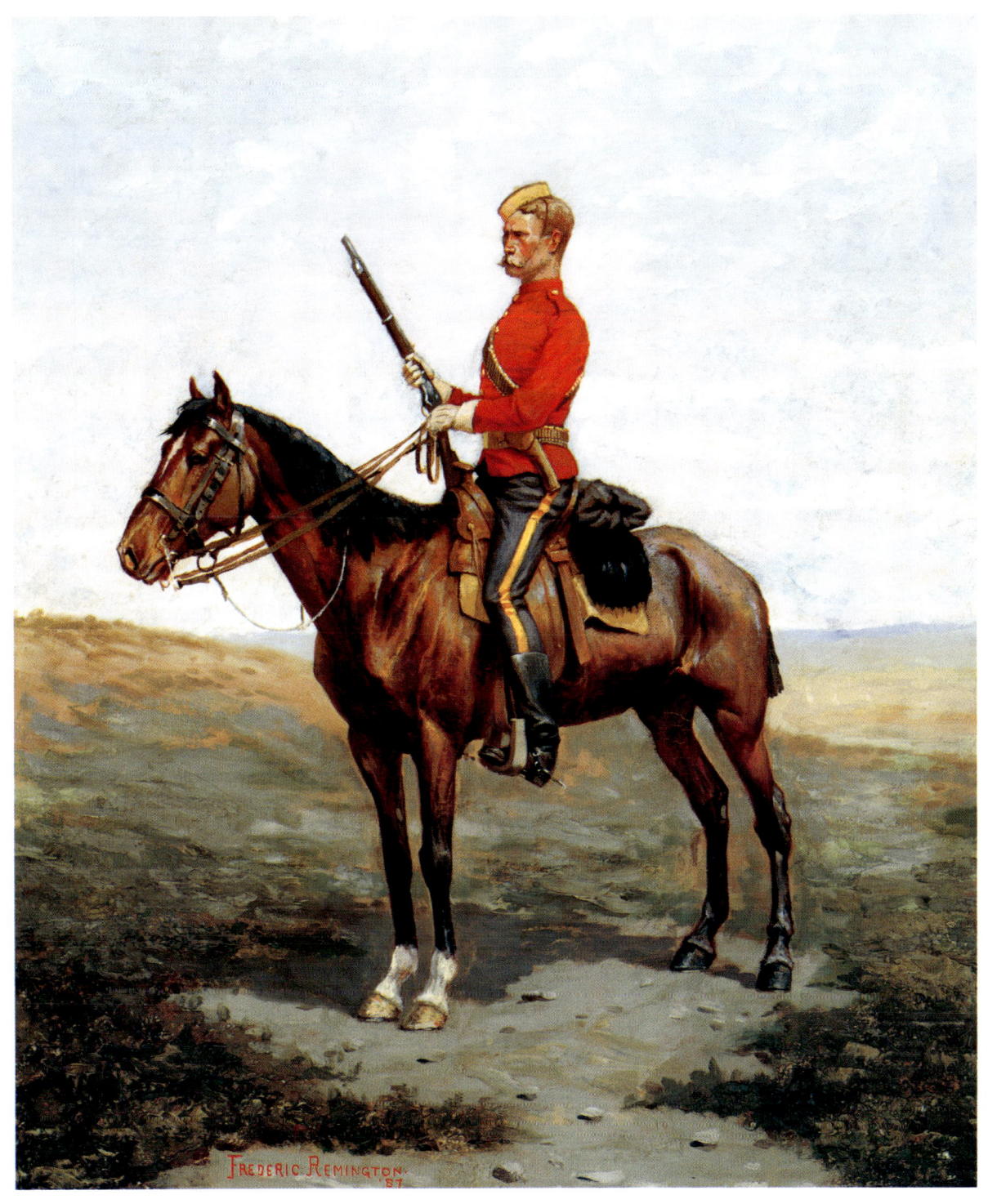

A MOUNTED INFANTRYMAN

1890

watercolor on paper on board

18 ¼ x 13 inches

inscriptions ll: *With compliments to/My friend May Ross.-/Frederic Remington./1890./No.6*

inscriptions verso: *To be returned U.S. Infantry in Montana under Gen. P. Miles, were mounted on captured Indian Ponies*
                              and went by the name of the 11th Cavalry.

PROVENANCE: Private collection; [Gerald Peters Gallery, Santa Fe, NM]

ILLUSTRATION: *Century Magazine* (March 1891), p. 644, wood engraving

LITERATURE: Harold McCracken, *Frederic Remington: Artist of the Old West* (Philadelphia: J. B. Lippincott Co., 1947), p. 125; Peter Hassrick & Melissa Webster, *Frederic Remington: A Catalogue Raisonné*, Buffalo Bill Historical Center, Cody, WY (1996), Vol. I, p. 352, pl. 1141.

In late autumn of 1890, Remington accepted a proposal from *Harper's Weekly* to accompany General Miles, Commander of the Army's Division of the Pacific, to the Cheyenne agency and Crow Reservation in Lame Deer, Montana. Such assignments allowed Remington to explore his profound interest in the historical contest between Indian and soldier, a theme that pervaded his work during the 1890s.

The format and style of *A Mounted Infantryman* is characteristic of Remington's military portrayals. In these works he typically depicts a single figure or equestrian subject isolated against a minimal background. There is no distracting activity, and the subject is shown at rest. This format allowed Remington to focus on the specifics of dress, gear, stance, and physical prototype—details which would communicate his firsthand observations of the military. The cleanly articulated naturalism of *A Mounted Infantryman* makes it one of the finest watercolors in this genre.

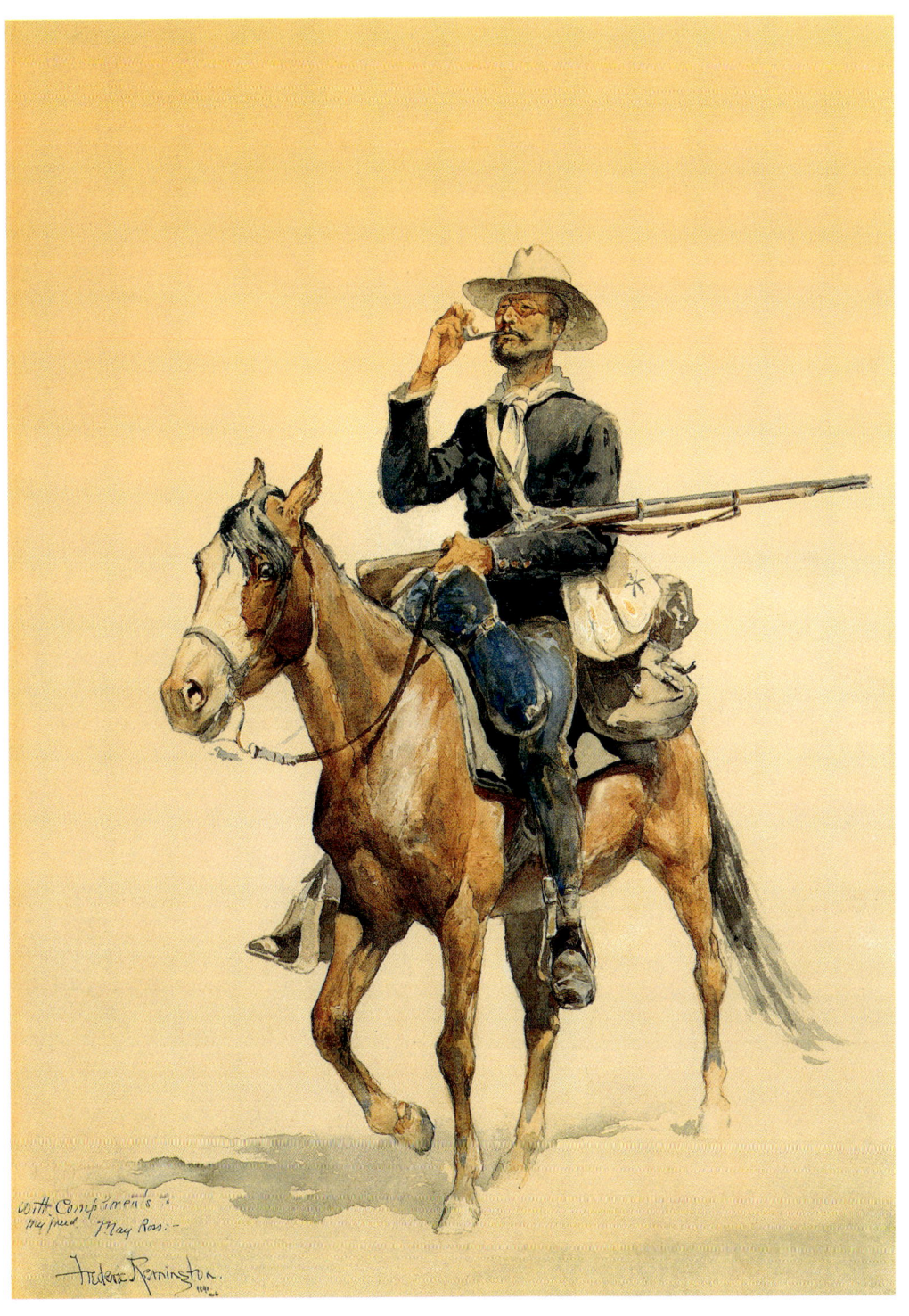

INDIAN SOLDIER IN THE CROW SCOUT CORPS

1890

watercolor on paper

23 ⅞ x 15 ⅝ inches

inscribed ll: *FREDERIC REMINGTON-/MONTANA., 90*

inscribed lr: *KURTZ*

PROVENANCE: Private collection, WY; [Mongerson Wunderlich, Chicago, IL]; Private collection

ILLUSTRATION: *Harper's Weekly* (December 27, 1890), p. 1005, halftone

LITERATURE: *Remington to Frederick B. Schell*, 1891, Denver Public Library, Denver, CO, Western History Dept.; Harold McCracken, *Frederic Remington: Artist of the Old West* (Philadelphia: J. B. Lippincott Co., 1947, p.136); Allen & Marilyn Splete, *Frederic Remington: Selected Letters* (New York: Abbeville Press, Inc., 1988); Peter Hassrick and Melissa Webster, *Frederic Remington, A Catalogue Raisonné*, Buffalo Bill Historical Center, Cody, WY (1996), ill. p. 348, pl. 1126

During the Sioux uprising of 1890, General Nelson Miles advised Remington to hurry back to the Dakota Territories to serve as the premier correspondent covering the Indian wars. Miles assigned Remington to the forefront of the action by attaching him to the command of Lieutenant W. Casey and his Northern Cheyenne Indian Scouts. The army enlisted two hundred and seventy-five Native American men, and many more served in a temporary capacity.

This watercolor, depicting an enlisted Crow scout, is stylistically related to *A Mounted Infantryman* (pg. 32). As with many of Remington's watercolors dating from this period, the figure is silhouetted against a stark, minimal background which focuses attention on the straightforward representation of horse and rider.

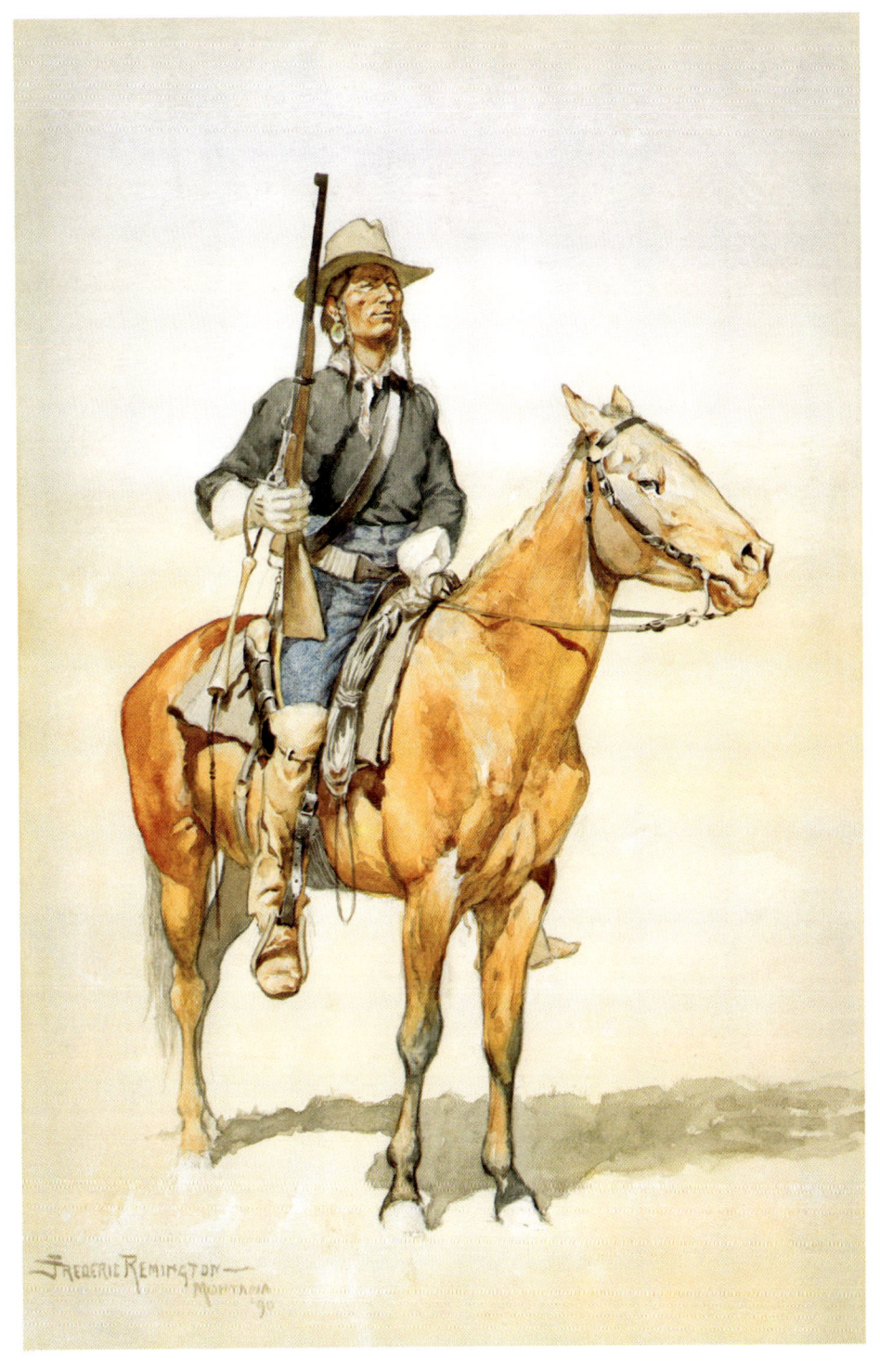

THE PICKET LINE: INFANTRY DRILLING IN THE WOODS: ENTRENCHMENT
AND FIRE DRILL
1898
pen and ink wash with white goache (*en grisaille*)
25 ¾ x 38 inches
signed ll: *Frederic Remington*

PROVENANCE: The artist; father of Dewitt R. Goodard; DeWitt R. Goodard, Maine; Mrs. George A. Parson, Maine; [Vose Galleries, Boston, MA]; [Kennedy Galleries Inc., New York, NY]; Private collection, TX; [Gerald Peters Gallery, Santa Fe, NM]; Los Angeles Athletic Club Art Collection, Los Angeles, CA; [Gerald Peters Gallery, Santa Fe, NM]; Private collection, TX; [Gerald Peters Gallery, Santa Fe, NM]

LITERATURE: Peter Hassrick & Melissa Webster, *Frederic Remington: A Catalogue Raisonné*, Buffalo Bill Historical Center, Cody, WY (1996), ill. p. 653, pl. 2301

As the son of a war hero, Remington longed to experience combat firsthand. Despite the authentic, almost documentary, feel of much of his work, the corpus of Remington's output as an action painter was largely based on second-hand knowledge of heroic feats and events of the Indian Wars. When revolution broke out in Cuba and it looked as though the United States and Spain might battle over Cuban freedom, Remington seized the opportunity to document the conflict firsthand. No doubt, the Spanish-American War would provide ample fresh material for his canvases. In *The Picket Line*, Remington utilizes a technique similar to that which he had employed in his Indian Wars pictures – omitting the adversary from the composition, and focussing his attention on one party of the combatants.

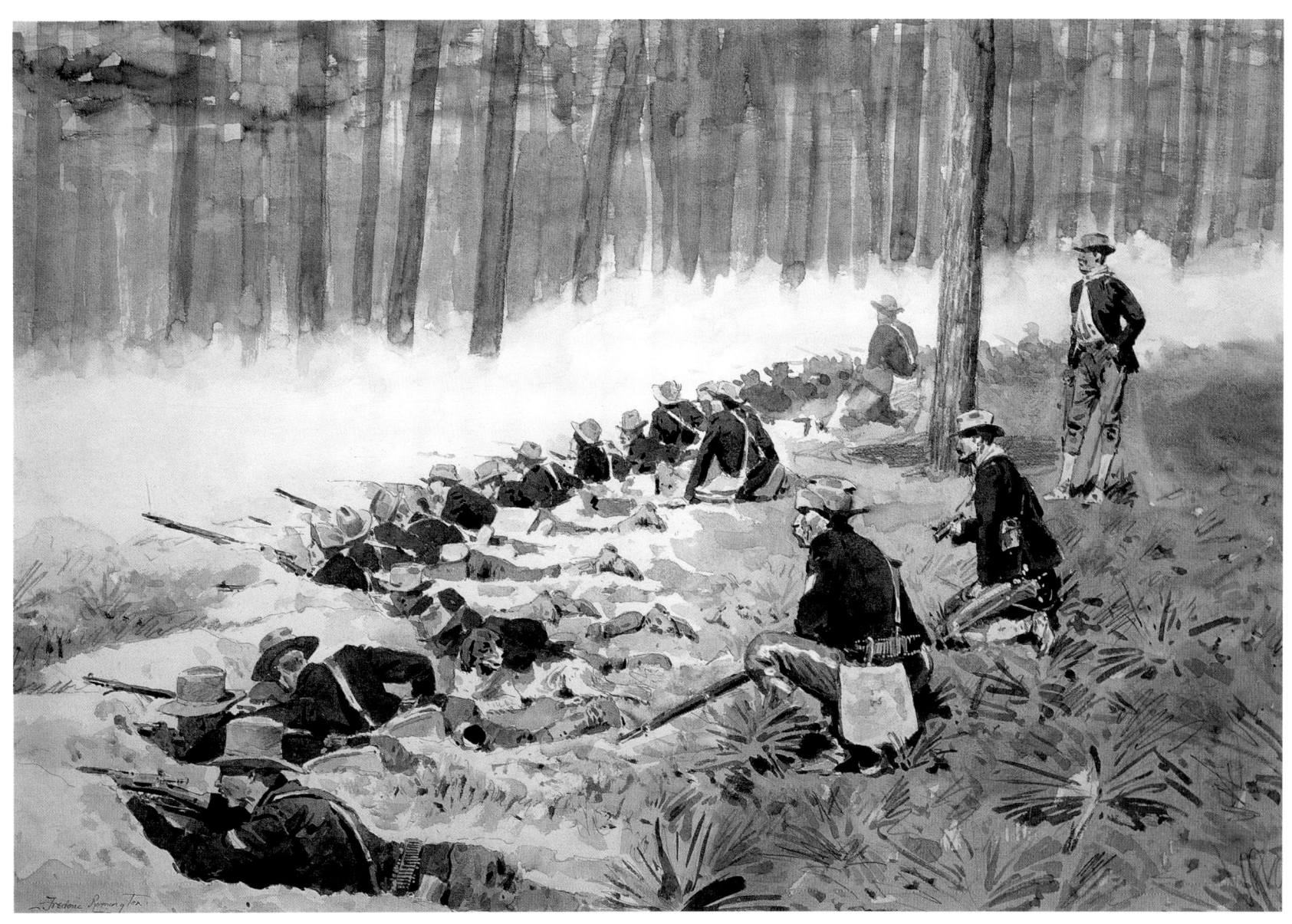

INDIAN SCOUTS IN THE MOONLIGHT

c. 1902

oil on canvas

30 x 20 inches

signed lr: *Frederic Remington*

PROVENANCE: [Newhouse Galleries, New York, NY]; Richard Manoogian, 1982; [J.N. Bartfield Galleries, New York, NY]; Private collection

LITERATURE: Harold McCracken, *The Frederic Remington Book: A Pictorial History of the West* (Garden City, NY: Doubleday & Co., Inc., 1966), p. 276, ill. p. 127, no. 171; Denver Art Museum (1981), ill. p. 54, detail p. 55; Grand Central Art Galleries (1984), p. 31, no. 64a, ill. p. 27; Peter Hassrick and Melissa Webster, *Frederic Remington: A Catalogue Raisonné*, Buffalo Bill Historical Center, Cody, WY (1996), ill. p. 745, pl. 2602

EXHIBITIONS: Denver Art Museum, Denver, CO (1981); Grand Central Art Galleries, New York, NY (1984)

After the turn of the century, Remington began to make adjustments in his style of painting, and to look with a different eye at the aura of the West. His pictures became less literal, and sought instead to elicit an emotional response from the viewer, enshrouding their subjects with a mysterious, sublime quality evocative of romantic vision.

For the first years of the twentieth century, Remington's paintings manifested Impressionist qualities. Instead of appearing clear and dry, his canvases now began to shimmer with reflections of moonlight. The world of night, full of mystery and melancholy, nurtured Remington's imagination. Paintings such as *Indian Scouts in the Moonlight* manifest freer, more painterly brushwork and liberal application of color. Remington was now devoting as much time to the study of nocturnal light and color as he had once dedicated to the accurate depiction of prairie sunlight.

Photograph courtesy of J.N. Bartfield Galleries, New York, NY

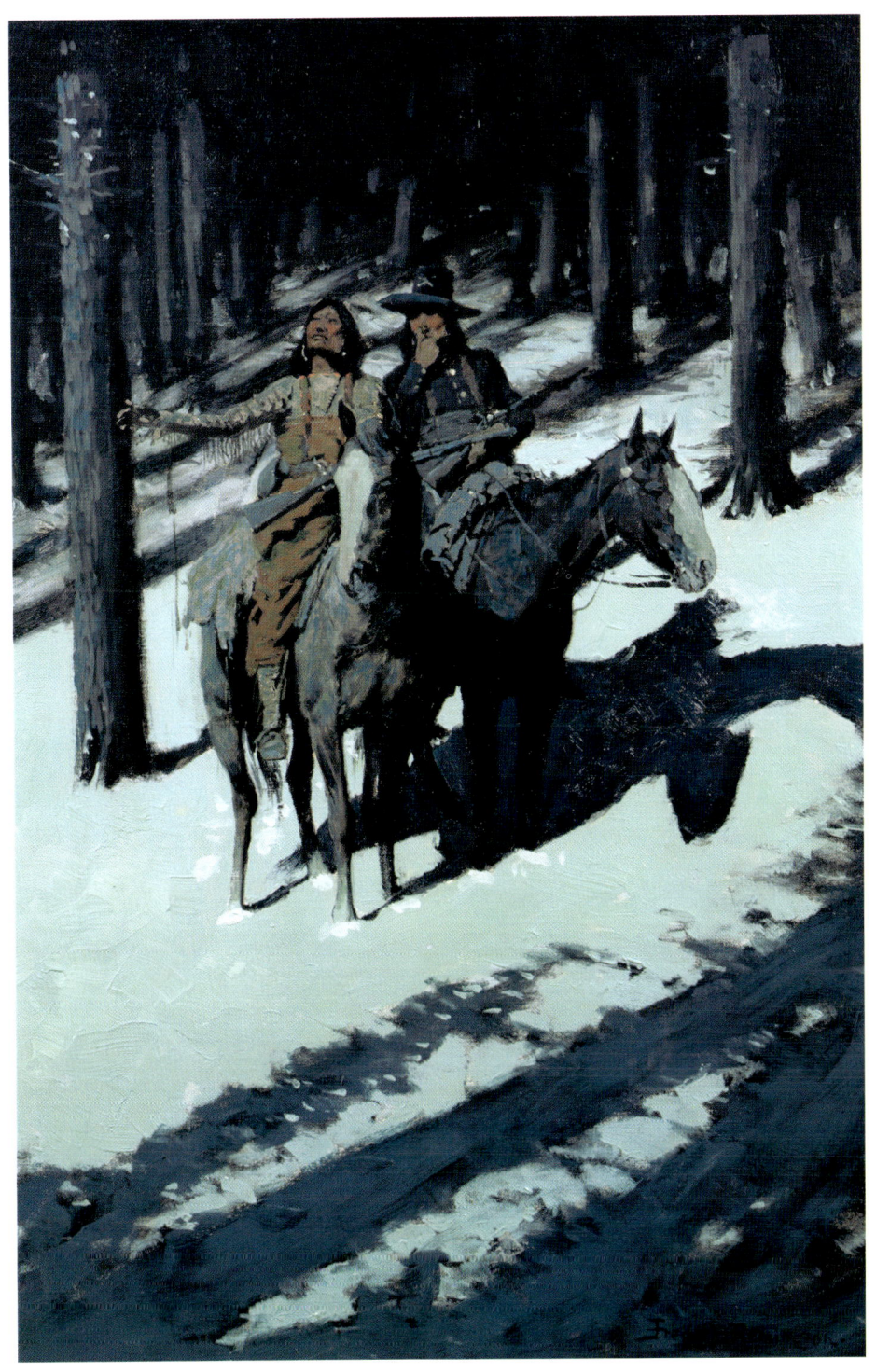

A RECONNAISSANCE
1902
oil on canvas
27 ¼ x 40 ⅛ inches
signed lr: *Frederic Remington/1902/copyright 1903*

PROVENANCE: The artist; *Collier's Weekly*; [David B. Findlay Galleries, New York, NY, 1952]; Amon G. Carter, Fort Worth, TX, 1952; Amon Carter Museum, Fort Worth, TX (1952-present)

ILLUSTRATION: *Collier's Weekly* (April 8, 1905), p. 18-19, halftone.

LITERATURE: Harold McCracken, *Frederic Remington: Artist of the Old West* (Philadelphia: J. B. Lippincott Co., 1947); Peter Hassrick, *Frederic Remington: Paintings, Drawings and Sculpture in the Amon Carter and Sid Richardson Foundation Collections* (New York: Harry N. Abrams, Inc., 1973), p.145, ill. p. 144; Harold & Peggy Samuels, *Frederic Remington: A Biography* (Garden City, NY: Doubleday & Co., Inc., 1982), p. 340; Harold & Peggy Samuels, *Remington: The Complete Prints* (New York: Crown Publishers, Inc., 1990), p. 94, 97, 150, 158, ill. p. 97, pl. 101; Peter Hassrick & Melissa Webster, *Frederic Remington: A Catalogue Raisonné*, Buffalo Bill Historical Center, Cody, WY (1996) ill. p. 766, pl. 2692

EXHIBITIONS: University of Utah, Salt Lake City, UT (1964); Mary Baldwin College, Stauton, VA (1964); Stanford Art Gallery, CA (1965); Portland Art Museum, Portland, OR (1965); Amon Carter Museum, Fort Worth, TX (1973); Birmingham Museum of Art, Birmingham, AL (1974); Mobile Art Gallery, Mobile, AL (1974); Lowe Art Museum, Coral Gables, FL (1975); Western Heritage, Littleton, CO (1978); Worcester Art Museum, Worcester, MA (1979); Phoenix Art Museum, Phoenix, AZ (1982)

A Reconnaissance shows a close affinity to Charles Rollo Peters's California nocturnes. Relative to earlier works, major changes are found in brush work and color—elements with which Remington had been struggling for almost a decade. The paint is more fluid, and Remington employs a significant degree of impasto. In *A Reconnaissance* the palette is muted and the tonal range restricted. The moon's light casts a bluish hue over the entire scene, in contrast to the full spectrum of color that sunlight would reveal. (Webster, "The Nocturnes of Frederic Remington," p. 7)

Photograph courtesy of Amon Carter Museum, Fort Worth, TX, 1961.245

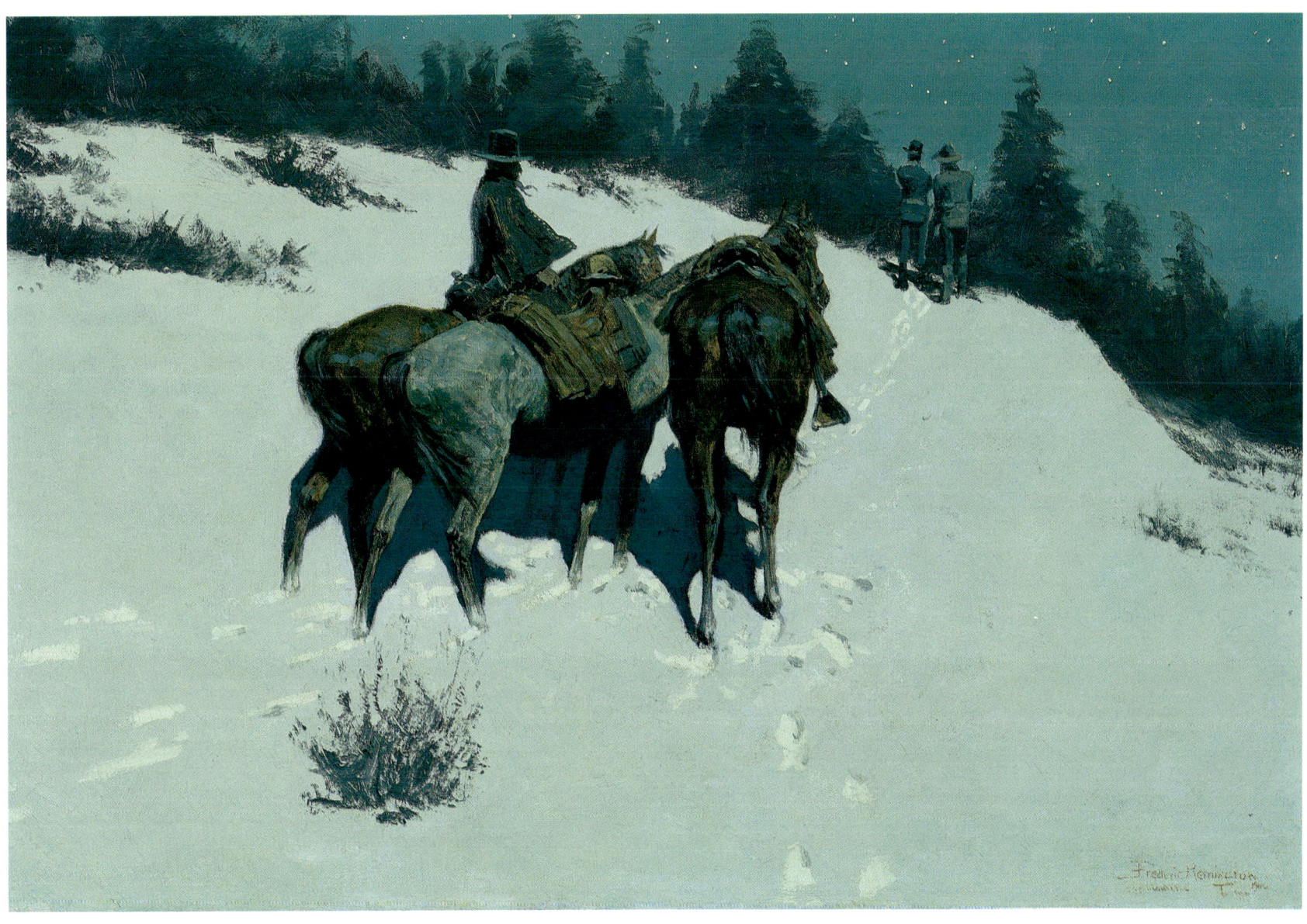

THE INTRUDERS

c. 1900
oil on canvas
27 x 47 inches
signed lr: *Frederic Remington*

PROVENANCE: Lawrence Green, New York, NY; [M. Knoedler & Co., NewYork, NY]; G.J. Fuerth, New York, NY; Mr. & Mrs. James Cox Brady, Far Hills, NJ; [Newhouse Galleries, New York, NY]; [Gerald Peters Gallery, Santa Fe, NM]; Private collection, TX; Private collection

LITERATURE: Harold McCracken, *The Frederic Remington Book: A Pictorial History of the West* (1966), pl. I, p. 276; *How The West Was Won*, Wildenstein Catalog, New York, NY (1968), pl. 31A; Peter Hassrick, *Frederic Remington: The Late Years*, Denver Art Museum, Denver, CO (1981), ill. p. 33; The Saint Louis Art Museum in conjunction with the Buffalo Bill Historical Center, *Frederic Remington: The Masterworks* (New York: Harry N. Abrams, Inc., 1988), pl. 19, p. 115, 126; James Ballinger, *Frederic Remington* (New York: Harry N. Abrams, Inc., 1989) p. 90, 91, ill. p. 112-13; *Frederic Remington*, Gerald Peters Gallery in association with Mongerson-Wunderlich (1991), ill. p. 46, 47; Peter Hassrick and Melissa Webster, *Frederic Remington: A Catalogue Raisonné*, Buffalo Bill Historical Center, Cody, WY (1996), ill. p. 713, pl. 2483

EXHIBITIONS: Wildenstein, New York, NY, *How The West Was Won: Paintings, Watercolors and Bronzes by Frederic Remington and Charles Russell* (1968); Denver Art Museum, Denver, CO, *Frederic Remington: The Late Years* (1981); St. Louis Art Museum, St Louis, MO, Buffalo Bill Historical Center, Cody, WY, The Museum of Fine Arts, Houston, TX, The Metropolitan Museum of Art, New York, NY, *Frederic Remington: The Masterworks* (1988-89).

The Intruders, one of the most significant of Remington's action canvases, explores a subject which was of interest to the artist throughout his career. For Remington, the heroic last stand of a frontier battle represented the strength and character of the intrepid settlers, and the motif appeared in several works, including *Last Lull in the Fight* (*Harper's Weekly*, March 30, 1889) and *Fight for the Water Hole* (Museum of Fine Arts Houston). In *The Intruders*, Remington focuses the painting's action on a group of outnumbered settlers, centrally arranged on the canvas in an inverted pyramid, while their adversaries circle in the distance. The clarity of the narrative is reinforced by the sharp, intense coloration and academic rendering of the figures— a style that is characteristic of Remington's major early works. The spatial relationships of ground and sky are ambiguous, with distances being somewhat difficult to gauge, all of which serves to focus the viewer's attention on the dramatic action of the foreground.

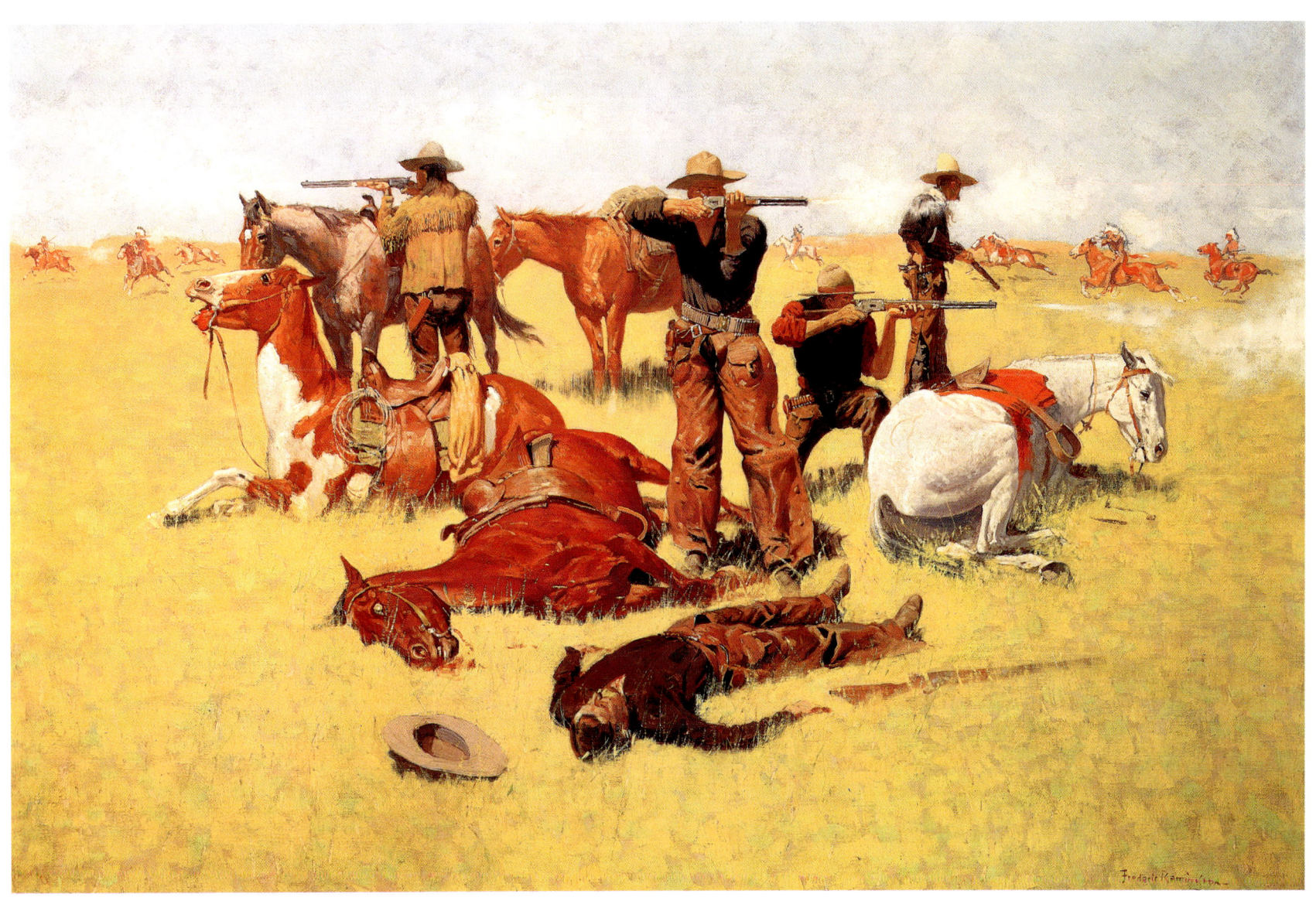

31

THE SCOUT: FRIENDS OR ENEMIES?

1902-05
oil on canvas
27 x 40 inches
signed lr: *Frederic Remington*

PROVENANCE: The artist; Lansing, Albany, NY; Ledyard Cogswell; Albany Institute of History and Art (J. Townsend Lansing bequest), Albany, NY; [John Levy Galleries, New York, NY]; [M. Knoedler & Co., New York, NY]; R. Sterling Clark; Sterling and Francine Clark Art Institute, Williamstown, MA

LITERATURE: Harold McCracken, *Portrait of the Old West* (New York: McGraw-Hill Book Co., Inc., 1952), ill. p. 204; Remington Art Memorial, *A Catalogue of the Frederic Remington Memorial Collection*, Ogdensburg, NY (1954), ill. p. 42; Harold McCracken, *The Frederic Remington Book: A Pictorial History of the West* (Garden City, NY: Doubleday & Co., Inc., 1966), p. 281, ill. p. 170; *How the West Was Won*, Wildenstein Catalogue, New York, NY (1968), ill. no. 5; Matthew Baigell, *The Western Art of Frederic Remington* (New York: Ballantine Books, 1976), ill. no. 8; *Berkshire Magazine* (Winter 1982); The Saint Louis Art Museum in conjunction with the Buffalo Bill Historical Center, *Frederic Remington: The Masterworks* (New York: Harry N. Abrams, Inc., 1988), p. 20, 127, ill. p. 82; James Ballinger, *Frederic Remington* (New York: Harry N. Abrams, Inc., 1989), p. 112, ill. p. 55; Peter Hassrick and Melissa Webster, *Frederic Remington: A Catalogue Raisonné*, Buffalo Bill Historical Center, Cody, WY (1996), ill. p. 745, pl. 2603

EXHIBITIONS: Museum of Fine Art, Dallas, TX (1936); M. Knoedler & Co., New York, NY (1952); City Art Museum, St. Louis, MO (1954); Clark Art Institute, Williamstown, MA (1955); Minneapolis Institute of Art, MN (1967); Clark Art Institute, Williamstown, MA (1967); Wildenstein Art Gallery, New York, NY (1968); St. Louis Art Museum, St. Louis, MO (1988); Buffalo Bill Historical Center, Cody, WY (1988); Museum of Fine Arts, Houston, TX (1988)

In his early night scenes, Remington was strongly influenced by the painter Charles Rollo Peters. Peters frequently employed large reflective surfaces in his compositions to serve as secondary light sources and as planes against which to silhouette figures and action. *The Scout: Friends or Enemies?* exemplifies an early nocturne in which Remington employed snow as the reflective surface and a bright spotlight to uniformly illuminate the landscape. The enigmatic title refers to an unresolved drama in which the mounted scout tries to determine the identity of the inhabitants of the distant camp. Consistent with the manner of Remington's late paintings, *The Scout: Friends or Enemies?* leaves the question posed by its title unanswered.

Photograph courtesy of the Sterling and Francine Clark Art Institute, Williamstown, MA

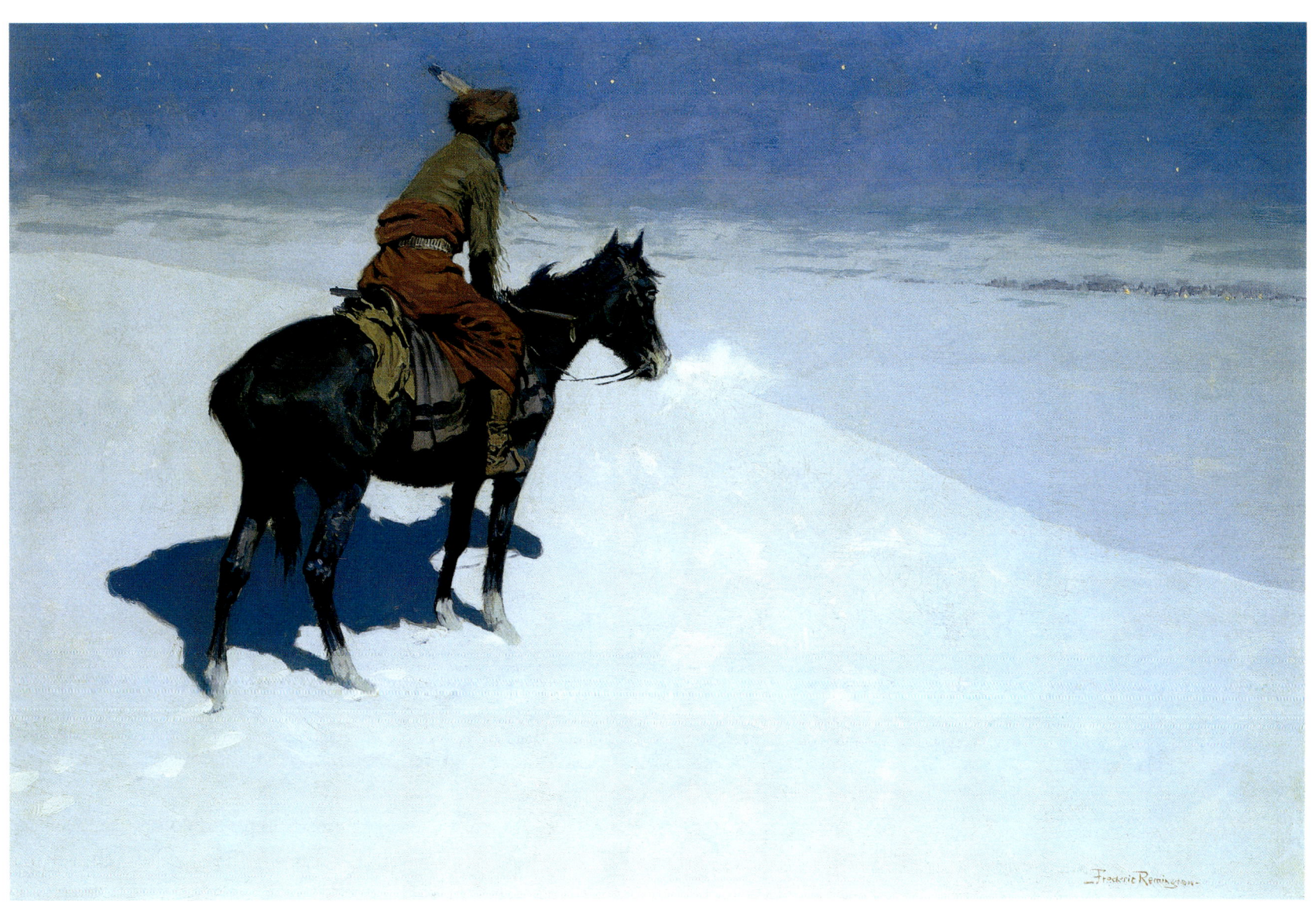

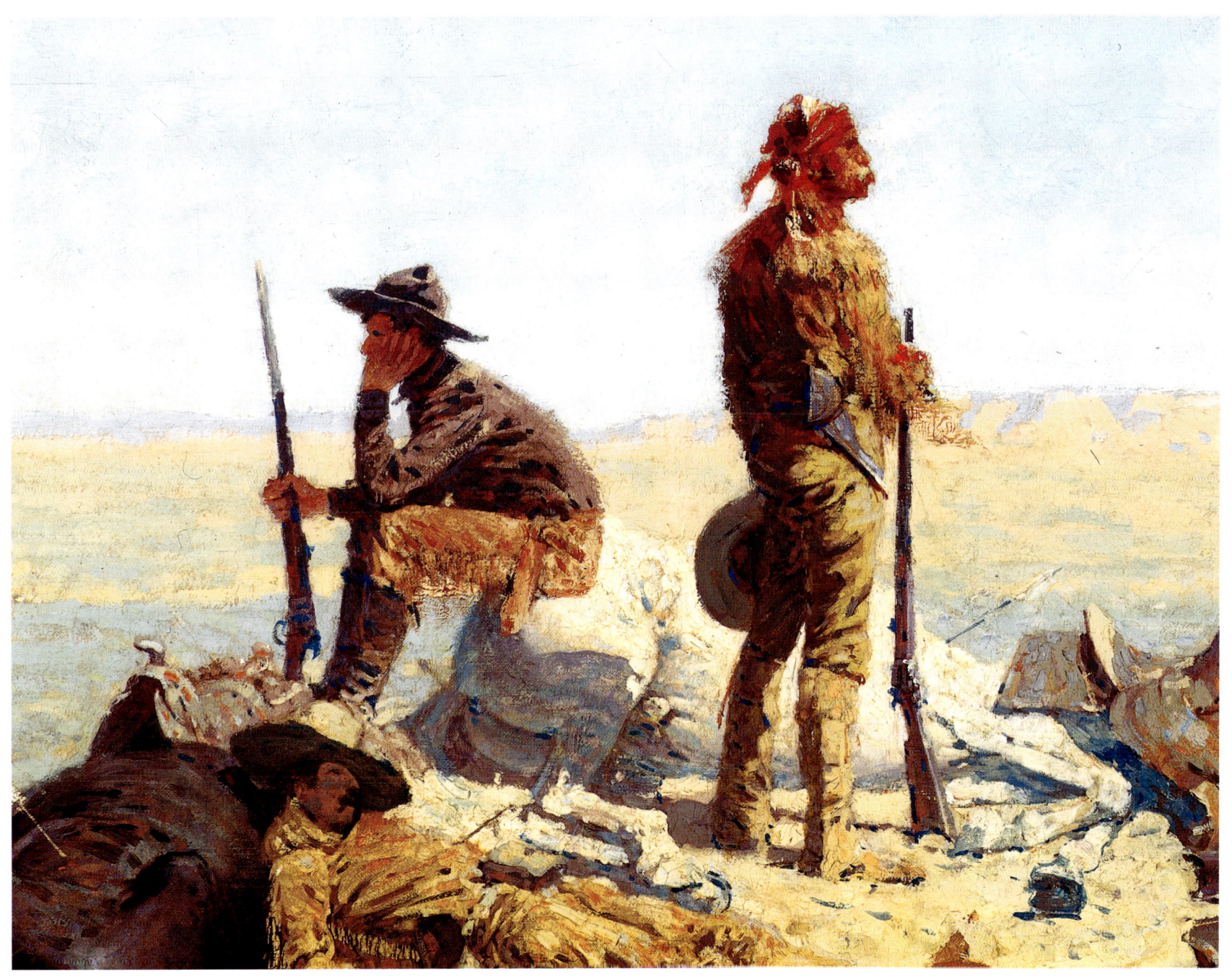

Detail of THE LAST LULL IN THE FIGHT (see page 37), 1903. Oil on canvas, 30 ¼ x 61 inches

THE LAST LULL IN THE FIGHT

alternate title: *The Last Stand*

c. 1903

oil on canvas

30 ¼ x 61 inches

signed lr: *Frederic Remington*

PROVENANCE: The artist; The artist's estate; [M. Knoedler & Co., New York, NY]; Edward Lawrence Doheny, Los Angeles, CA; Private collection; [Gerald Peters Gallery, Santa Fe, NM]

EXHIBITIONS: *Special Exhibition of Recent Paintings by Frederic Remington*, The Noé Gallery, New York, NY (1904); Union League Club, New York, NY (1906); M. Knoedler & Co., New York, NY (1907); Reinhardt's Gallery, Chicago, IL (1908); M. Knoedler & Co., New York, NY (1913)

LITERATURE: Noé Gallery Catalogue (1904), no.1; *New York Times* (March 15, 1904), p.8; Union League Club Catalogue (1904), no. 23; M. Knoedler & Co. Catalogue (1907), no. 13; Reinhardt's Gallery Catalogue (1908), n.p.; *New York Sun* (Dec. 27, 1909); Harold and Peggy Samuels, *Frederic Remington: A Biography* (New York: Doubleday & Co., 1982), pp. 124, 126, 315, 355, 380, 396; *Frederic Remington: The Masterworks*, The Saint Louis Art Museum in conjunction with the Buffalo Bill Historical Center, Cody, WY (1988), pp. 69, 72, 73, 81; James K. Ballinger, *Frederic Remington* (New York: Harry Abrams, Inc., 1989), pp.46, 113; Peter Hassrick and Melissa Webster, *Frederic Remington: The Catalogue Raisonné*, Buffalo Bill Historical Center, Cody, WY (1996), pl. 2695, p.767

The Last Lull in the Fight is one of the truly great and pivotal paintings in Frederic Remington's celebrated career. The theme, drawn from tales of Comanche resistance of the early 1860s on the Llano Estacado, resonates with the powerful determinism and fatalism that were central to Remington's art from early in his career. It speaks not only to the compelling contest for settlement of the West, but also to Remington's insightful and potent assertion that the forces of civilization (symbolized here by the beleaguered cowboys) would not necessarily always prevail against native peoples defending their lands and their way of life.

This painting is a late, yet remarkable version of an earlier work of the same title that gave Remington his first taste of fame, both in the United States and internationally. That initial version (now lost) was painted in 1888 and exhibited in the American Pavilion at the famed 1889 Paris Universal Exposition— the same event for which the Eiffel Tower was constructed. Remington's painting was received enthusiastically by both the American jury and French audiences, and was awarded a Silver Medal for second place out of all the American entries. This accolade, along with the positive critical acclaim lavished upon his painting *A Dash for the Timber* that year at the National Academy, provided the real launch for Remington's artistic career. Although it is not certain, it is presumed that the early version of *The Last Lull in the Fight* was sold in Europe. The subject was considered to be of such importance that it was illustrated as a two-page spread in *Harper's Weekly* on March 30, 1889. The painting's theme remained a vital part of Remington's reservoir of western imagery, leading him to produce this second version in 1903, at a point in his career when he was beginning to make serious strides to enhance and modernize his artistic style.

The year 1903 saw the advent of dramatic changes in Remington's career. He signed an exclusive contract with *Collier's* to provide twelve color oils per year to be reproduced in the magazine on a monthly basis. As a result, his paintings (of which *The Last Lull in the Fight* is a particularly fine example) became increasingly rich in color, more broadly painted, lighter in palette, and more harmonious in overall composition in the Impressionist mode. The influence of lessons from Remington's friends and fellow artists – J. Alden Weir, John Twachtman, and Childe Hassam– became apparent at this time.

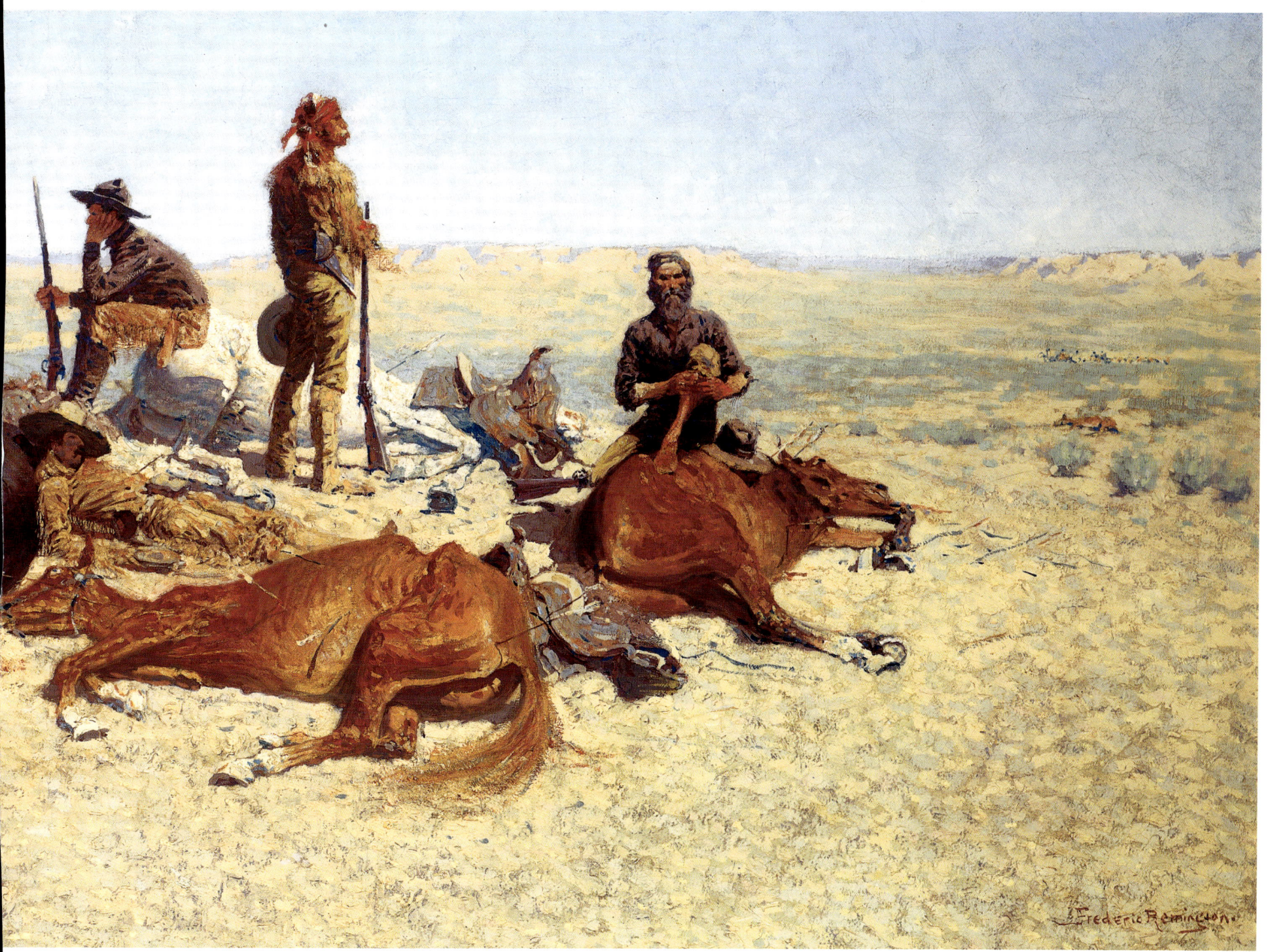

In 1910, the art critic and historian Royal Cortissoz referred to the change that took place in Remington's work as "one of the most interesting noted in some years...by observers of American art." What was seen, according to Cortissoz, was "a truer adjustment of 'values' and an improvement in the quality of painted surface." The dappled strokes of paint, the subtle juxtaposition of hues, and the reduced contrast of color values provide a resolved yet exhilarating paint surface.

The Last Lull in the Fight is animated by a superbly powerful pathos and a sense of dramatic portent. The light and shade are managed expertly, the modeling of the horses and drawing of the human figures are adroitly handled, the textures are vigorously presented, and the color scheme is carefully and masterfully integrated. This large, ambitious painting provides powerful evidence of Remington's evolving talent and leaves no question as to his natural gift as a painter.

The late version of *The Last Lull in the Fight* was first exhibited at The Noé Gallery in New York City in the spring of 1904. On March 15 of that year *The New York Times* commented that the painting evidenced a refreshingly broader handling than heretofore seen in the artist's work. When the painting was exhibited three years later at Knoedler's, it was selected to go in the gallery's front window. Critics claimed that this and other works in the exhibition represented a significant transformation for Remington. *American Art News* asserted in its review that:

> *Mr. Remington has worked out and away from his former hard and dry*
> *color and his pictures have a new softness and almost a delicacy of color*
> *at times, while they still possess that vrai-semblance which makes them so*
> *interesting and at times dramatic.*

Knoedler sold *The Last Lull in the Fight* in 1914 to an enthusiastic California collector, Edward Lawrence Doheny. It has come to the present owners by descent through the Doheny family. Doheny was recognized about a decade later for commissioning a set of murals for his library in Los Angeles from the Montana-based artist, Charles M. Russell. *The Last Lull in the Fight* is the largest and most important late Remington work still in private hands. It is featured as a color plate in the recently published (1996) catalogue raisonné on the artist.

Peter Hassrick

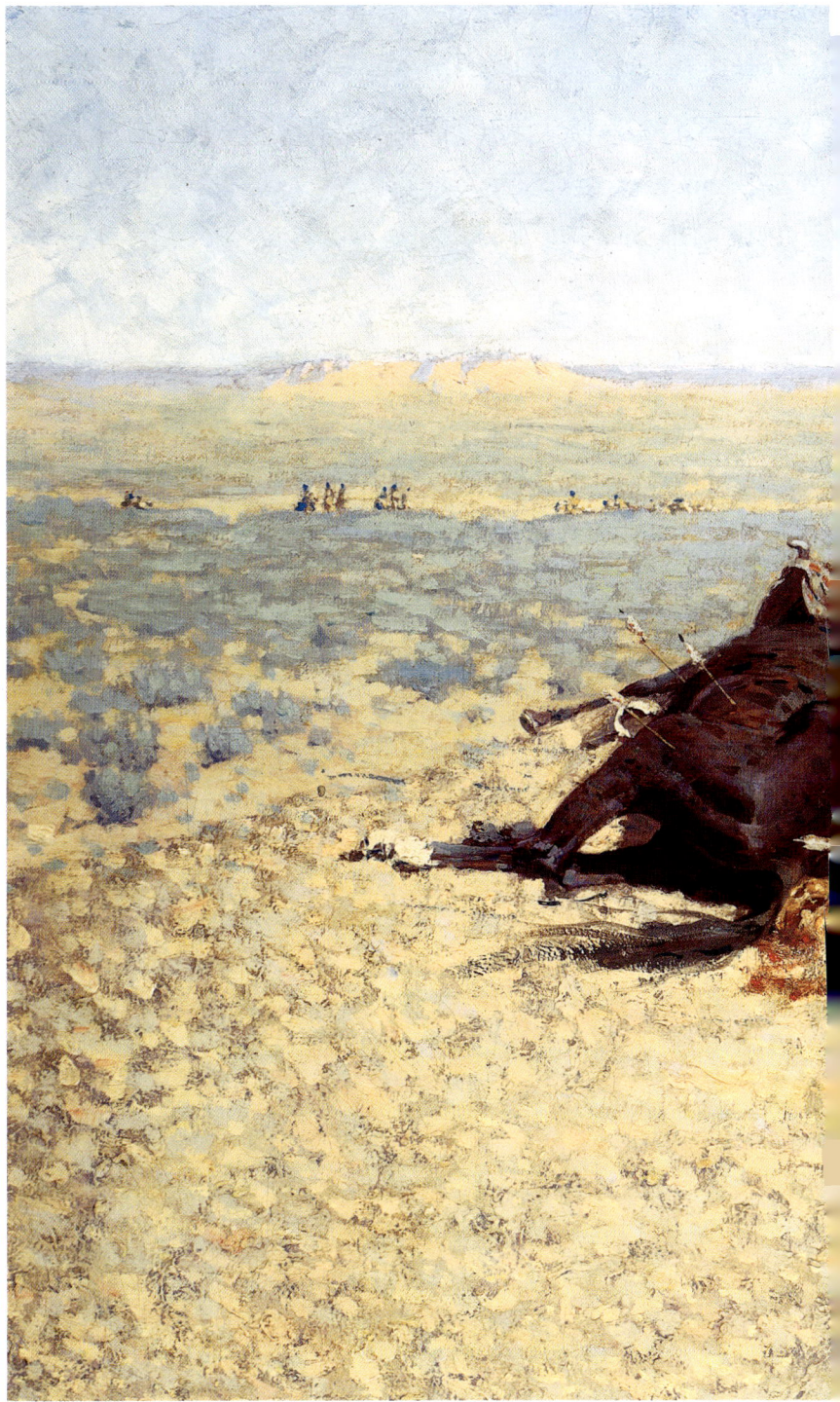

FIGHT FOR THE STOLEN HERD
c. 1903
oil on canvas
30 x 50 inches
signed lr: *Frederic Remington-*

PROVENANCE: [M. Knoedler & Co., New York, NY]; James Cox Brady, New York, NY, 1979; by descent through the family; [Newhouse Galleries, New York, NY]; Private collection, CO; [Gerald Peters Gallery, Santa Fe, NM, 1991] Private collection, TX, 1991

LITERATURE: Harold McCracken, *The Frederic Remington Book: A Pictorial History of the West* (1966), pl. 285; Peter Hassrick and Melissa Webster, *Frederic Remington: A Catalogue Raisonné*, Buffalo Bill Historical Center, Cody, WY (1996), p. 767, pl. 2694

EXHIBITIONS: *Frederic Remington*, Gerald Peters Gallery in association with Mongerson-Wunderlich, Santa Fe, NM, 1991

One of Remington's most dramatic and energetic images, *Fight for the Stolen Herd* depicts a large group of cowboys in active pursuit of a herd of ponies apparently stolen by a group of Indians. Several of the cowboys fire at the fleeing Indians, one of whom raises a buffalo hide, a common signal for battle and the hunt. Remington constructs a complex frieze of horses and riders which extends across the entire canvas, with figures cropped at either side suggesting that the group extends beyond the space defined by the canvas. This cropping implies not only the rapid movement forward of the horses, but a continuum of action.

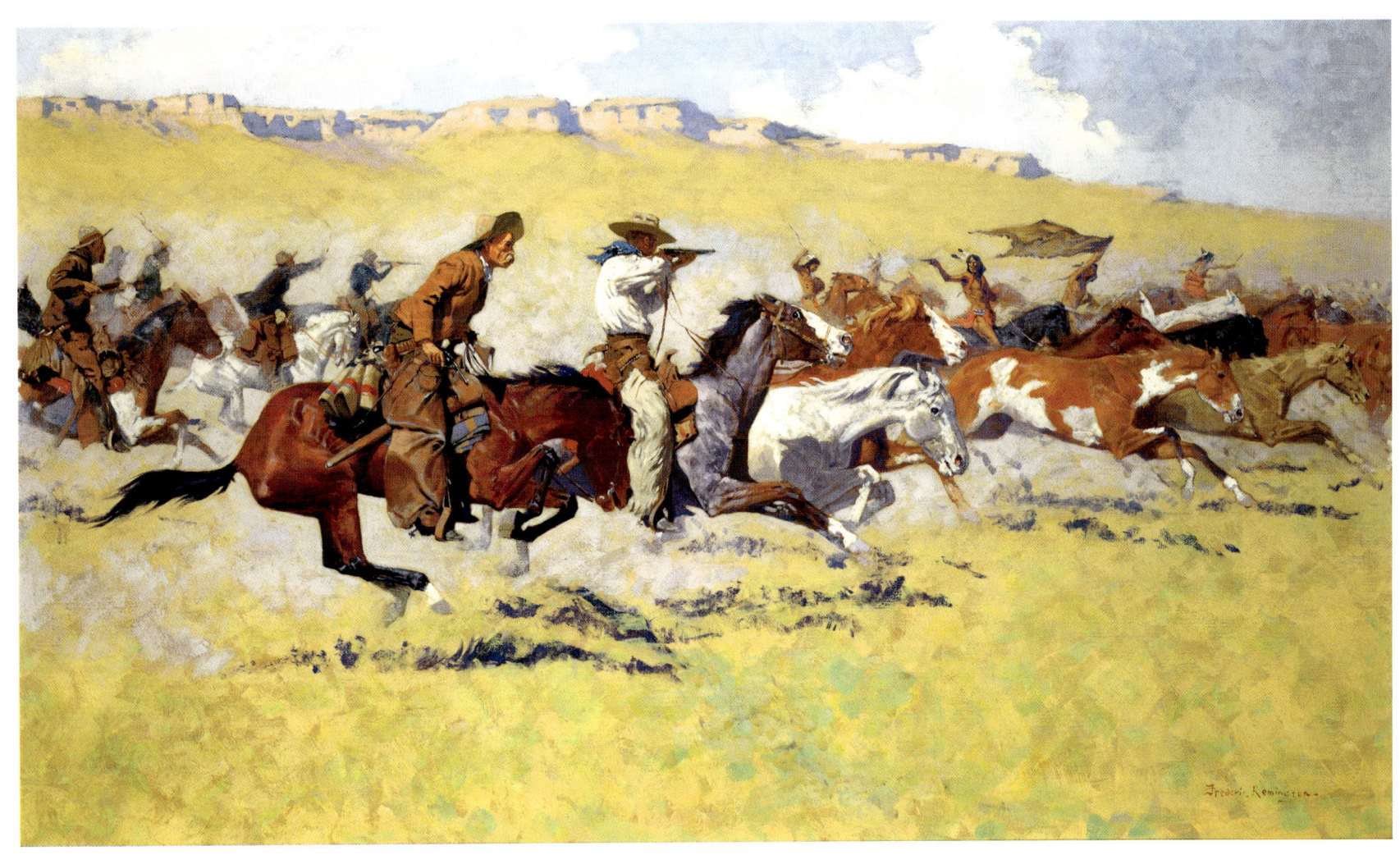

PONY TRACKS IN THE BUFFALO TRAILS
1904
oil on canvas
30 ⅛ x 51 ⅛ inches
signed lr: *Frederic Remington*

PROVENANCE: The artist; [Macbeth Galleries, New York, NY, 1937]; Bartlett Arkell, Canajoharie, NY; gift to Canajoharie Library and Art Gallery, Canajoharie, NY, 1937-54; [Grand Central Art Galleries, New York, NY, 1954]; Amon G. Carter, Fort Worth, TX, 1954; Amon Carter Museum, Fort Worth, TX; [Gerald Peters Gallery, Santa Fe, New Mexico, 1996]; Private collection, 1997

ILLUSTRATION: *Collier's Weekly* (October 8, 1904), p. 16-17, color halftone

LITERATURE: Harold McCracken, *The Frederic Remington Book* (Garden City, NY: Doubleday & Co., 1966); Peter Hassrick, *Frederic Remington: The Amon Carter & Sid Richardson Collections* (New York: Harry N. Abrams, Inc. 1973), p. 152; James Ballinger, *Frederic Remington* (New York: Harry N. Abrams, Inc. 1989), ill. pp. 116-17; James West Davidon & Mark H. Lytle, *The United States, A History of the Repulic* (Englewood Cliffs, NJ: Prentice Hall 1990); Rick Stewart, *Frederic Remington, Masterpieces from the Amon Carter Museum*, Amon Carter Museum, Fort Worth, TX (1992), p. 46-47; Peter Hassrick and Melissa Webster, *Frederic Remington: A Catalogue Raisonné*, Buffalo Bill Historical Center, Cody, WY (1996), p. 793, pl. 2732

EXHIBITIONS: New York Historical Society, *Frederic Remington: Artist of the Old West*, New York, NY (Nov. 1, 1947-Jan.1, 1948); Memorial Student Center, Texas A & M University (traveling exhibition), *Remington/Russell Exhibition*, College Station, TX (Nov. 12-Dec. 10, 1962), Midland Public Library, Midland TX (April 1-30, 1963), Art Museum of South Texas, Corpus Christi, TX (Sept. 5 - Oct.2, 1963); Birmingham Museum of Art, *The Opening of the West*, Birmingham, AL (Oct. 2-Dec. 1, 1963); Mary Baldwin College, *Remington/Russell Exhibition* (traveling exhibition), Staunton, VA (May 24-June 8, 1964), University of Utah, Salt Lake City, UT (Nov.1-30, 1964), Portland Art Museum, Portland, OR (Jan. 15-Feb.15, 1965), Stanford, California Art Gallery and Museum (March 29-April 18, 1965); Reynolda House, Winston-Salem, OH (1966); Amon Carter Museum, Fort Worth, TX (1973); Amon Carter Museum, Fort Worth, TX (1994)

In order to satisfy his contract with *Collier's* for at least one major painting every month, Remington found renewed inspiration in old themes. Although *Pony Tracks in the Buffalo Trails* seems to have been loosely based on the artist's sojourn in the Sioux country fourteen years earlier, his new style of painting evoked a different emotional response. This painting exhibits a reduced value range, softer lines, and a greater sense of atmosphere when compared to a painting like *Missing* completed only five years prior. *Pony Tracks in the Buffalo Trails* was also published as a print by P.F. Collier and Son in *A Portfolio of Drawings* By Frederic Remington.

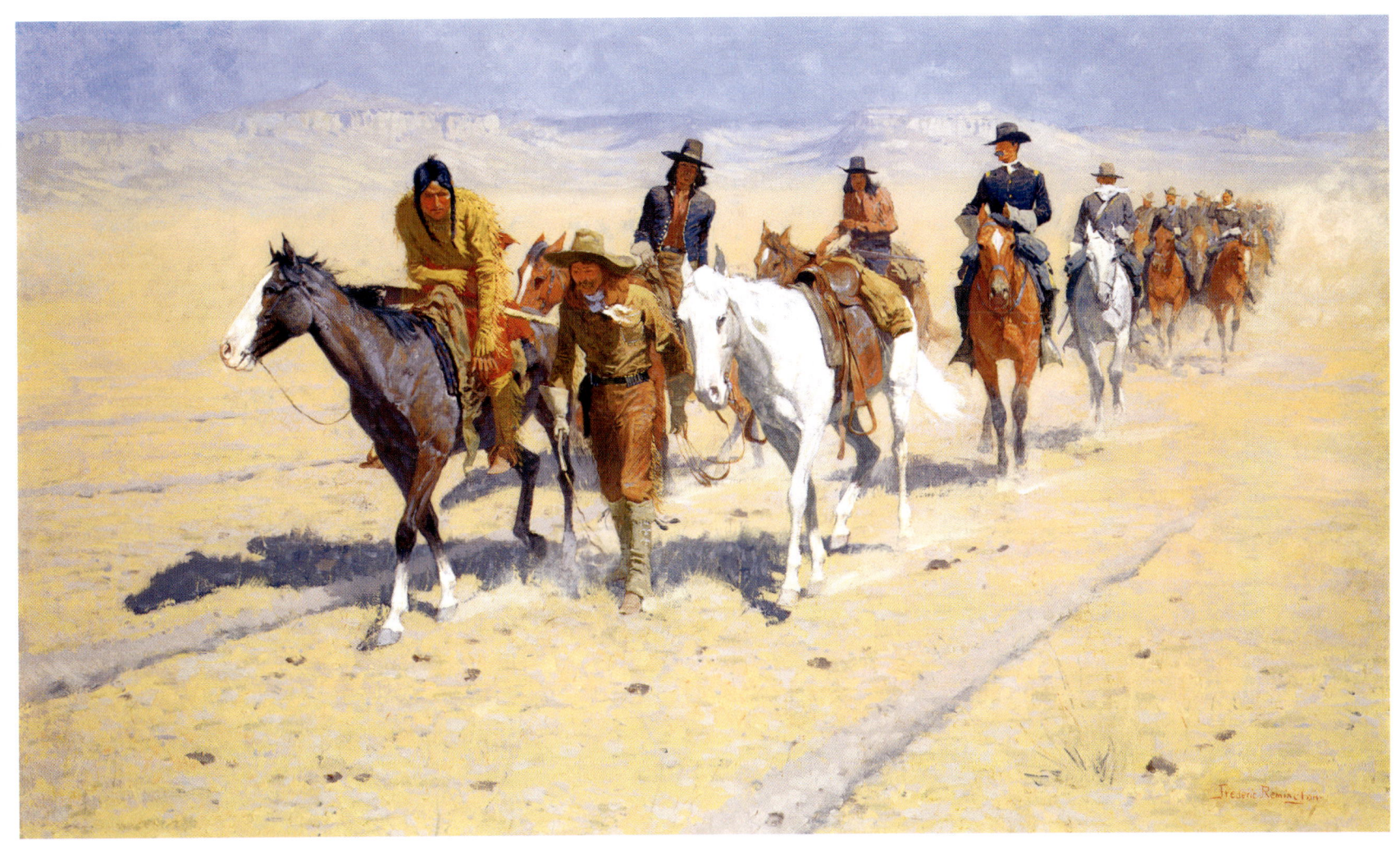

COLD MORNING ON THE RANGE
c. 1904
oil on canvas
27 x 40 inches
signed lr: *Frederic Remington-*

PROVENANCE: The artist; Harry Folsom (Yale friend), New York, NY; Charlotte Saunders (Folsom's daughter), New York, NY; Rudolf G. Wunderlich, New York, NY; [Gerald Peters Gallery, Santa Fe, NM]; USF & G, Baltimore, MD; The Anschutz Collection, Denver, CO

LITERATURE: *New York Times* (March 15, 1904), p. 8; "Rediscovering America," *Time Magazine* (July 7, 1980), p. 23; James Ballinger, *Frederic Remington* (New York: Harry N. Abrams, Inc., 1989), ill. p. 108, 109, 112; *Antiques* (May 1991), ill. p. 854; *Frederic Remington*, Gerald Peters Gallery in conjunction with Mongerson-Wunderlich, Santa Fe, NM (1991), ill. p. 17 and detail on cover; Peter Hassrick and Melissa Webster, *Frederic Remington: A Catalogue Raisonné*, Buffalo Bill Historical Center, Cody, WY (1996), ill. p. 772, pl. 2713

EXHIBITIONS: Noé Art Galleries, *Special Exhibition of Recent Paintings by Frederic Remington*, New York (1904); Gerald Peters Gallery, *Frederic Remington*, Santa Fe, NM (1991); Mongerson-Wunderlich, Chicago, IL (1991)

During the mid-1890's, one of Frederic Remington's favorite subjects was the bucking horse, representing both a test of man's strength and a symbol of man's control over the frontier. Remington explored this theme extensively in his writings and paintings, adapting it to a new aesthetic or style of painting. *Cold Morning on the Range* is close in subject and composition to *Turn Him Loose, Bill* (Baigell, *The Western Art of Frederic Remington*, pl. 10). The picture is centered around the focal image of the horse and rider, with the landscape providing a simple and minimal background.

Photograph courtesy of the Anschutz Collection, Denver, CO

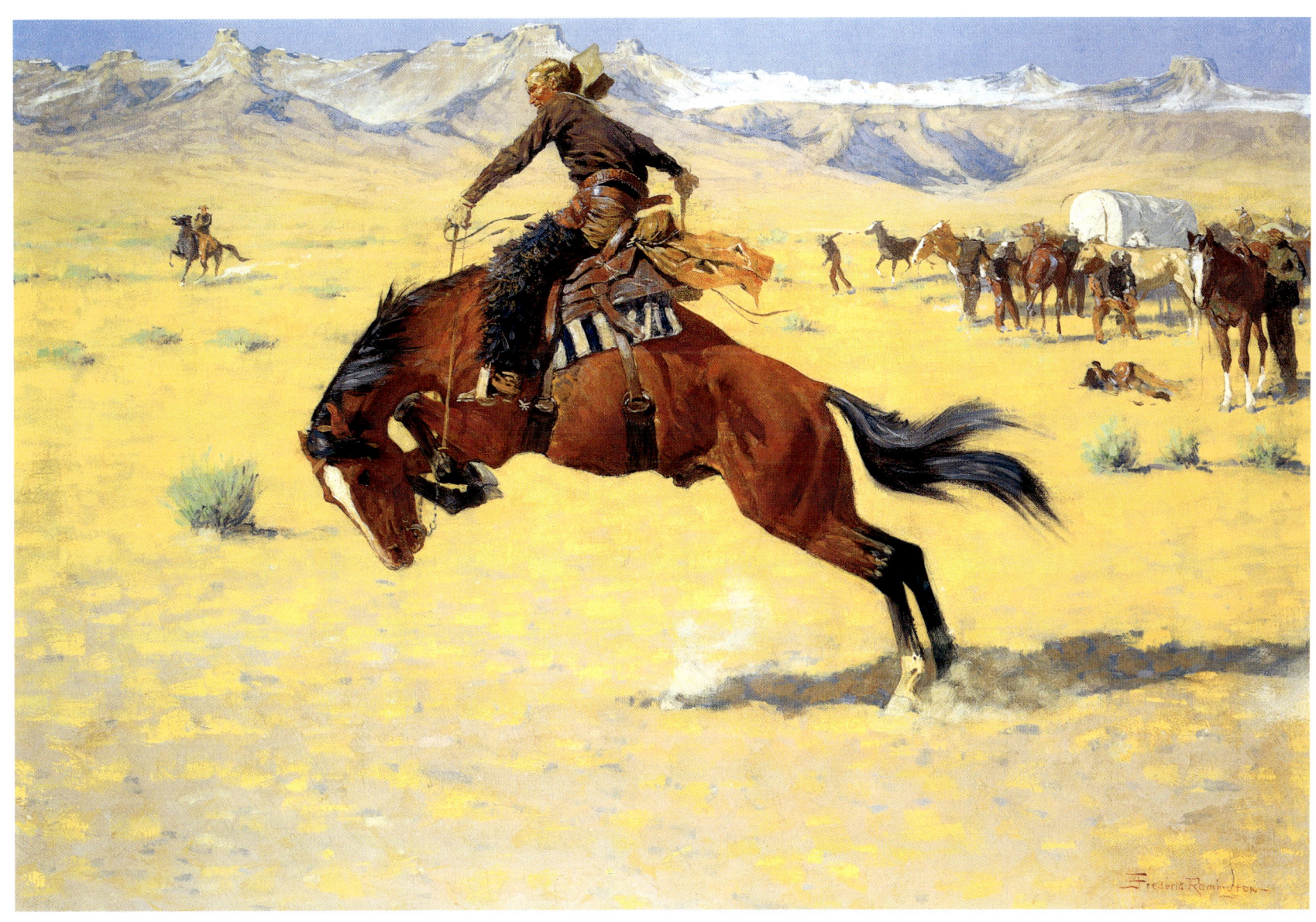

43

THE APACHES!
1904
oil on canvas
25 x 30 inches
signed ll: *Frederic Remington/copyrighted 1904.*

PROVENANCE: The artist; Estate of Henry Smith, New York, NY; [The American Art Association, New York, NY]; E.L. King, Michigan; Irwin Jacobs, Minneapolis, MN; [James Maroney, Inc., New York, NY]; Richard Manoogian, Grosse Pointe, MI; [Gerald Peters Gallery, Santa Fe, NM]; Private collection

LITERATURE: Special Exhibition of Recent Paintings by Frederick [sic] *Remington*, Noé Art Galleries, New York, NY (1905), no. 4; *Antiques Magazine* (May 1980), ill. p. 989; Peter Hassrick, *Frederic Remington: The Late Years*, Denver Art Museum, Denver, CO (1981), ill. p. 20, detail p. 17; Peter Hassrick and Melissa Webster, *Frederic Remington: A Catalogue Raisonné*, Buffalo Bill Historical Center, Cody, WY (1996), p. 771, pl. 2711

EXHIBITIONS: *Special Exhibition of Recent Paintings by Frederick* [sic] *Remington*, Noé Art Galleries, New York, NY (1905); American Art Gallery, New York, NY (1924); *Frederic Remington: The Late Years*, Denver Art Museum, Denver, CO (1981); Dixon Gallery and Gardens, Memphis, TN (1991); Lakeview Museum, Peoria, IL (1992); National Cowboy Hall of Fame, Oklahoma City, OK (1992); Phoenix Art Museum, Phoenix, AZ (1993); Montgomery Museum of Fine Art (1993); Hunter Museum of Art (1993); Telfair Academy of Art (1993); Norton Gallery and School of Art (1993); Dallas Museum of Art, Dallas, TX (1994); Columbus Museum of Art, Columbus, OH (1994); Arkansas Art Center (1994)

Gradually but emphatically, Remington's images began to forsake detailed, firsthand observation in favor of a more impressionistic, personal style reflective of his nostalgia for the West of the past. Closely observed fact gave way to generalization, and Remington's vision expanded to encompass a wide overview, rather than a specific recounting of individual events. This move from the finite to the generic was best marked by Remington's acceptance of a contract with *Collier's* magazine in 1903. The lucrative deal offered $1,000 for each painting that Remington submitted for reproduction—but also gave the artist total freedom to select his own subjects. He agreed to provide *Collier's* with a minimum of twelve paintings per year.

In *The Apaches!* Remington utilized value and large planes of color to convey broader pictorial concepts than had been possible in his earlier, more literal illustrative style. The composition focuses our attention to the central figures, the shadows, and the architectural elements in the background.

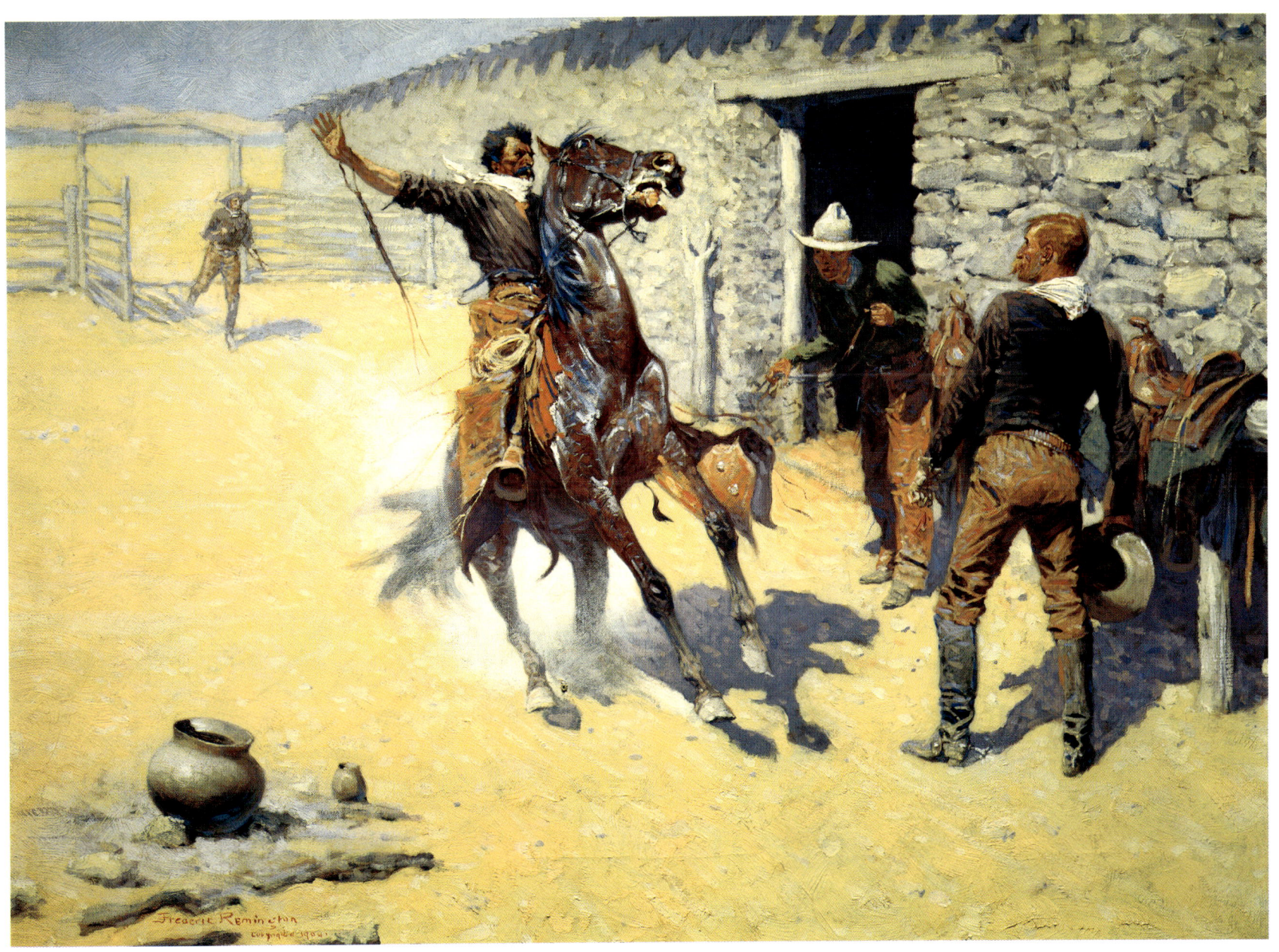

THE BELATED TRAVELER

1905-06

oil on canvas

20 x 26 inches

signed lr: *Frederic Remington*

      ll: *copyright 1906 by Frederic Remington*

PROVENANCE: The artist; [Noé Art Gallery, New York, NY]; Lee French; Barbara Davidson, Apple Valley, CA; [J.N. Bartfield Galleries, New York, NY]; Private collection

LITERATURE: *A Catalogue of the Frederic Remington Art Memorial Collection*, Remington Memorial Art Museum, Ogdensburg, NY (1954), p. 29; Peter Hassrick & Melissa Webster *Frederic Remington, A Catalogue Raisonné*, Buffalo Bill Historical Center, Cody, WY (1996), p. 795, pl. 2742

The Belated Traveler is a quiet, mysterious scene that marks a definite stride toward tonalist esthetics and Remington's mastery of night effects. The elegiac snow scene depicts a solitary traveler seeking refuge from the wintry night. The ample, shadowy figure strongly resembles Remington, who often included himself in paintings of this period.

This painting is one of approximately fifteen that Remington copyrighted in January of 1906. Although Remington's contract with *Collier's Weekly* to produce monthly illustrations did not expire until January 1909, he apparently created the artworks in this group as fine art rather than as illustrations: He exhibited them, but did not submit them to the magazine for reproduction.

Photograph courtesy of J.N. Bartfield Galleries, New York, NY

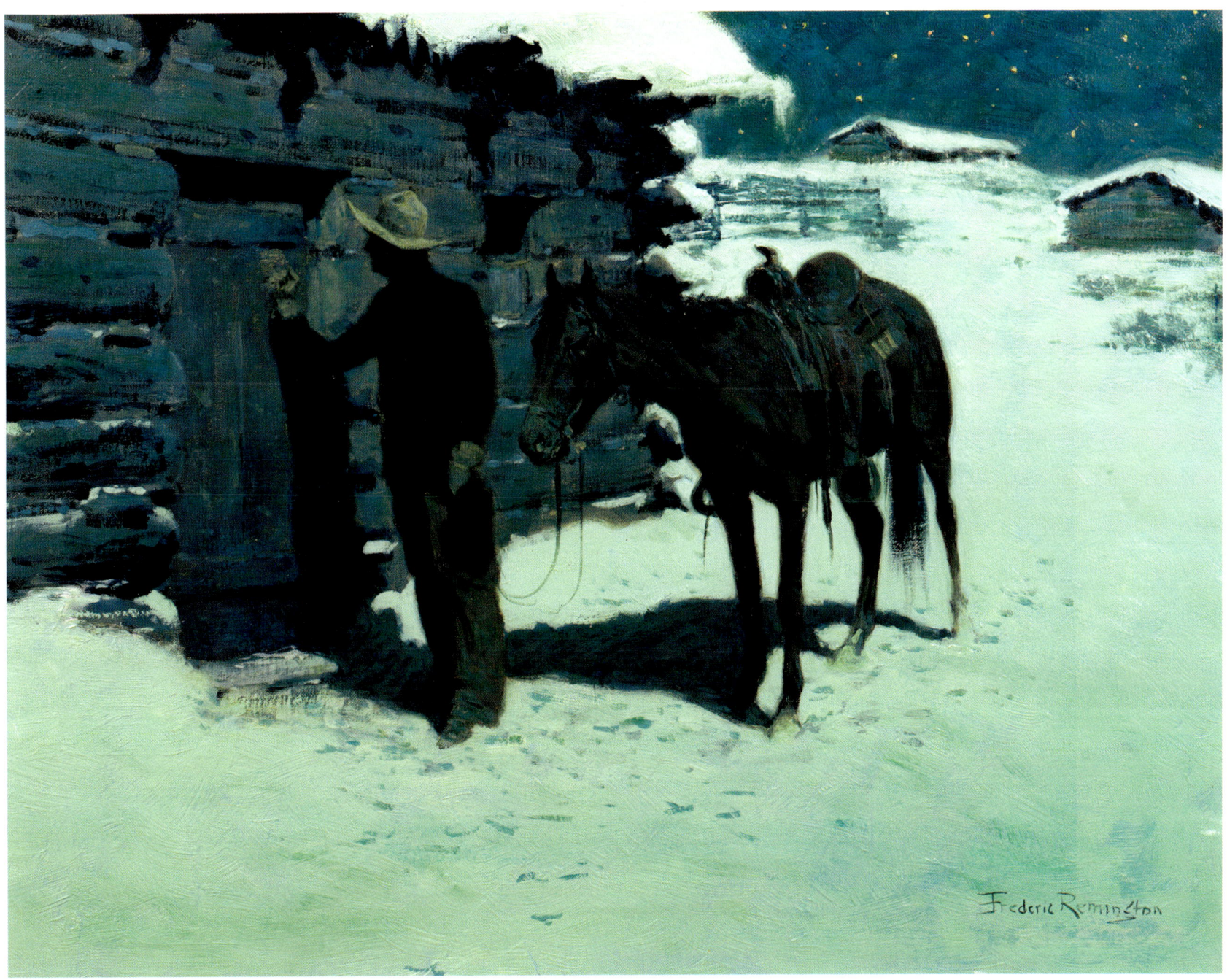

AGAINST THE SUNSET
1906
oil on canvas
22 x 30 inches
signed lr: *Frederic Remington*

PROVENANCE: The artist; [M. Knoedler & Co., New York, NY]; Goelet Gallatin, New York, NY; [M. Knoedler & Co., New York, NY, 1909]; Mr. Reinhart, Milwaukee, WI, 1910; [Kennedy Galleries Inc., New York, NY]; Gulf States Paper Company, Tuscaloosa, AL; [James Graham & Sons, New York, NY]; Private collection; [Peterson Gallery, Beverly Hills, CA]; [Gerald Peters Gallery, Santa Fe, NM]; Private collection

LITERATURE: Matthew Baigell, *The Western Art of Frederic Remington* (New York: Ballentine Books, 1976), pl. 26; Denver Art Museum, *Frederic Remington: The Late Years* (1981), ill. p. 56; Palm Springs Desert Museum, *The West as Art* (1982), pl. 120; Harold and Peggy Samuels, *Frederic Remington: A Biography* (Garden City, NY: Doubleday & Co., Inc., 1982), p. 377-79; Lonn Taylor and Ingrid Maar, *The American Cowboy*, American Folklife Center (Washington, D.C., 1983), ill. p. 101; "Cowboy's and Indians: The New Game for Collectors and Galleries," *Signature Magazine* (September 1983), ill. p. 54; *Antiques* (January 1984), ill. p. 55; *Antiques* (July 1984), ill. p. 57; *Antiques* (January 1985), ill. p. 121; *Antiques* (August 1986), ill. p. 231; James K. Ballinger, *Frederic Remington* (New York: Harry N. Abrams, Inc., 1989), 127-28, ill. p. 129; *Frederic Remington*, Gerald Peters Gallery in association with Mongerson-Wunderlich, Santa Fe, NM (1991), pp. 66-67; Peter Hassrick and Melissa Webster, *Frederic Remington: A Catalogue Raisonné*, Buffalo Bill Historical Center, Cody, WY (1996), p. 807, pl. 2788

EXHIBITIONS: M. Knoedler & Co., *Paintings by Frederic Remington*, New York, NY (1906); The Denver Art Museum, *Frederic Remington: The Late Years*, Denver, CO (1981); Palm Springs Desert Museum, *The West as Art*, Palm Springs, CA (1982); The Library of Congress, *The American Cowboy*, Washington, D.C. (1983)

Although Remington was widely known for his action paintings, his later works are among the most compelling and personal statements within his oeuvre. Details became secondary to mood as he found freedom in color and simplification of form. *Against the Sunset* is an exercise in color harmonies and perceptual phenomenon. Remington's notations and diaries from the period reveal an interest in exploring the interaction of colors to depict images which transcend the simple facts of observed reality. The horizontal format and brilliant backlighting provide a dramatic stage for the heroic proportions of the lone cowboy. The horse and rider no longer represent specific characters in a historical narrative, but rather iconic symbols of the waning culture of the frontier.

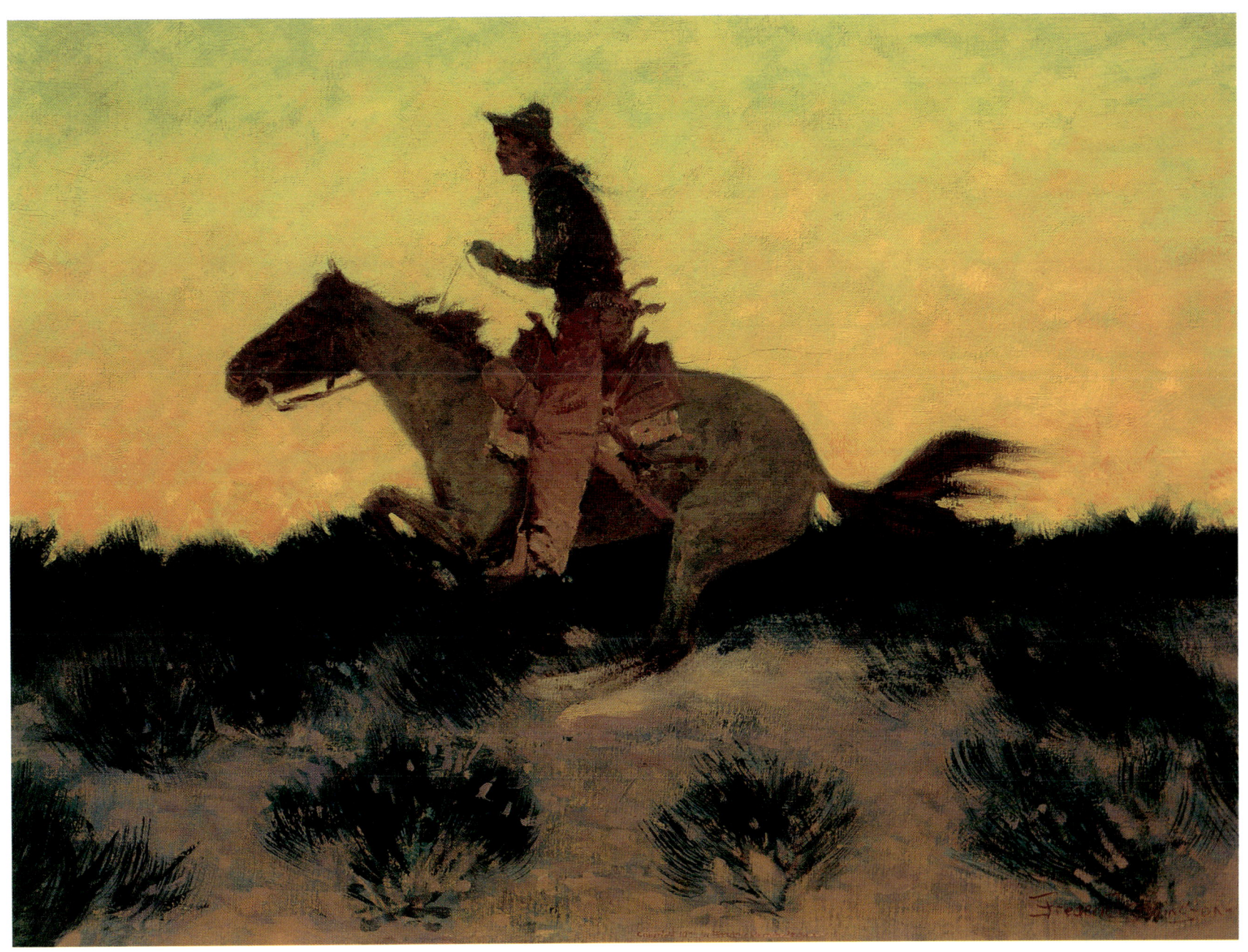

TAINT IN THE WIND
1906
oil on canvas
27 ⅛ x 40 inches
signed lr: *Frederic Remington*
signed lc: *© 1906 by Frederic Remington*

PROVENANCE: The artist; Grant B. Schley, New York, NY; Robert Dudley Winthrop, Old Westbury, Long Island, NY; Beekman Winthrop, Old Westbury, Long Island, NY; Robert Winthrop, New York, NY; [Scott & Fowles, New York, NY]; [Newhouse Galleries, New York, NY]; Sid Richardson Collection of Western Art, Fort Worth, TX

LITERATURE: *American Art News* (December 1906); *New York Times* (December 23, 1906); *A Catalogue of the Frederic Remington Memorial Collection*, Remington Art Memorial, Ogdensburg, NY (1954), p. 29; Peter Hassrick, *Frederic Remington: Painting, Drawings and Sculpture in the Amon Carter and Sid W. Richardson Foundation Collections* (New York: Harry N. Abrams, Inc., 1973), p. 159; Peter Hassrick, "Remington in the Southwest," *Southwestern Historical Quarterly*, vol. 76, no.3 (January 1973), p. 46; Brian Dippie, *Remington and Russell* (Austin, TX: Univ. of Texas Press, 1982), p. 44; Harold and Peggy Samuels, *Frederic Remington: A Biography* (Garden City, NY: Doubleday & Co., Inc., 1982), p. 377-79; James Ballinger, *Frederic Remington* (New York: Harry N. Abrams, Inc., 1989), p. 127, 132-33; Peter Hassrick and Melissa Webster, *Frederic Remington: A Catalogue Raisonné*, Buffalo Bill Historical Center, Cody, WY (1996), p. 809, pl. 2801

EXHIBITIONS: M. Knoedler & Co., Inc., New York, NY (1906); Union League, New York, NY (1908); Amon Carter Museum, Fort Worth, TX (1973); Eastern Europe (1973); Poland (1974); Takashimaya, Tokyo (1976); Takashimaya, Osaka (1976); Grand Rapids Art Museum, MI (1977); Amon Carter, Fort Worth, TX (1978); Amarillo Art Center, Amarillo, TX (1979); Amon Carter, Fort Worth, TX (1979); Wichita Falls Museum, Wichita, TX (1979); New Orleans, LA (1979); Amon Carter Museum, Fort Worth, TX (1980)

One of the recurring themes in Remington's art is that of the moment when a quiet stagecoach ride is abruptly disturbed by some unseen foe. The instant affords Remington the opportunity to exercise his forte: the portrayal of horses in various states of frenzy. James Ballinger traces the painter's progress by comparing *Taint in the Wind* with its earlier precedent *Old Stage Coach of the Plains*, 1901. The utilization of white sand and a white horse in the new picture reflects a compositional method Remington learned from Charles Rollo Peters, a master at employing reflective light sources in his nocturnal scenes. By contrast, *Old Stage Coach of the Plains* employs no reflective light source, forcing Remington to overlight the picture, and, by putting the moon behind the subject, there is no detail toward the viewer, resulting in black blocks of paint.

Photograph courtesy Sid Richardson Collection of Western Art, Fort Worth, TX

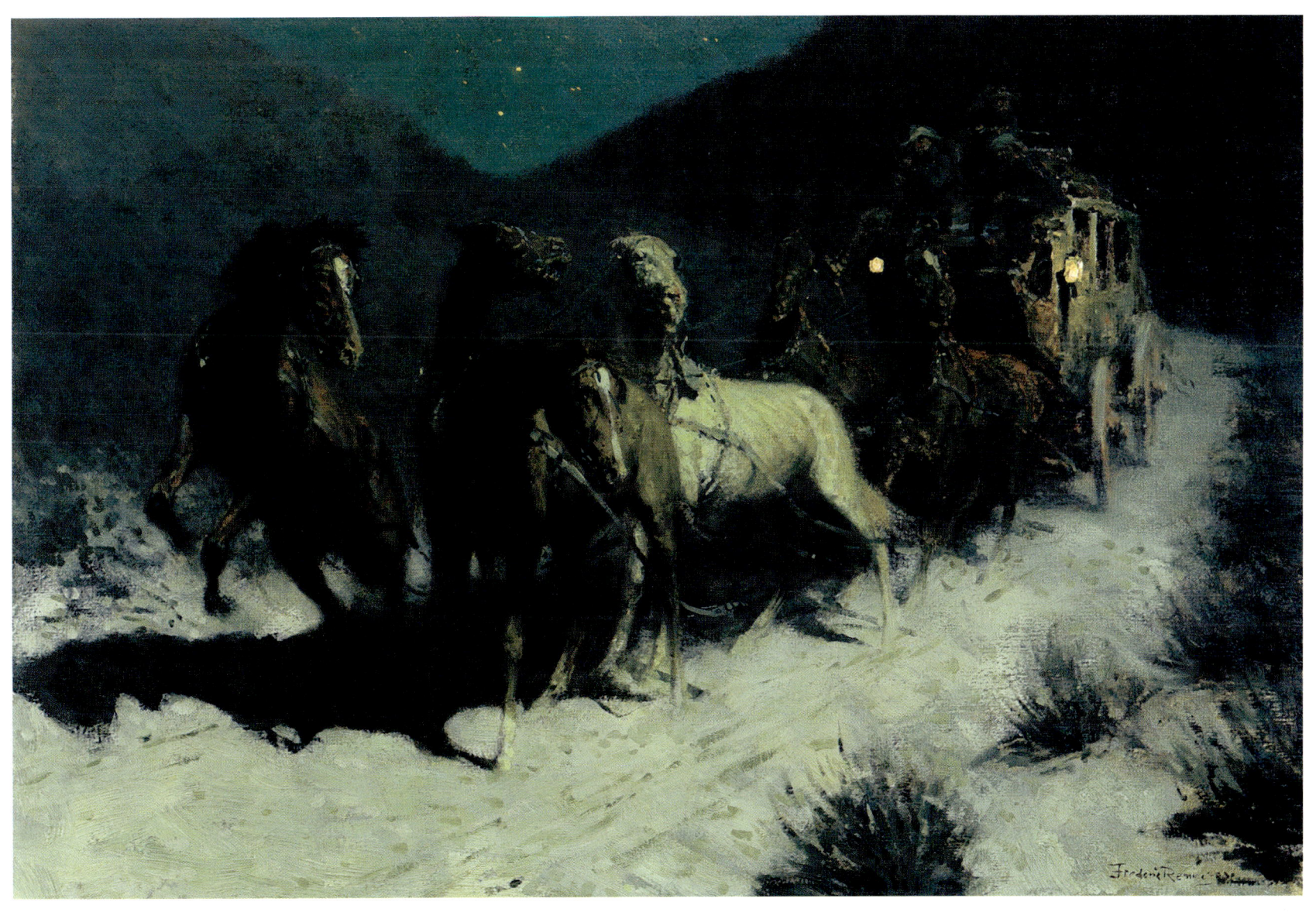

51

WAITING IN THE MOONLIGHT

1907

oil on canvas

27 x 30 inches

unsigned

PROVENANCE: Artist's estate; Eva Remington's estate; Frederic Remington Art Museum, Ogdensburg, NY

LITERATURE: Remington Art Museum, *The Remington Art Museum: 50th Anniversary*, Ogdensburg, NY: Archie Lee Stobie & Mildred E. Dillenbeck (1973), n.p., ill.; James Ballinger, *Frederic Remington's Southwest*, Phoenix Art Museum, Phoenix, AZ (1992), p. 86, ill. p. 88; Peter Hassrick & Melissa Webster, *Frederic Remington: A Catalogue Raisonné*, Buffalo Bill Historical Center, Cody, WY (1996), p. 816, pl. 2833

In *Waiting in Moonlight*, Remington skillfully differentiates between forms within a narrow tonal spectrum. The focal point is a white rectangular form—the lower skirt of the woman's dress, which brilliantly reflects the moon's light. The skirt is not completely white; it is dappled with a pale green that permeates the entire composition. The figures, veiled in an atmospheric cloak of grey-green as revealed in the moon's sheen, are made anonymous by their own shadows and by brush work that purposely obscures detail. (Webster, "The Nocturnes of Frederic Remington," p. 13)

Photograph courtesy Frederic Remington Art Museum, Ogdensburg, NY

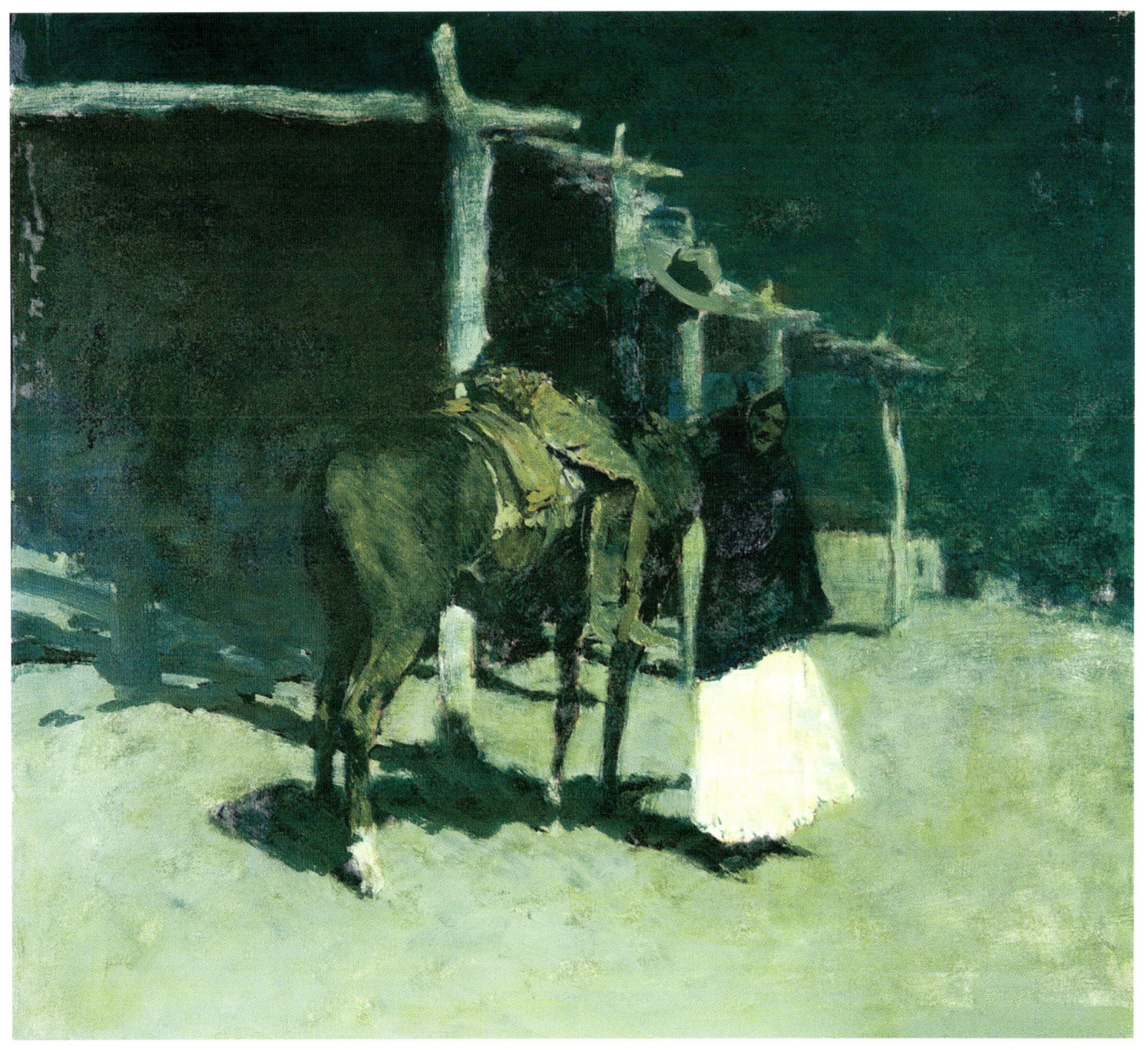

FIRED ON
1907
oil on canvas
27 ⅛ x 40 inches
signed lr: *Frederic Remington-*
       lc: *Copyright 1907 by Frederic Remington-*

PROVENANCE: The artist; [M. Knoedler & Co., New York, NY]; William T. Evans; (gifted to) National Museum of American Art, Smithsonian Institution, Washington, D.C.

LITERATURE: "New Remington Paintings and Etchings by Charles Henry White at the Montross Gallery," *New York Times* (Dec. 5, 1907), p. 8, col. 6; *American Art News* (Dec. 7, 1907); *A Special Exhibition of Recent Paintings by Frederic Remington and Portraits by A. de Ferraris of Vienna*, Reinhardt's Annex Gallery, Chicago, IL (1908); *Second Exhibition of Oil Paintings and Sculpture by American Artists*, The Corcoran Gallery of Art, Washington, D.C. (1908), no. 379; *The Twenty-Second Annual Exhibition of Oil Paintings and Sculpture by American Artists*, The Art Institute of Chicago, Chicago, IL (1909), p. 33, no. 216; *Frederic Remington Centennial Exhibition and Paintings, Drawings, and Sculpture by other Notable Documentary Artists of the Old West and Plains Indian Art*, Buffalo Bill Historical Center, Cody, WY (1961), p. 8; Harold McCracken, *The Frederic Remington Book: A Pictorial History of the West* (Garden City, NY: Doubleday & Co., Inc., 1966), p. 276, ill. p. 163, no. 228; Allen & Marilyn Splete, *Frederic Remington: Selected Letters* (New York: Abbeville Press, Inc., 1988), p. 435, 450; *Frederic Remington: The Masterworks*, The Saint Louis Art Museum in conjunction with the Buffalo Bill Historical Center (New York: Harry N. Abrams, Inc., 1988), p. 37, 149, ill. p. 141, pl. 32; James K. Ballinger, *Frederic Remington's Southwest*, Phoenix Art Museum, Phoenix, AZ (1992), ill. p. 84-85; Peter Hassrick & Melissa Webster, *Frederic Remington, A Catalogue Raisonné*, Buffalo Bill Historical Center, Cody, WY (1996), p. 812, pl. 2817

EXHIBITIONS: M. Knoedler & Co., New York, NY (1907); Reinhardt's Annex Gallery, Chicago, IL (1908); Corcoran Gallery of Art, Washington, D.C. (1909); Art Institute of Chicago, Chicago, IL (1909); Virginia Museum, Richmond, VA (1936); Museum of Modern Art, New York, NY (1943); The White House, Washington, D.C. (1954); Joslyn Museum, Omaha, NB (1954); Virginia Museum, Richmond, VA (1957); National Collection of Art, Washington, D.C. (1959); El Paso Museum of Art, El Paso, TX (1960); Buffalo Bill Historical Center, Cody, WY (1961); National Gallery of Art, Washington, D.C. (1961); Paine Art Center, Oshkosh, WI (1967); IBM Gallery, New York, NY (1967); Clark Art Institute, Williamstown, MA (1967); Minneapolis Institute of Arts, MN (1967); Amon Carter Museum, Ft. Worth, TX (1973); National Academy of Design, New York, NY (1975); Military Academy, West Point, NY (1979); New Orleans Museum of Art, New Orleans, LA (1979-80); Denver Art Museum, Denver, CO (1981); Rockwell Museum, Corning, NY (1984); Buffalo Bill Historical Center, Cody, WY (1988); St. Louis Art Museum, St. Louis, MO (1988); The Metropolitan Museum of Art, New York, NY (1989); Museum of Fine Arts, Houston, TX (1989); Joslyn Museum, Omaha, NB (1992); Memphis Brooks Museum of Art (1992); Phoenix Art Museum, Phoenix, AZ (1992)

In Remington's later years, many exemplary paintings flowed from the wellspring of his creative genius. *Fired On*, in which gunshots have halted six horsemen at the edge of a body of water, stands out as one of the most noteworthy. In December, 1907, critic Royal Cortissoz, described the painting as the artist's consummate masterpiece to date:

"This was the painter's ultimate drama, accomplished through bold brushwork and a subdued tonal key. Most significantly, the study of...moonlight appears to have reacted upon the very grain of his art, so that all along the line, in drawing, in brush work, in color, in atmosphere, he has achieved greater freedom and breadth. He is, too, as spirited as ever, painting in the picture called *Fired On* one of the most truly dramatic compositions he has ever put to his credit..." (*New York Tribune*, December 4, 1907)

Photograph courtesy of National Museum of American Art, Washington, D.C./Art Resource, NY

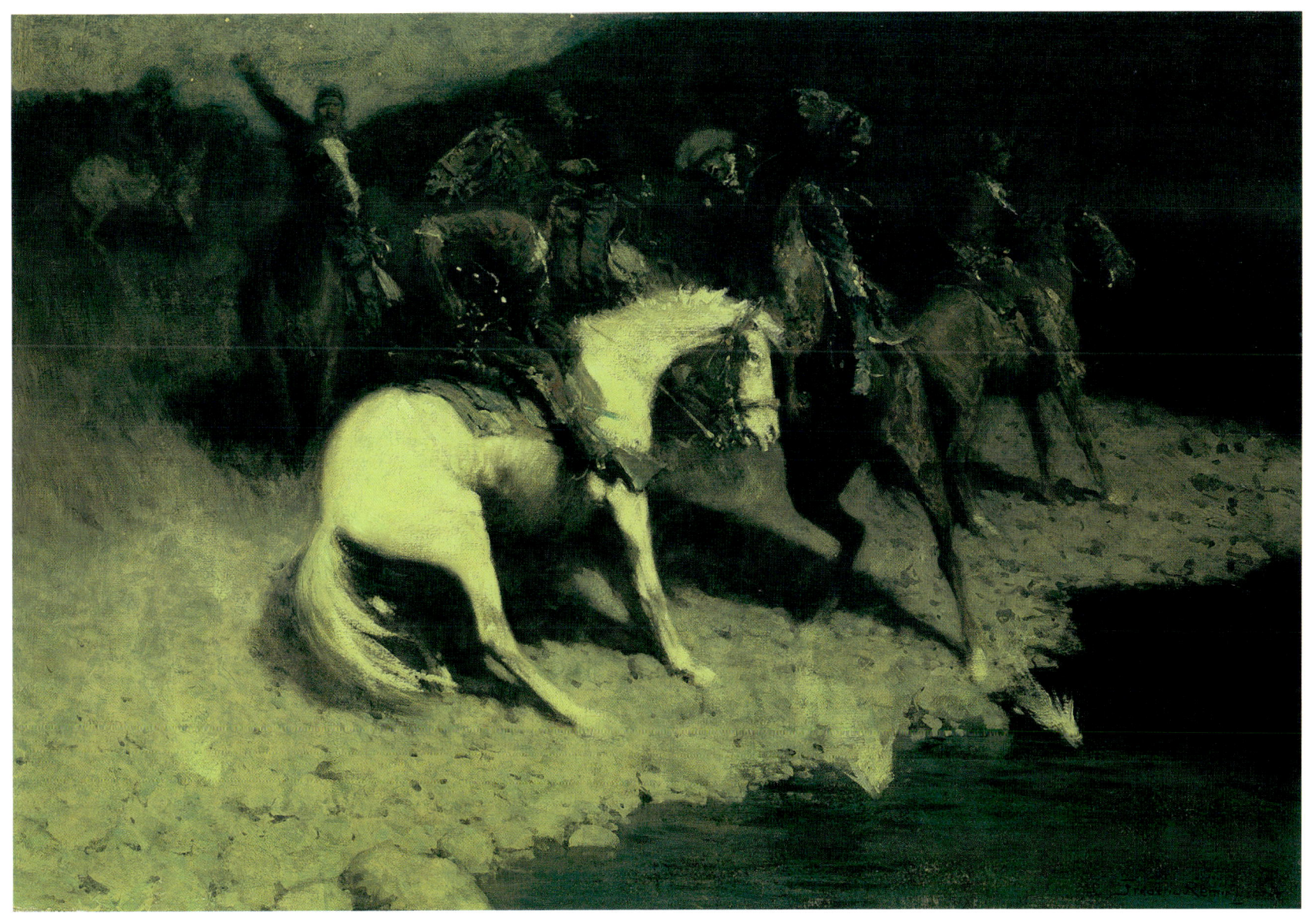

DOWNING THE NIGH LEADER

1907

oil on canvas

30 x 50 inches

signed lr: *Frederic Remingon/1907*

PROVENANCE: The artist; [M. Knoedler & Co., New York, NY, 1907]; Mr. William M. Wood, Boston, MA, 1908; [?]; Mr. Lincoln Ellsworth, Mrs. Lincoln Ellsworth; [J. N.Bartfield Galleries, New York, NY]; Museum of Western Art, Denver, CO; Cindy and Alan F. Horn

ILLUSTRATION: *Collier's Weekly* (April 20, 1907), p. 10, color halftone

LITERATURE: "Notes and Reviews," *The Craftsman*, vol. 13 (October, 1907), p. 119; *Current Literature* (November 1907), ill. p. 525; *New York Press* (December 4, 1907); *American Art News* (December 7, 1907), p. 6, col. 1; Reinhardt's Annex Gallery, *A Special Exhibition of Recent Paintings by Frederic Remington and Portaits by A. de Ferrais of Vienna*, Chicago, IL (1908); Giles Edgerton, "Frederic Remington, Painter and Sculptor: A Pioneer in Distinctive American Art," *The Craftsman*, vol. 15 (March 1909), p. 658-670; Harold McCracken, *Frederic Remington: Artist of the Old West* (Philadelphia: J. B. Lippincott Co., 1947), p. 127, 151; Remington Art Memorial, *A Catalogue of the Frederic Remington Memorial Collection*, Ogdensburg, NY (1954), p. 29, 30, ill. p. 36; Harold McCracken, *The Frederic Remington Book: A Pictorial History of the West* (Garden City, NY: Doubleday & Co., Inc., 1966), p. 278, ill. p. 63; Peter Hassrick, *The Way West: Art of Frontier America* (New York: Harry N. Abrams, Inc., 1977), p. 177, ill. pl. 182; Peggy & Harold Samuels, *Frederic Remington: A Biography* (Garden City, NY: Doubleday & Co., Inc., 1982), p. 386, 392, 396, 433; *Frontier Spirit*, Museum of Western Art, Denver, CO (1983), p. 73-75, no. 51; The Saint Louis Art Museum in conjunction with the Buffalo Bill Historical Center, *Frederic Remington: The Masterworks* (New York: Harry N. Abrams, Inc., 1988), p. 148, ill. p. 140; James Ballinger, *Frederic Remington* (New York: Harry N. Abrams, Inc., 1989), p. 132, 122, ill. p. 132-33; Peggy & Harold Samuels, *Remington: The Complete Prints* (New York: Crown Publishers, Inc., 1990), p. 11, 112, 118, 148, 160, ill. p. 112, fig. 8, pl. 122; Peter Hassrick and Melissa Webster, *Frederic Remington: A Catalogue Raisonné*, Buffalo Bill Historical Center, Cody, WY (1996), p. 817, pl. 2835

EXHIBITIONS: M. Knoedler & Co., New York, NY (1907); Reinhardt's Annex Gallery, Chicago, IL (1908); St. Louis Art Museum, St. Louis, MO (1988); Buffalo Bill Historical Center, Cody, WY (1988); Museum of Fine Arts, Houston, TX (1988); Metropolitan Museum of Art, New York, NY (1989); Autry Museum of Western Heritage, Los Angeles, CA (1997)

By 1906, critics had begun to recognize Remington's diligent experiments with the effects of color and light. It is important to note that his later work evidences a significant commitment to impressionism, and he served the cause as well as a fundamentally figurative artist possibly could. In these late years, he increasingly befriended members of the group of impressionist painters known as The Ten: Robert Reid, Willard Metcalf, Childe Hassam, and his old acquaintnce J. Alden Weir. Their influence is particularly striking in paintings such as *Downing the Nigh Leader*, in which the landscape is generalized, suggesting that color, rather than topographical nuance, was all that mattered to Remington. (Hassrick p. 13)

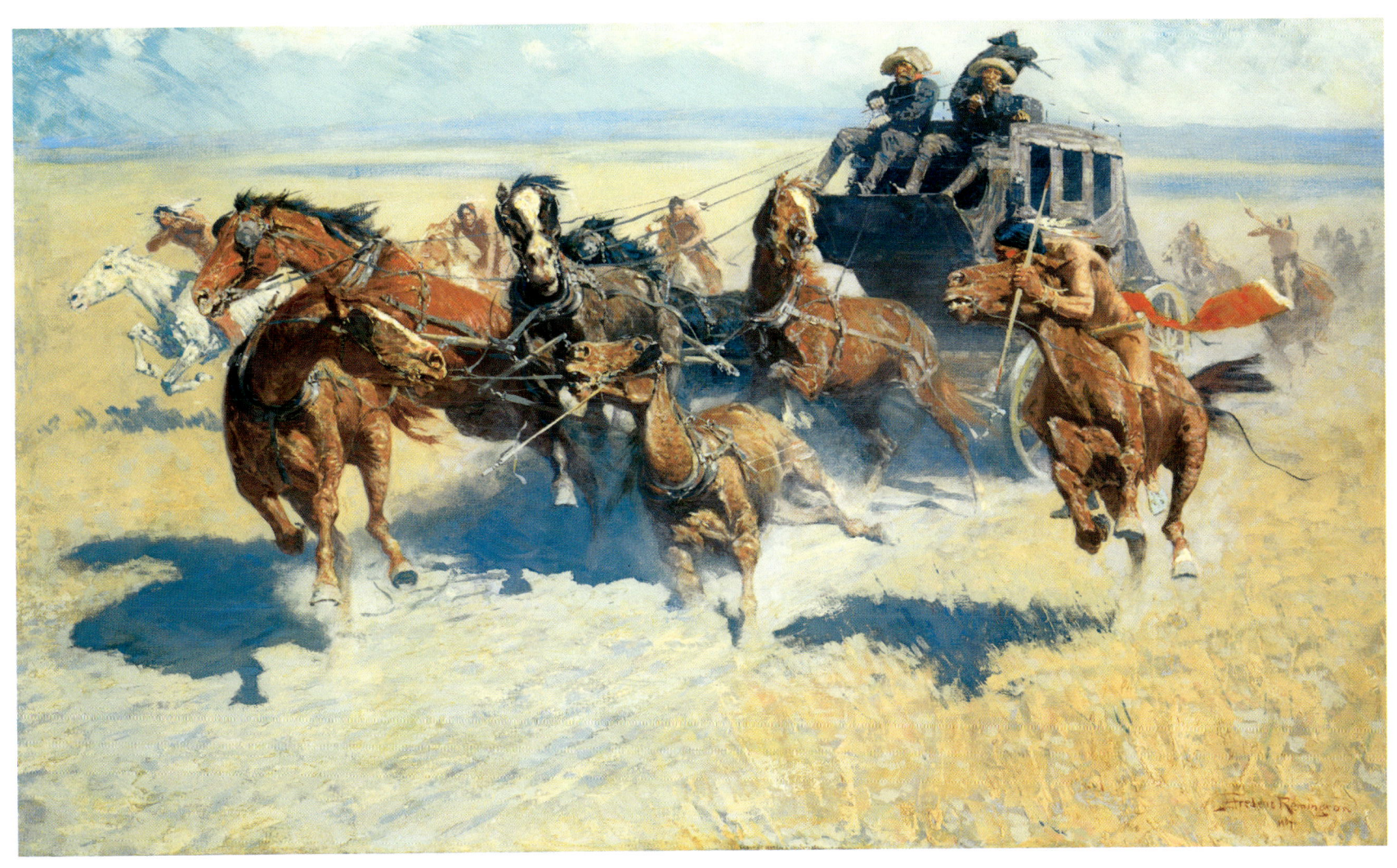

POOL IN THE DESERT
1907-1908
oil on canvas
27 x 40 inches
signed lr: *Frederic Remington-/1907*

ILLUSTRATION: *Collier's Weekly* (October 22, 1910), p.8, color halftone

PROVENANCE: The artist; [M. Knoedler & Co., New York, NY, May 1909]; [?]; [Kennedy Galleries Inc., New York, NY]; Col. A. Rogers, Hyde Park, New York; descended through family to Anne Stradling, Patagonia, AZ; Museum of the Horse, Patagonia, AZ; The Hubbard Museum, Museum of the Horse, Ann Stradling Collection, Ruidoso Downs, NM

LITERATURE: *Craftsman* (January 1909); Harold McCracken, *Frederic Remington, Artist of the Old West*, (Philadelphia: J.B. Lippincott Co., 1947), p. 127; Allen & Marilyn Splete, *Frederic Remington: Selected Letters* (New York: Abbeville Press, Inc., 1988), p. 438; Harold & Peggy Samuels, *Remington: The Complete Prints* (New York: Crown Publishers, Inc., 1990), p. 135, 150, 161, ill. p. 135, pl. 139; Peter Hassrick & Melissa Webster, *Frederic Remington: A Catalogue Raisonné*, Buffalo Bill Historical Center, Cody, WY (1996) p. 814, pl. 2824

EXHIBITIONS: M. Knoedler & Co., New York, NY (1908); Buffalo Bill Historical Center, Cody, WY (Spring 1996); Gene Autry Western Heritage Museum, Los Angeles, CA (Fall 1996); Eiteljorg Museum of American Indian and Western Art, Indianapolis, IN (Winter 1996); National Cowboy Hall of Fame and Western Heritage Center, Oklahoma City, OK (Summer 1997)

The Indian peoples of North America provided enticing subjects for Remington to the very end of his career. For Remington and many of his fellow artists, as well as for the American public, the Indians were symbolic of the rapidly vanishing way of life of the Western Frontier, where nature reigned supreme and independence and self-reliance were primary virtues. In *Pool in the Desert*, Remington realized the full potential of an exotic narrative unfolding beneath the stark clarity of the western light. Though essentially narrative in its impact, *Pool in the Desert* is very much an impressionist work. Remington's method was to build the figures through traditional techniques and then overlay the dappled brushwork, thus creating the subtle and highly evocative atmospheric effects of the final piece. Having reworked an earlier version of *Pool in the Desert* that appeared in *Collier's Weekly*, Remington's March 29, 1908, diary entry reflects his satisfaction with the finished paining: "I have got some color and heat in it and I used Force..."

Photograph courtesy of The Hubbard Museum, Museum of the Horse, Ruidoso, NM

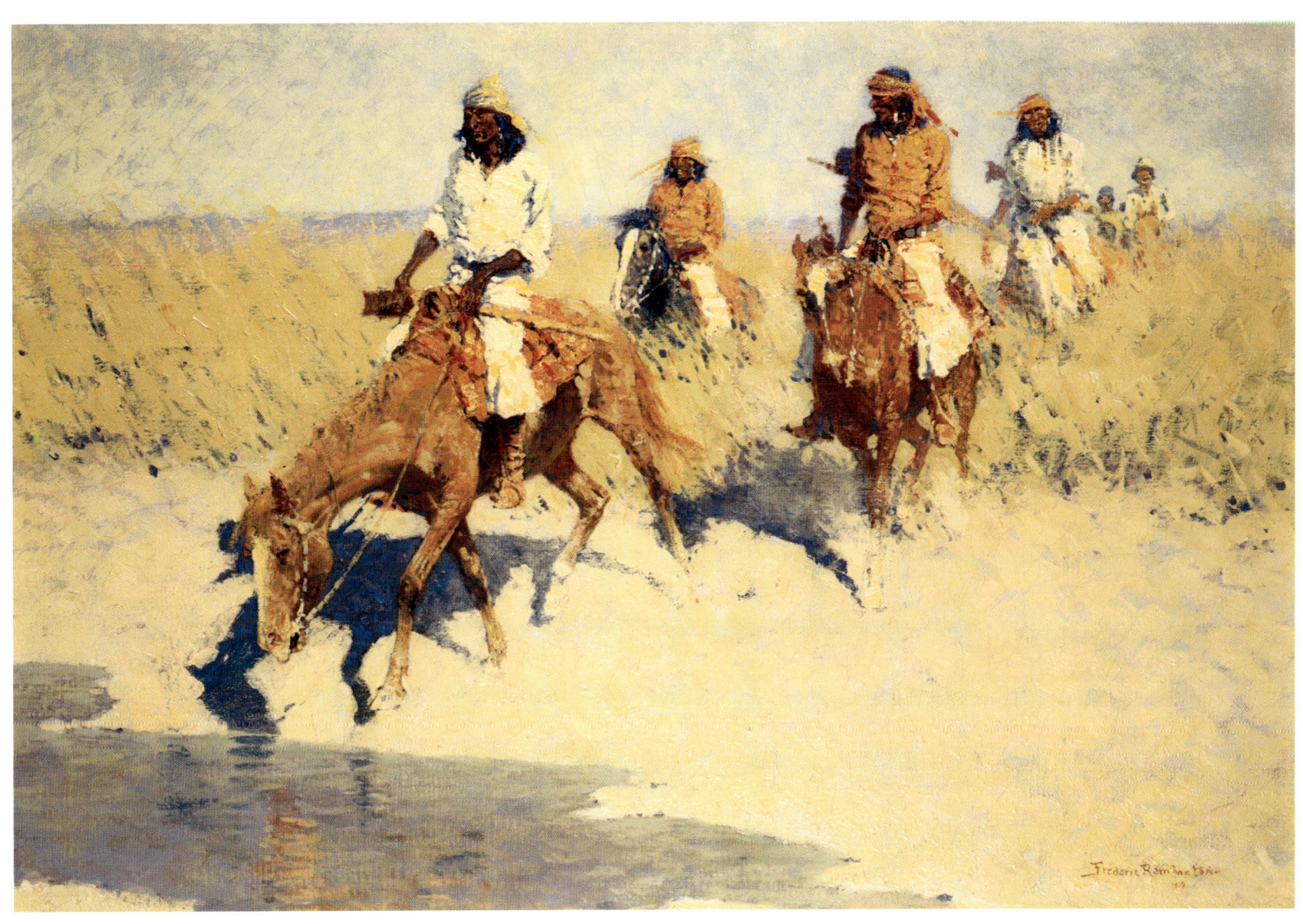

THE GRASS FIRE
1908
oil on canvas
27 ⅛ x 40 ⅛ inches
signed lr: *Frederic Remington/1908-*
      ll: *Copyrighted [illegible] by P.F. Collier*

PROVENANCE: The artist; [M. Knoedler & Co., Inc., New York, NY]; [?]; [David B. Findlay Galleries, New York, NY, 1949]; Amon G. Carter, Fort Worth, TX; Amon Carter Museum, Fort Worth, TX, 1949-present

ILLUSTRATION: *Colllier's Weekly* (April 3, 1909), p. 8, color halftone

LITERATURE: Harold McCracken, *Frederic Remington: Artist of the Old West* (Philadelphia: J.B. Lippincott Co., 1947), p. 127; *A Catalogue of the Frederic Remington Memorial Collection*, Remington Art Memorial, Ogdensburg, NY (1954), p. 30; Harold McCracken, *The Frederic Remington Book: A Pictorial History of the West* (Garden City, NY: Doubleday & Co., Inc., 1966), p. 279, ill. p.98, no.125; Peter Hassrick, *Frederic Remington: Paintings, Drawings, and Sculpture in the Amon Carter and Sid Richardson Foundation Collections* (New York: Harry N. Abrams, Inc., 1973), p.162, ill. p. 163; Peter Hassrick, "Remington in the Southwest," *Southwestern Historical Quarterly*, vol. 76, no. 3 (January, 1973), p. 297-314; Harold & Peggy Samuels, *Remington: The Complete Prints* (New York: Crown Publishers, Inc., 1990), p. 122, 124, 126, 148, 160, ill. p. 126; Peter Hassrick & Melissa Webster, *Frederic Remington: A Catalogue Raisonné*, Buffalo Bill Historical Center, Cody, WY (1996), p. 828, pl. 2888

EXHIBITIONS: M. Knoedler & Co., New York, NY (1908); Roswell Museum, Roswell, NM (1963); McAllen State Bank (1964); University of Utah, Salt Lake City, UT (1964); Portland Art Museum, Portland, OR (1965); Stanford Art Gallery, Stanford, CA (1965); Austin State Capitol, Austin, TX (1969); Tyler Museum of Art, Tyler, TX (1972); Amon Carter Museum, Fort Worth, TX (1973); Minneapolis Institute of Arts, Minneapolis, MN (1973); World's Fair, Spokane, WA (1974); Grunwald Center, Los Angeles, CA (1976); Angelo State University, San Angelo, TX (1977); Western Heritage Museum, Littleton, CO (1978); Worcester Art Museum, Worcester, MA (1979); Gilcrease Institute, Tulsa, OK (1982); Amon Carter Museum, Fort Worth, TX (1994)

In *The Grass Fire*, Remington does not employ a uniform diffusion of light, but rather utilizes it sporadically to great dramatic effect. In baroque fashion, a stream of light cuts diagonally across the painting, throwing the foreground and background into utter darkness, except for the extreme lower left corner, where flickers of flame leap up. The fire illuminates the figures from below, etching the forms sharply in a manner similar to the fashion in which Degas utilized stage lights in his pictures of the ballet. The result is a theatrical and eerie lighting that creates unusual highlights and casts unexpected black shadows, distorting the features of the Indians. (Webster, "The Nocturne Paintings of Frederic Remington," p. 16)

Photograph courtesy of Amon Carter Museum, Fort Worth, TX (1961.228)

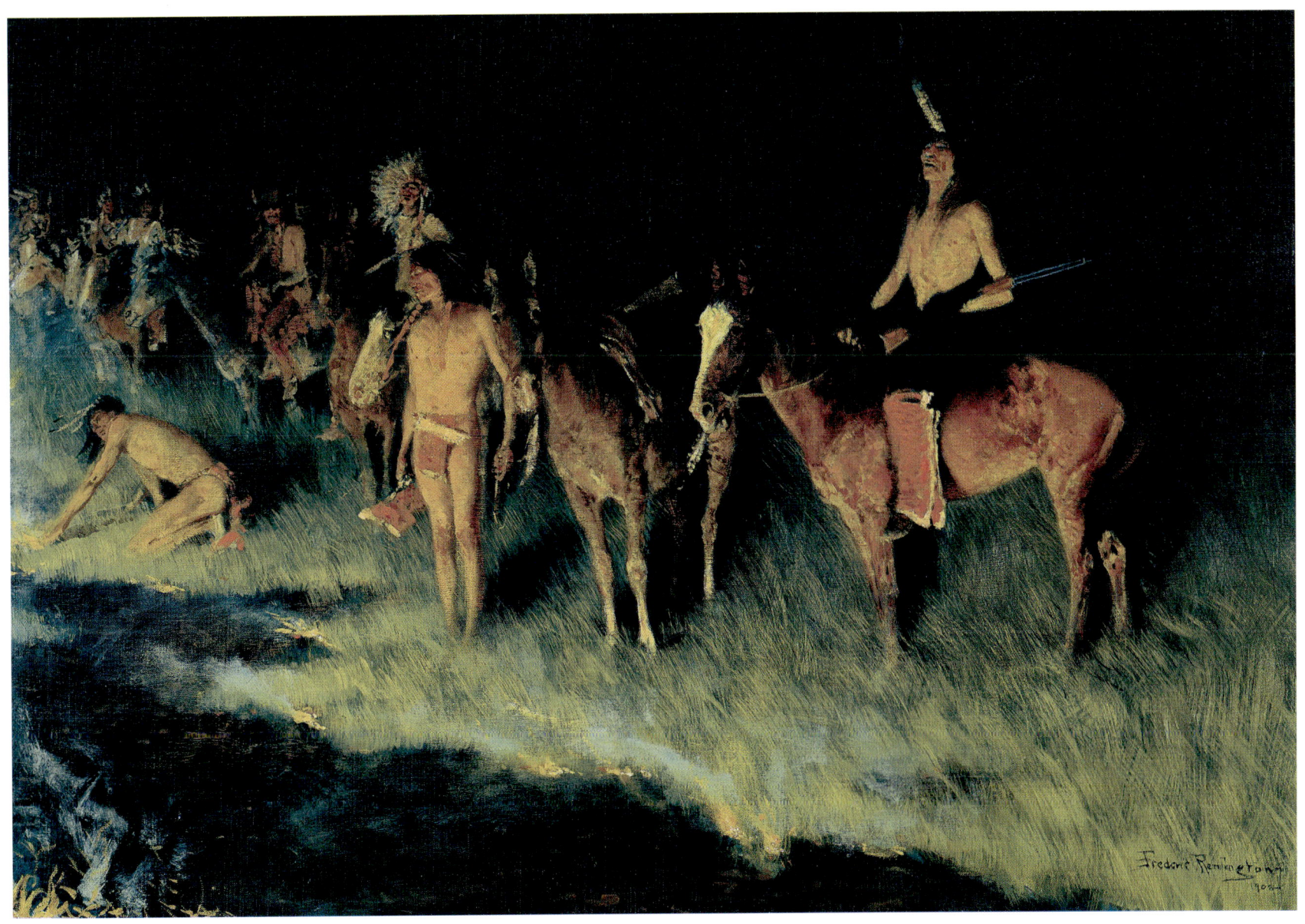

NIGHT HALT OF THE CAVALRY

1908

oil on canvas

27 x 40 inches

signed lr: *Frederic Remington/'08*

PROVENANCE: Artist's Estate [?]; [Rosenstock Arts, Denver, CO, 1987]; Museum of Western Art, Denver, CO; [Gerald Peters Gallery, Santa Fe, NM]; Private collection

LITERATURE: *New York Herald* (November 30, 1908); *New York Times* (December 2, 1908), p.8; *American Art News* (December 5, 1908), p. 6; "Gallery Notes. Remington Paintings on View-Exhibit at Corcoran Gallery." *The Craftsman*, vol. 15 (January, 1909), p. 501-502; Harold McCracken, *The Frederic Remington Book: A Pictorial History of the West* (Garden City, NY: Doubleday and Co. Inc., 1966), pl. 200; Harold & Peggy Samuels, *Frederic Remington: A Biography* (Garden City, NY: Doubleday & Co., Inc., 1982), p. 414; *Frontier Spirit*, Museum of Western Art, Denver, CO (1983), p. 78-80, no. 53; Allen & Marilyn Splete, *Frederic Remington: Selected Letters* (New York: Abbeville Press, Inc., 1988), p. 428; *Frederic Remington: The Masterworks*, Saint Louis Art Museum in conjunction with the Buffalo Bill Historical Center (New York: Harry N. Abrams, 1988), p. 36, 53, pl. 37; *Frederic Remington*, Gerald Peters Gallery in association with Mongerson-Wunderlich, Santa Fe, NM (1991), p. 114-115; Alexander Nemerov, *Frederic Remington and Turn-of-the-Century America* (New Haven, CT: Yale University Press, 1995), pp. 156-158; Peter Hassrick and Melissa Webster, *Frederic Remington: A Catalogue Raisonné* Buffalo Bill Historical Center, Cody, WY (1996), p. 823, pl. 2862

EXHIBITIONS: *Paintings by Frederic Remington on Exhibition at the Galleries of M. Knoedler & Co.*, New York, NY (1908); The Denver Art Museum, Denver, CO (1981); *Frederic Remington: The Masterworks*, St. Louis Art Museum, St. Louis, MO (traveling exhibition 1988-89); Buffalo Bill Historical Center, Cody, WY (1988); Museum of Fine Arts, Houston, TX (1988); The Metropolitan Museum of Art, New York (1989); *Frederic Remington*, Gerald Peters Gallery, Santa Fe, NM; (traveling exhibition) Mongerson Wunderlich Gallery, Chicago, IL

Remington's nighttime scenes, with their mysterious figures that seem to dissolve even as they emerge from the atmospheric haze, evoke impressions of a romantic, vanished world. It is as though the brilliant illumination in Reminton's moonlight exists only to proclaim its fleetingness— as though the figures are brought into view only to portend their fading. *Night Halt of the Cavalry* presents a perfect example of such a scene. Like many of Remington's late paintings, *Night Halt* accentuates the cavalrymen's states of mind rather than their actions. Stillness pervades the scene, encompassing both the soldiers and their horses. The painting represents the dramatic transformation from Remington's early interest in cavalry charges and last stands to his late emphasis on quiescence. (Nemerov p. 156-157)

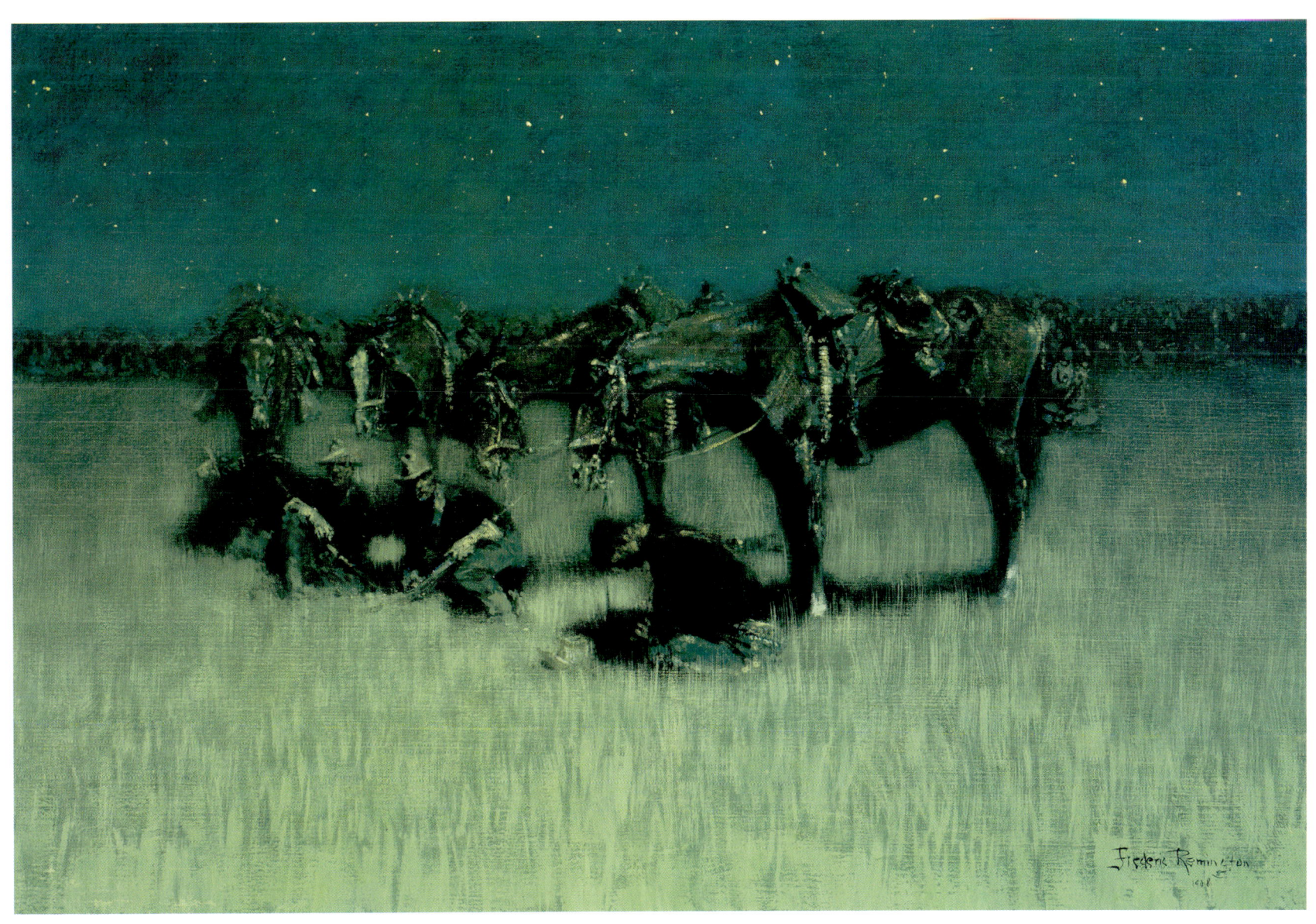

APACHE MEDICINE SONG
1908
oil on canvas
27 ⅛ x 29 ⅞ inches
signed lr: *Frederic Remington/1908*

PROVENANCE: The artist; Robert Dudley Winthrop, Old Westbury, Long Island, NY, 1909; Beekman Winthrop, Old Westbury, Long Island, NY; Robert Winthrop, New York; [Scott & Fowles, New York, NY]; [Newhouse Galleries, New York, NY]; Sid Richardson Collection of Western Art, Fort Worth, TX

LITERATURE: Giles Edgerton, "Frederic Remington, Painter and Sculptor: A Pioneer in Distinctive American Art," *Craftsman 15* (March 1909): 669; *Arts Quarterly* (1979), Vol. 1, issue B; Harold & Peggy Samuels, *Frederic Remington: A Biography* (Garden City, NY: Doubleday & Co., Inc., 1982), p. 421; Brian Dippie, *Remington & Russell* (Austin, TX: Univ. of Texas Press, 1982), p.46, ill. p. 47; Alexander Nemerov, *Frederic Remington & Turn-of-the-Century America* (New Haven, CT: Yale Univeristy Press, 1995), ill. pl.1; Peter Hassrick & Melissa Webster, *Frederic Remington: A Catalogue Raisonné*, Buffalo Bill Historical Center, Cody, WY (1996), p. 819, pl. 2844

EXHIBITIONS: Doll & Richards Gallery, Boston, MA (1909); Amon Carter Museum, Fort Worth, TX (1964); Wichita Falls Museum, Wichita, TX (1967); Univ. of Texas, Austin, TX (1971); LBJ Library, Austin, TX (1971); Tyler Museum of Art, Tyler, TX (1972); Amon Carter Museum, Fort Worth, TX (1973); Sakowitz Festival, Houston, TX (1973); Texas A&M, College Station, TX (1974); Takashimaya, Osaka (1976); Takashimaya, Tokyo (1976); Amon Carter Museum, Fort Worth, TX (1976); Witte, San Antonio, TX (1977); Amon Carter Museum, Fort Worth, TX (1979); Military Academy, West Point, NY (1979); Amarillo Art Center, Amarillo, TX (1979); Wichita Falls Museum, Wichita, TX (1979); Abilene Fine Arts Museum, Abilene, TX (1980); Amon Carter Museum, Fort Worth, TX (1980)

Painted at the end of the centuries-old realist tradition, at the moment when the long-assumed mimetic abilities of paint were irrevocably thrown into question, *Apache Medicine Song* announces its own evolutionary eclipse. The forces creeping to replace it, like the shadows of the unseen tree at the bottom of the canvas, are vague and quasi-representational. Again, like the shadows, these forces evoke objects for which the only evidence is the shadows or images themselves, thereby elevating an unremarkable occurrence, such as an evening around a campfire, to ritualistic status. Here Remington hints at a new kind of art, one altogether distant from the old realist belief in a one-for-one correspondence between the painted image and the real world. (Nemerov, p. 52)

Photograph courtesy Sid Richardson Collection of Western Art, Fort Worth, TX

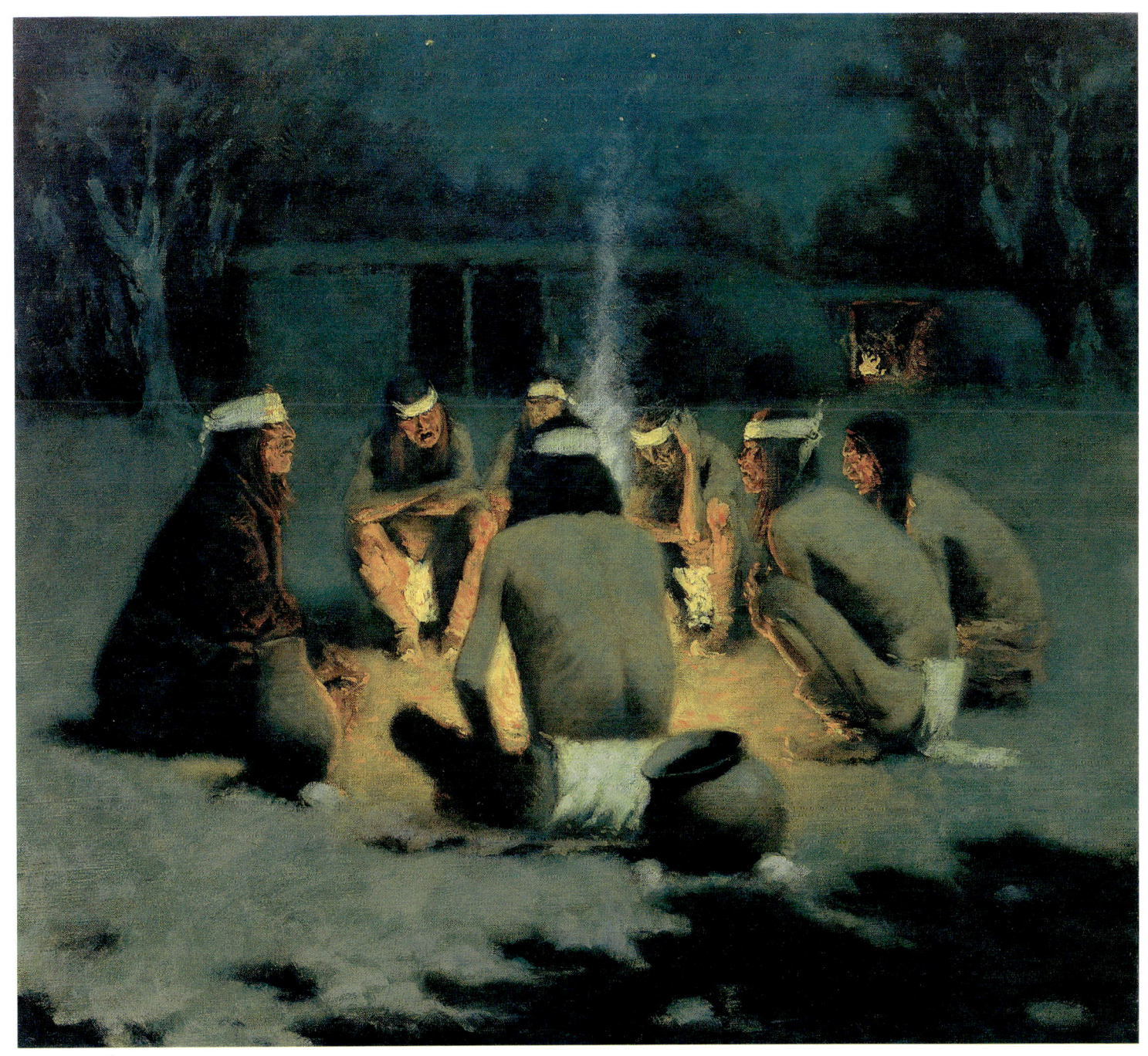

SCARE IN A PACK TRAIN
1908
oil on canvas
27 x 40 inches
signed ll: *Frederic Remington/1908.*

PROVENANCE: The artist; [M. Knoedler & Co., Inc., New York, NY]; Mrs. James C. Greenway, Greenwich, NY; Lauder Greenway, New York, NY; Sid Richardson Collection of Western Art, Fort Worth, TX

LITERATURE: *New York Herald* (November 30, 1908); "Gallery Notes. Remington Paintings on View-Exhibit at Corcoran Gallery." *New York Times* (December 2, 1908); *American Art News*, vol. 8 (Dec. 5, 1908); *A Catalogue of the Frederic Remington Art Memorial Collection*, Ogdensburg, NY (1954), p. 30; *Frederic Remington: An Exhibition Honoring Harold McCracken*, Buffalo Bill Historical Center, Cody, WY (1974), ill. p. 76, no. 112; Harold & Peggy Samuels, *Frederic Remington: A Biography* (Garden City, NY: Doubleday & Co., Inc., 1982), p. 418; Peter Hassrick & Melissa Webster, *Frederic Remington: A Catalogue Raisonné*, Buffalo Bill Historical Center, Cody, WY (1996), p. 824, pl. 2867

EXHIBITIONS: *Paintings by Frederic Remington on Exhibition at the Galleries of M. Knoedler & Co.*, New York, NY (1908); Wildenstein & Co., New York, NY (1968); *Frederic Remington: An Exhibition Honoring Harold McCracken*, Buffalo Bill Historical Center, Cody, WY (1974); Denver Art Museum, Denver, CO (1981)

By 1900, Remington was well established as an illustrator, but struggled to gain acceptance as an artist of serious merit. Throughout the 1900s, he reexamined his aesthetic approach, and turned from his strongly narrative, illustrative traditions to a greater concern with the pictorial effects of light, color, and atmosphere. His advances were received with great critical acclaim at Knoedler & Company's one-man exhibit in December, 1908, in which *Scare in a Pack Train* was included. *The Globe* summarized Remington's technical advances: "Mr. Remington has greatly improved. He handles his pigment with surer brush, in a bigger way and a more logical manner, with greater simplicity than hitherto. His color is purer, more vibrant, more telling, and his figures are more in atmosphere."

Photograph courtesy Sid Richardson Collection of Western Art, Fort, Worth, TX

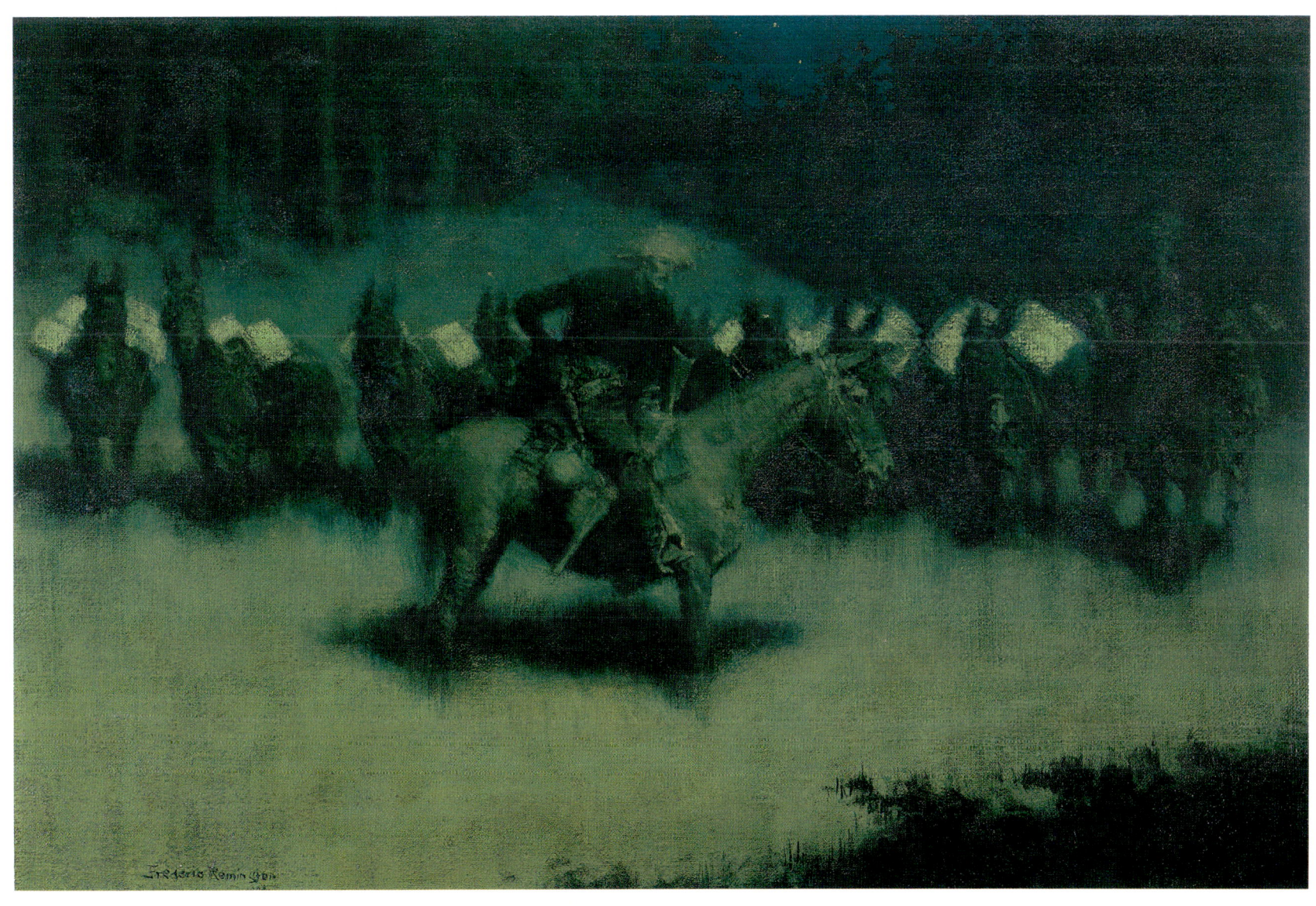

APACHE SCOUTS LISTENING
1908
oil on canvas
27 x 40 inches
signed lr: *Frederic Remington/1908.*

PROVENANCE: Estate of the artist; [M. Knoedler & Co., New York, NY, 1910]; Mr. Robert McClellan, London; [David Findlay Jr. Inc., New York, NY]; Cindy and Alan E. Horn

LITERATURE: *The Craftsman*, vol. 15 (January 1909), p. 501-502; Philip Hale, "Art," *The Boston Herald* (Jan. 9, 1909) vol. 125, p.6, col. 7; *Chicago Record Herald* (February 7, 1909); Harold & Peggy Samuels, *Frederic Remington: A Biography* (Garden City, NY: Doubleday & Co., Inc., 1982), p. 421; *Frederic Remington: The Masterworks*, The Buffalo Bill Historical Center in conjunction with The Saint Louis Art Museum (New York: Harry N. Abrams, Inc. 1988), ill. p. 150, pl. 36; Alexander Nemerov, *Frederic Remington and Turn-of-the-Century America* (New Haven, CT: Yale University Press, 1995), pp. 200-201; Peter Hassrick & Melissa Webster, *Frederic Remington: A Catalogue Raisonné*, Buffalo Bill Historical Center, Cody, WY (1996), ill. pp. 819, & in color pl. 91

EXHIBITIONS: M. Knoedler & Co., *Paintings by Frederic Remington on Exhibition at the Galleries of M. Knoedler & Co.*, New York, NY (1908); *Exhibition of Paintings by Frederic Remington*, Doll & Richards, Boston, MA (1909); O'Brien's Art Gallery, Chicago, IL (1909); C.M. Russell Museum, Great Falls, MT (1990); Smithsonian Institute, Washington, D.C. (1991); Denver Art Museum, Denver, CO (1991); St. Louis Art Museum, St. Louis, MO (1992); Los Angeles County Museum of Art, Los Angeles, CA (1996)

In Apache Scouts Listening, a group of frontiersmen and Apaches strain to see and hear an unidentified presence approaching in the darkness. The impenetrable shadows, evoking a threatening realm beyond the space defined by the painting, are a motif that recurs in many of Remington's late works. The technique relates to his desire late in life to activate the viewer's imagination: "Do your hardest work outside the picture and let your audience take away something to think about—to imagine."

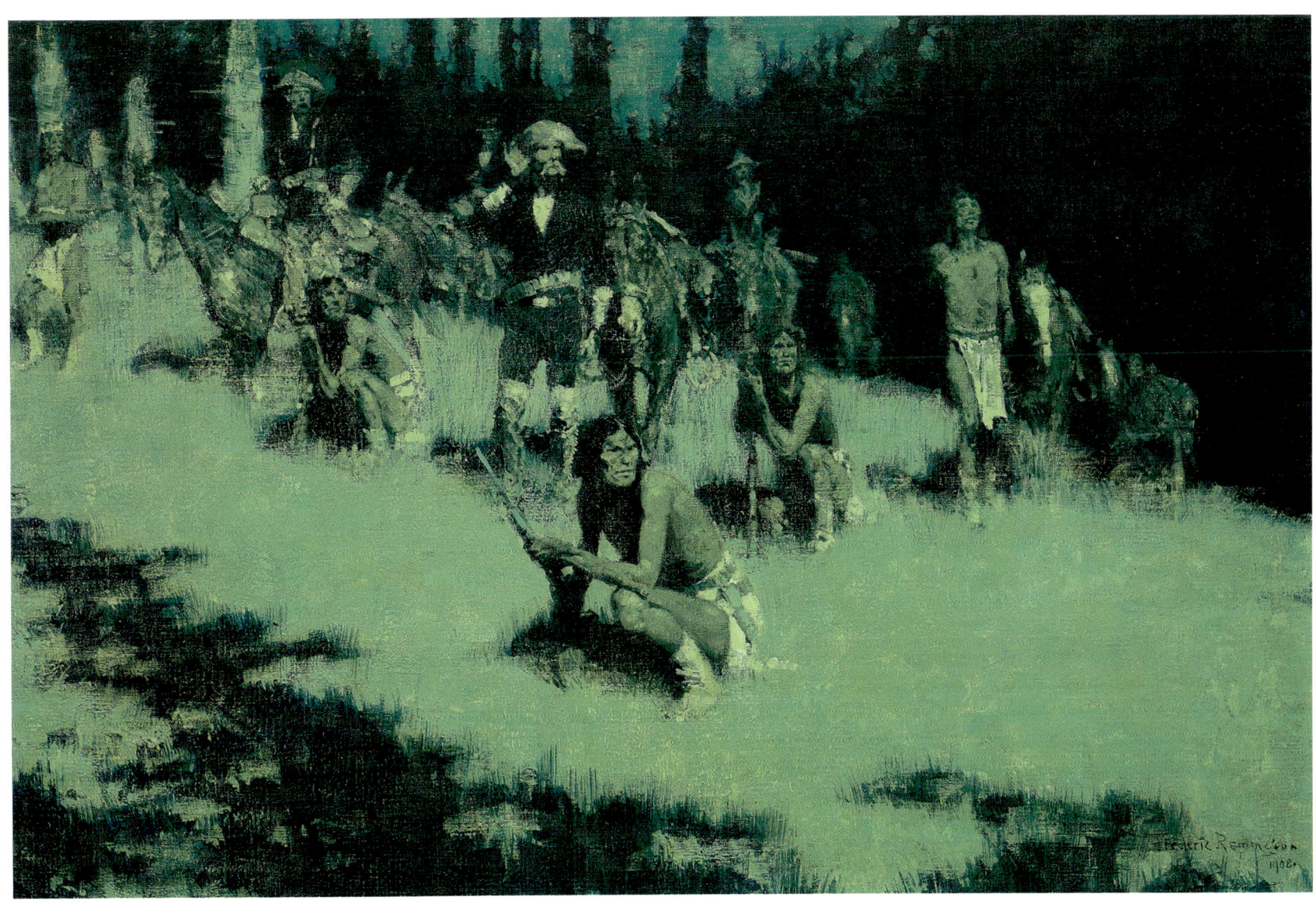

SHOTGUN HOSPITALITY

1908

27 ½ x 40 inches

oil on canvas

signed lr: *Frederic Remington/1908-*

PROVENANCE: The artist; [M. Knoedler & Co., Inc., New York, NY]; Judge Horace Russell, Class of 1865; Hood Museum of Art, Dartmouth College, Hanover, NH

ILLUSTRATION: *Colliers Weekly*, (September 17, 1910), p. 12, color halftone

LITERATURE: M. Knoedler & Co., *Paintings by Frederic Remington*, New York (1908), no. 6; *New York Herald* (November 30, 1908); *New York Times* (December 2, 1908); *New York Evening Post*, p.9, col. 6; *American Art News* (December 5, 1908); *New York Daily Tribune* (December 6, 1908), part II, p. 2, col.1; Harold McCracken, *Frederic Remington: Artist of the Old West* (Philadelphia: J. B. Lippincott Co., 1947), p. 127; Harold McCracken, *The Frederic Remington Book: A Pictorial History of the West* (Garden City, NY: Doubleday & Co., Inc., 1966), p. 278, ill. p. 67, no. 80; Dr. Watson Parker, *Frederic Remington*, Paine Art Center & Arboretum, Oshkosh, WI (1967); *How the West was Won: Frederic Remington and Charles Russell* (New York: Wildenstein & Co., 1968), n.p. pl. 15; Robert Farmer, *Remington Portfolio-Epilogue: Indian Painting Project by Dartmouth* (Watertown, NY: *Watertown Daily Times*, Dec. 1970); Peter Hassrick, *Frederic Remington*, Amon Carter Museum, Fort Worth, TX (1973), ill. p. 42, no. 76; Peter Hassrick, *Frederic Remington: The Late Years*, Denver Art Museum, Denver, CO (1981), ill. p. 48-49; Barbara McAdam, "American Paintings in the Hood Museum of Art, Dartmouth College," *Antiques* (Nov. 1985), ill. p. 1026; *Interciencia* (May/June, 1988), Vol. 13, cover ill., no. 3; Allen & Marilyn Splete, *Frederic Remington: Selected Letters* (New York: Abbeville Press, Inc., 1988), p. 403; David Murphy, "The Hood Museum of Art at Dartmouth," *Dartmouth Review* (March 7, 1990), Vol. 10, Issue 18, ill. p. 9; Peggy & Harold Samuels, *Remington, The Complete Prints* (New York: Crown Publishers, Inc., 1990), p. 134, 150, 161, ill. p. 134; *American Art* (National Museum of American Art, Smithsonian Inst. with Oxford Univ. Press, Winter/Spring 1991), Vol. 5, no.1-2, p. 52; William Truettner, ed., *The West as America: Reinterpreting Images of the Frontier, 1820-1920* (National Museum of American Art by the Smithsonian Inst. Press, 1991); Federica Pirani & Maria Elisa Tittoni, *The American West: l'arte della Frontiera Americana 1830-1920* (Venzia: Marsilio Editori, 1993), ill. p. 183; Alexander Nemerov, *Frederic Remington and Turn-of-the Century America* (New Haven, CT: Yale University Press, 1995) pp. 205-206; Rebecca Bailey, "What Is There to Teach About Art?" *Dartmouth Alumni Magazine*, Vol. 88, No. 8 (South Burlington: The Lane Press Inc., May, 1996), pp. 36-45, ill. p. 44; Peter Hassrick & Melissa Webster, *Frederic Remington: A Catalogue Raisonné*, Buffalo Bill Historical Center, Cody, WY (1996), p. 824, ill. pl. 2869

EXHIBITIONS: M. Knoedler & Co., Inc., New York, NY *Paintings by Frederic Remington* (Dec. 1908-Jan., 1909); Paine Art Center and Arboretum, Oshkosh, WI, *A Retrospective Exhibit of Painting and Sculpture* (Aug.-Sept., 1967-traveling exhibit); Minneapolis Institute of Art, Minneapolis, MN (Oct.-Nov., 1967); Sterling and Francine Clark Art Institute, Williamstown, MA (Dec., 1967) Wildenstein & Co. Galleries, New York, NY, *How the West was Won: Frederic Remington and Charles Russell* (March-June, 1968); Amon Carter Museum, Fort Worth, TX, *Work of Frederic Remington* (Jan.-March, 1973); Strauss Gallery, Hopkins Center Art Galleries, Dartmouth College (Aug. 1973); Buffalo Bill Historical Center, Cody, WY, *Frederic Remington: An Exhibition Honoring Harold McCracken* (May-Sept., 1974); Strauss and Barrows Galleries, Hopkins Center Art Galleries, Dartmouth College, *Light in Art* (Dec., 1977-Jan., 1978); Carpenter Galleries, Dartmouth College (Feb., 1978); New Orleans Museum of Art, New Orleans, LA, *Paintings & Sculpture by Frederic Remington and Charles Russell* (Nov. 1979-Feb.,1980); Carpenter Gallery, Hopkins Center Art Galleries, Dartmouth College (June, 1980-June, 1981); Denver Art Museum, Denver, CO, *Frederic Remington: The Late Years* (July-Aug., 1981); Jaffe-Friede Gallery, Hopkins Center Art Galleries, Dartmouth College, *The Dartmouth Collection: 19th & 20th Century Paintings* (Sept.-Nov., 1982); Sack Gallery, Hood Museum of Art, Dartmouth College (May-Nov., 1993); Palazzo delle Esposizioni, Rome, Italy, *The American West: l'arte della Frontiera Americana 1830-1920* (Dec., 1993-Feb., 1994); Harrington Gallery Teaching Exhibition, Hood Museum of Art, *Images of the West: Selections from the Permanent Collection* (July-Aug., 1994); Israel Sack Gallery, Hood Museum of Art, Dartmouth College (Feb., 1995-June, 1997)

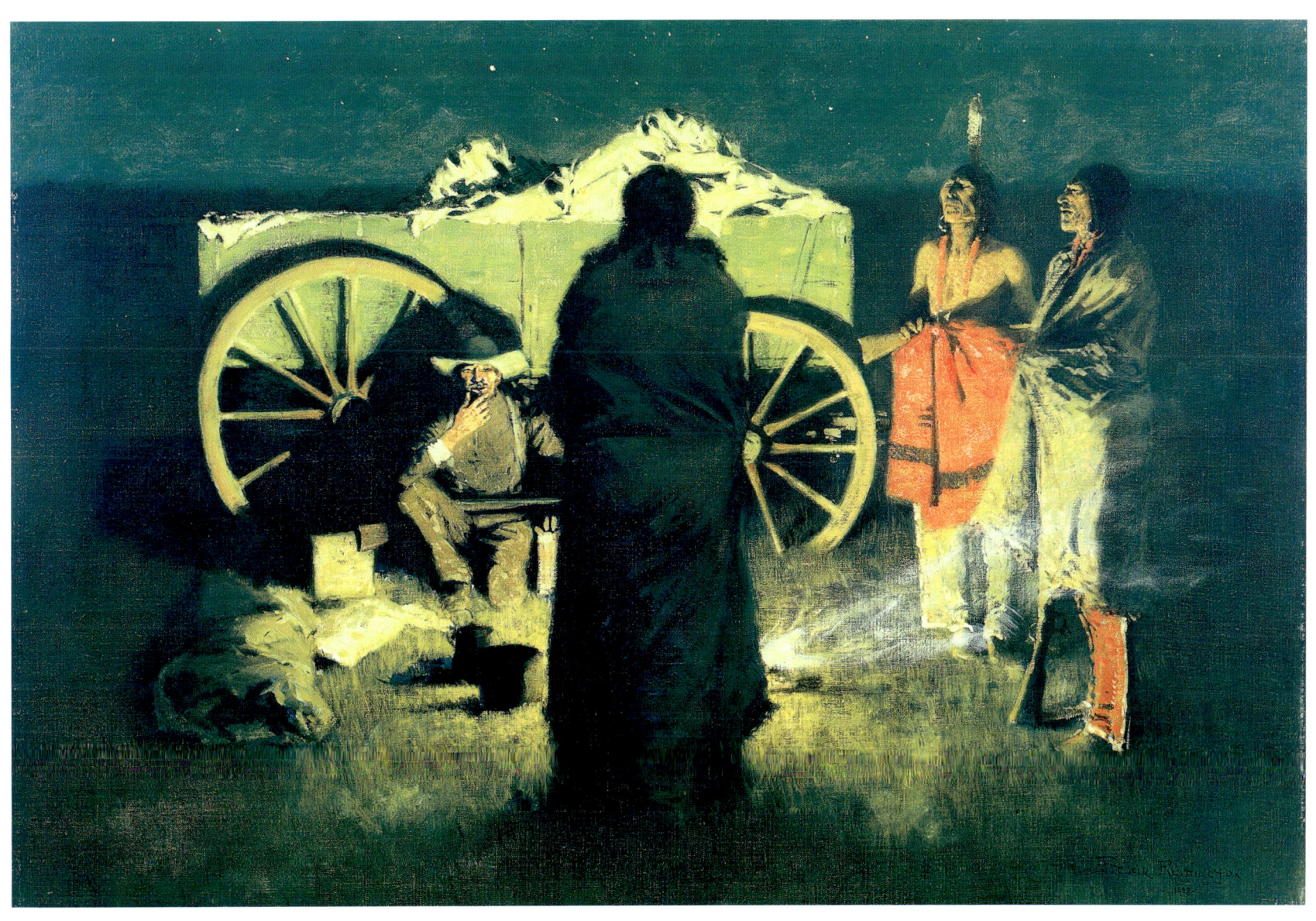

71

AMONG THE LED HORSES
1909
oil on canvas
27 x 40 inches
signed & dated ll: *Frederic Remington/1909-*

PROVENANCE: Artist's estate; [M. Knoedler & Co., New York, NY, 1910]; William C. Sproul, Chester, PA, 1910; [M. Knoedler & Co., New York, NY]; Private collection, Denver, CO (purchased c. 1950; descended through family), Denver, CO; William Foxley; [Gerald Peters Gallery, Santa Fe, NM, 1993]; Sid Richardson Collection of Western Art, Fort Worth, TX

ILLUSTRATION: *Scribner's Magazine* (February, 1910), p. 191, halftone

LITERATURE: M. Knoedler & Co., *Paintings by Frederic Remington*, New York, NY (1909); *New York Evening Post* (Dec. 9, 1909), p. 9, col. 3; *New York Herald* (Dec. 9, 1909); *New York Herald* (Dec. 26, 1909); Royal Cortissoz, *American Artists*, New York, NY (1923), p. 238-39; Earle 1924, p. 265; Downey (1941), ill. opp. p. 30; Harold McCracken, *Frederic Remington: Artist of the Old West* (Philadelphia: J. B. Lippincott Co., 1947), p. 143; Remington Art Memorial, *A Catalogue of the Frederic Remington Memorial Collection*, Ogdensburg, NY (1954); Harold McCracken, *The Frederic Remington Book: A Pictorial History of the Old West* (Garden City, NY: Doubleday and Co. Inc., 1966), ill. p. 145; Peter Hassrick, *Frederic Remington: The Late Years*, Denver Art Museum, Denver, CO (1981) ill. p. 50-51; Peter Hassrick and Melissa Webster, *Frederic Remington: A Catalogue Raisonné*, Buffalo Bill Historical Center, Cody, WY (1996), ill. p. 829, pl. 2891

EXHIBITIONS: M. Knoedler & Co., *Paintings by Frederic Remington*, New York, NY (1909); Denver Art Museum, *Frederic Remington: The Late Years*, Denver, CO (July 11-Aug. 30, 1981)

In *Among the Led Horses*, a horse has been felled by some unseen foe. The instant of stunned and frantic reconnoitering, frozen in time by the artist's hand, brings into focus the dramatic saga of the Indian Wars. Remington reveals his knowledge of equine anatomy in the tight composition that centers around the heads and graceful necks of four chestnut-colored horses. Beneath the full flood of western light, Remington has captured the essence of life-and-death confrontation, which remained an integral part of his statement throughout his career. The pounding action of earlier works is replaced in *Among the Led Horses* by the compositional device of centricity, by vigorous and painterly surface treatment, and by the suggestion, rather than articulation of drama. (Hassrick, p. 50)

Photograph courtesy of Sid Richardson Collection of Western Art, Fort Worth, TX

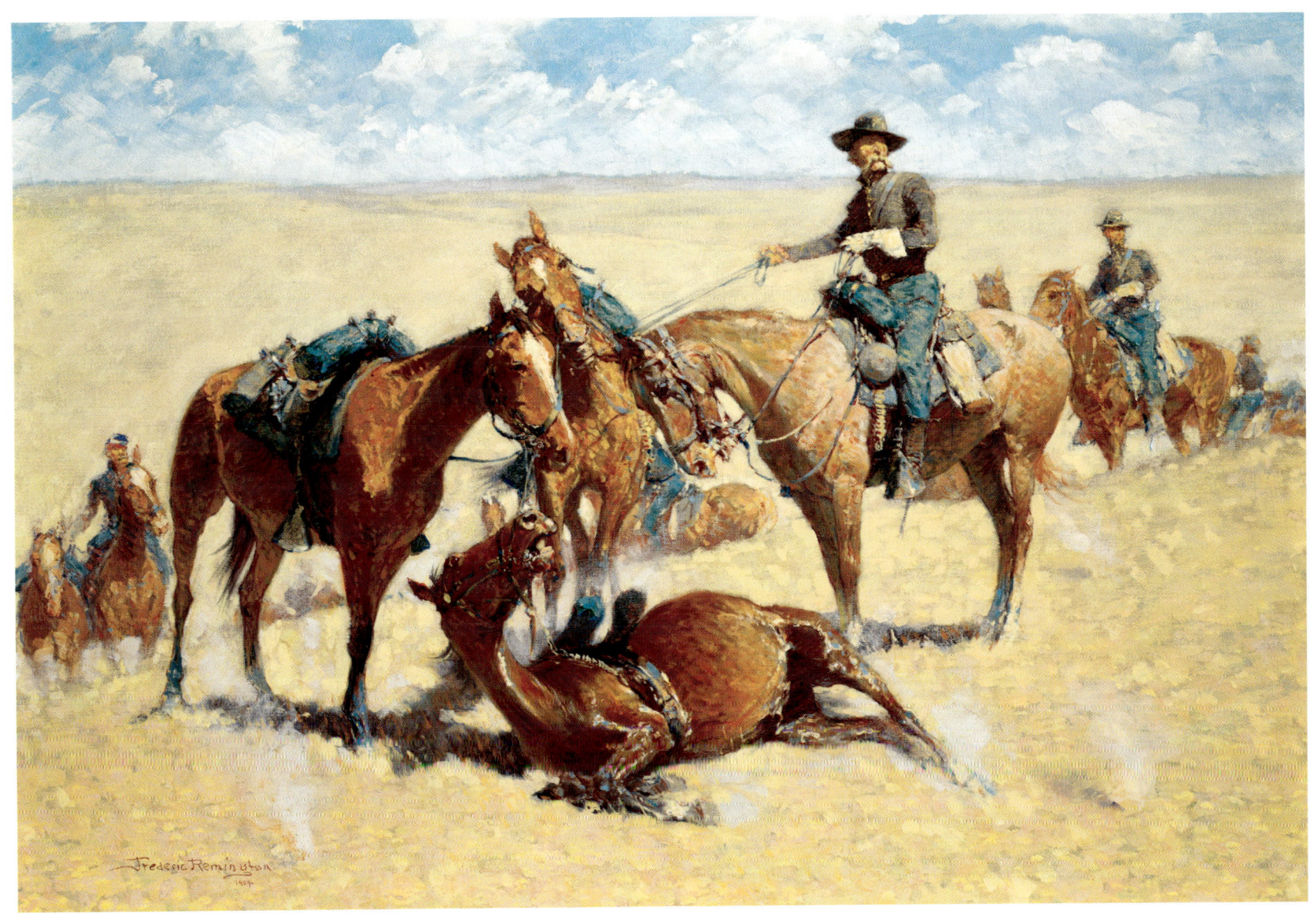

THE HUNTER'S SUPPER

1909

oil on canvas

27 x 30 inches

signed lr: *Frederic Remington/Big Horn Mountains./1909.*

ILLUSTRATION: *Scribner's Magazine* (February 1910), p. 187, halftone

PROVENANCE: The artist; [M. Knoedler & Co., New York, NY]; John C. Howard, Ogdensburg, NY, 1909; [M. Knoedler & Co., New York, NY]; [?]; [Kennedy Galleries Inc., New York, NY, 1962]; National Cowboy Hall of Fame and Western Heritage Center, Oklahoma City, OK

LITERATURE: "New Paintings Shown by Mr. Remington," *New York Herald* (December 9, 1909), p. 5; Harold McCracken, *Frederic Remington: Artist of the Old West* (Philadelphia: J. B. Lippincott Co., 1947), p. 143; *Kennedy Quarterly*, 1962, p. 81, no. 116, ill. cover; Harold McCracken, *The Frederic Remington Book: A Pictorial History of the West* (Garden City, NY: Doubleday & Co., Inc., 1966), p. 283, ill. p. 221; *Frederic Remington: An Exhibition Honoring Harold McCracken*, Buffalo Bill Historical Center, Cody, WY (1974), ill. p. 53, no. 67; Matthew Baigell, *The Western Art of Frederic Remington* (New York: Ballatine Books, 1976), ill. n.p.; National Cowboy Hall of Fame, *Persimmon Hill*, 1980, p. 38, ill. p. 50-51; Harold and Peggy Samuels, *Frederic Remington: A Biography* (Garden City, NY: Doubleday & Co., Inc., 1982), p. 434; Allen P. and Marilyn D. Splete, *Frederic Remington: Selected Letters* (New York: Abbeville Press, Inc., 1988); Peter Hassrick and Melissa Webster, *Frederic Remington: A Catalogue Raisonné*, Buffalo Bill Historical Center, Cody, WY (1996), ill. pl. 97, & p. 831, pl. 2904

EXHIBITIONS: [M. Knoedler & Co., Inc., New York, NY]; Amon Carter Museum, Fort Worth, TX (1973); Buffalo Bill Historical Center, Cody, WY (1974)

Several nocturnes executed in the last year of Remington's life depict quiet and personal moments in the lives of his subjects. In *The Hunter's Supper*, the campfire offers refuge from the loneliness of the vast and empty prairie. The alienation that pervades the scene is eloquently represented in the ghostly faces of the cowboys, who appear as apparitions from a by-gone era. Though it offers comfort and companionship to the cowboys, there is a strong sense of the camp's physical isolation from the rest of the world. The mood of the painting may reflect the sentiment Remington had expressed the prior year, that the modern United States was "someone else's America, but it isn't mine."

Photograph Courtesy National Cowboy Hall of Fame and Western Heritage Center, Oklahoma City, OK

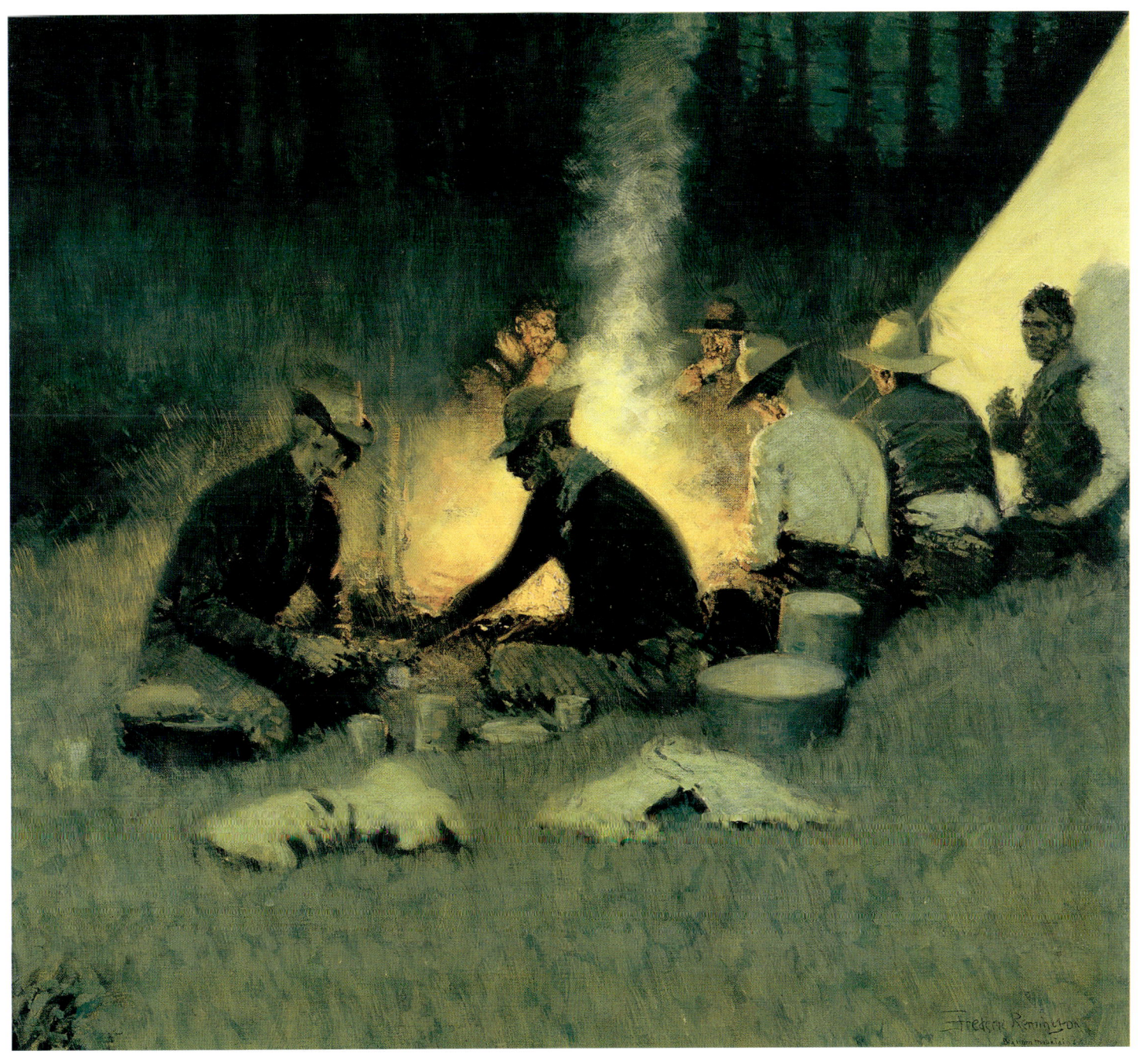

THE SUNDANCE

1909
oil on canvas
27 x 40 inches
signed ll: *Frederic Remington/1909*

PROVENANCE: Artist's estate; Eva Remington's estate; Frederic Remington Art Museum, Ogdensburg, NY

LITERATURE: *A Catalogue of the Frederic Remington Memorial Collection*, Remington Art Memorial, Ogdensburg, NY (1954), p. 31; Allen & Marilyn Splete, *Frederic Remington: Selected Letters* (New York: Abbeville Press, Inc., 1988), p. 435, 436; Harold & Peggy Samuels, *Frederic Remington: A Biography* (Garden City, NY: Crown Publishers, Inc., 1990), p. 436; Peter Hassrick & Melissa Webster, *Frederic Remington: A Catalogue Raisonné*, Buffalo Bill Historical Center, Cody, WY (1996), p. 835, pl. 2923

EXHIBITIONS: M. Knoedler & Co., New York, NY; Museum of Fine Arts, Dallas, TX (1936); Wildenstein, New York, NY (1968)

The migratory habits of the buffalo were a central concern of life for the Plains Indians, and much of their tribal life— both spiritual and temporal— revolved around the the all-important buffalo. As a result, hunting and territory issues formed the axis of Plains Indian life, and not surprisingly, many of their most important ceremonial occasions centered on enhancing hunting prowess and ensuring success in both warfare and the pursuit of the buffalo. Among the Plains Indians, the Sun Dance ceremony was an important ritual marking the transition from childhood to adulthood for boys. By enduring this painful ordeal, boys proved themselves worthy of the status of manhood in their tribe.

Photograph courtesy Frederic Remington Art Museum, Ogdensburg, NY

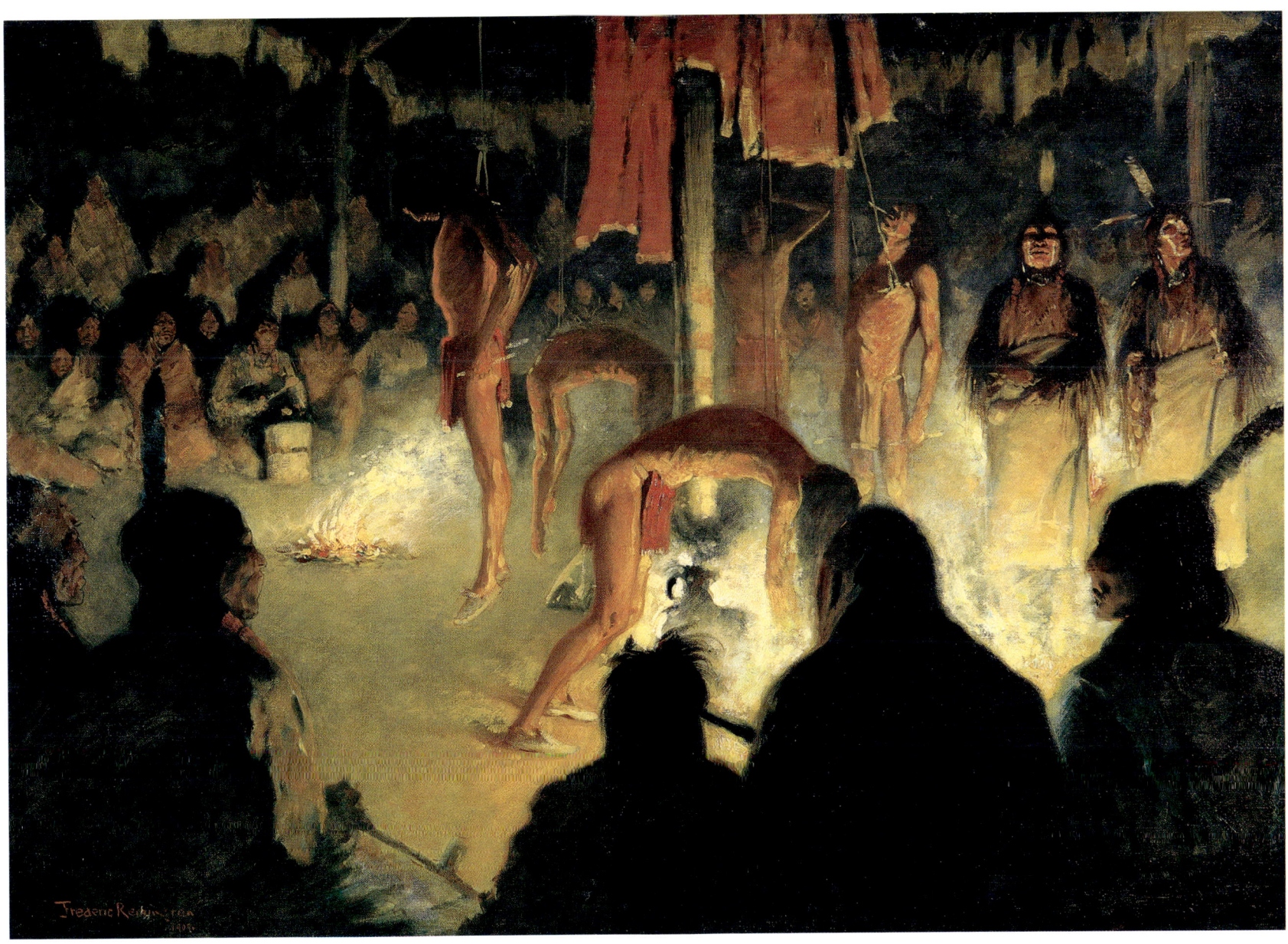

THE WINTER CAMPAIGN
1909
oil on canvas
27 x 40 ⅛ inches
signed lr: *Frederic Remington/1909*

ILLUSTRATION: *Scribner's Magazine*, February 1910, p. 183, halftone

PROVENANCE: The artist; [M. Knoedler & Co., New York, NY]; R.L. Skofield, 1909; [Parke-Bernet Galleries, Inc., New York, NY, February 1, 1940]; Mr. Edward S. Moore, 1940; [James Graham & Sons, New York, NY]; The Rockwell Foundation, Corning, NY, 1987; The Rockwell Museum, Corning, NY

LITERATURE: *New York Daily Tribune* (December 7, 1909): p. 7, col. 1; *New York Times* (December 8, 1909), p. 10, col. 7; Cortissoz 1923, p. 240-242; Earle 1924, p. 265; Sothebys Parke-Bernet 1940, lot 51, ill.; Harold McCracken, *Frederic Remington: Artist of the Old West* (Philadelphia: J. B. Lippincott Co., 1947); Allen & Marilyn Splete, *Frederic Remington: Selected Letters* (New York: Abbeville Press, Inc., 1988); Peter Hassrick and Melissa Webster, *Frederic Remington: A Catalogue Raisonné*, Buffalo Bill Historical Center, Cody, WY (1996), p. 837, pl. 2929

EXHIBITIONS: M. Knoedler & Co., Inc., New York, NY (1909); Rockwell Foundation, Corning, NY (1984)

Remington's one-man show at M. Knoedler & Company in December, 1909, was the most critically acclaimed exhibition of his career. Perhaps the most celebrated painting in the exhibition was *The Winter Campaign*. One critic noted how the painting, "expresses, as only Remington can, the oneness of feeling of animals and men in the face of nature's menace of death." Indeed, many of Remington's tonalist paintings reveal his late-life preoccupation with death and the mourning of a by-gone era. In *The Winter Campaign*, the moon's glow casts a chilly, blue light that reflects brightly off the snow and dully, but clearly, illumines the solidly delineated horses. The band of horses effectively separates the viewer from the cavalrymen's world, thereby heightening the fugitive mood of the painting.

Photograph courtesy of Rockwell Museum, Corning, New York. Clara S. Peck Fund purchase. Photographer James O. Milmoe

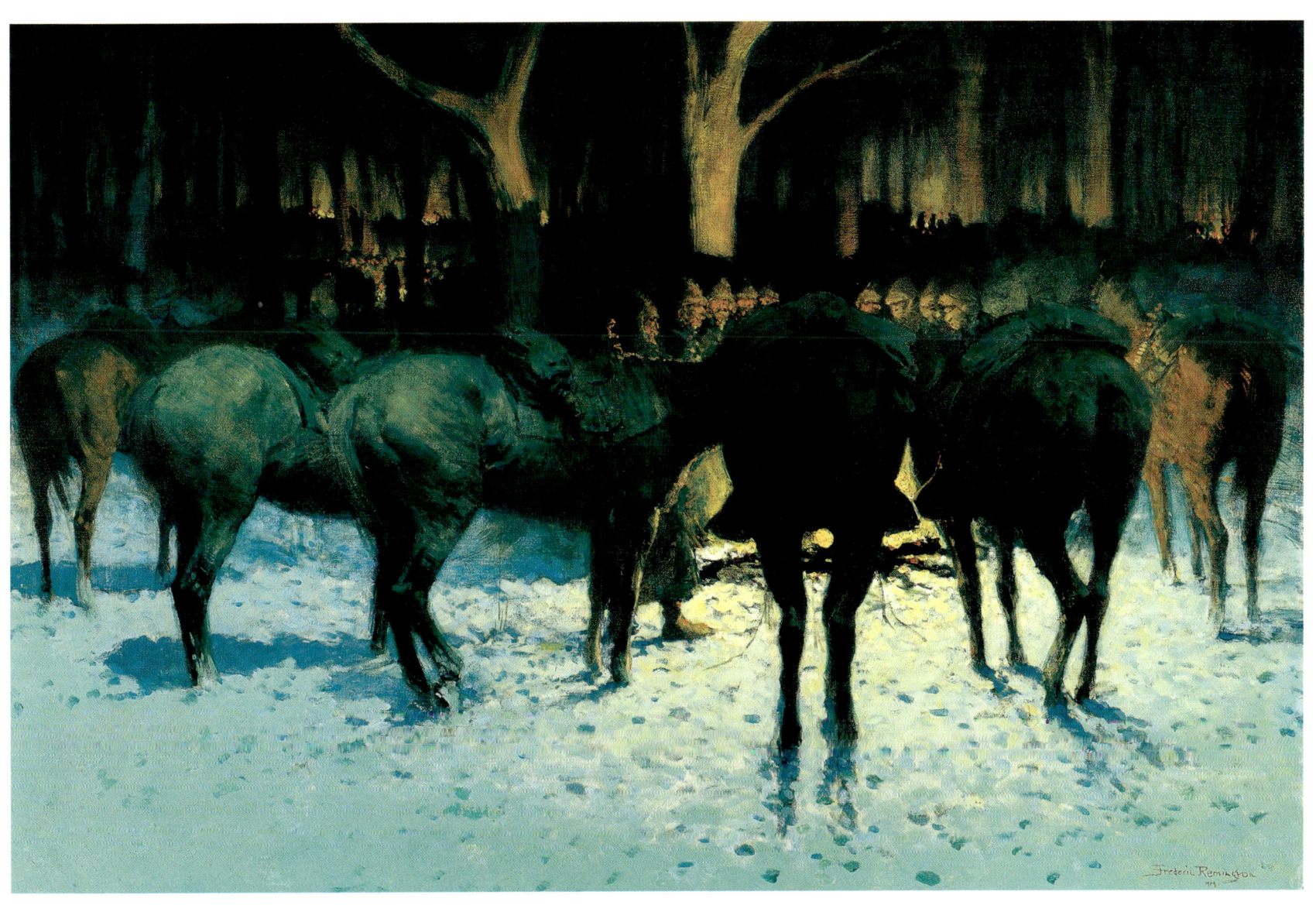

79

THE LOVE CALL

1909

oil on canvas

31 x 28 inches

signed lr: *Frederic Remington/1909—*

ILLUSTRATION: *Scribner's Magazine* (February 1910), p. 188, halftone

PROVENANCE: The artist; [M. Knoedler & Co., Inc., New York, NY]; Mr. & Mrs. William A. Paine, Boston 1909; [M. Knoedler & Co., Inc., New York, NY]; Mr. Robert Gross, California; [David Findlay, New York, NY]; George Bates, Cary, IL, since 1960; private collection; [J. N. Bartfield Galleries, New York, NY, 1996]; Sid Richardson Collection of Western Art, Fort Worth, TX

REFERENCES: M. Knoedler & Co., Inc., New York, NY (1909), no. 14; *New York Daily Tribune* (December 7, 1909), p. 7, col. 1; *New York Herald* (December 26, 1909); Panama-Pacific Expo 1915, vol. 2, p. 359, no. 2948; Newhaus (1915), p. 56; Cortissoz 123, p. 237; Harold McCracken, *Frederic Remington: Artist of the Old West* (Philadelphia: J. B. Lippincott Co., 1947); *A Catalogue of the Frederic Remington Memorial Collection,* Remington Art Memorial, Ogdensburg, NY (1954), p. 31; *Antiques* (May 1966), ill. p. 636; Peggy & Harold Samuels, *Frederic Remington: A Biography* (Garden City, NY: Doubleday & Co., Inc., 1990); *Frederic Remington: The Masterworks,* The Saint Louis Art Museum in conjunction with the Buffalo Bill Historical Center (New York: Harry N. Abrams, Inc., 1988), p. 163; Peter Hassrick and Melissa Webster, *Frederic Remington: A Catalogue Raisonné,* Buffalo Bill Historical Center, Cody, WY (1996) p. 831, pl. 2906

EXHIBITIONS: M. Knoedler & Co., Inc., New York, NY (1909); Panama-Pacific Exposition, San Francisco, CA, (1915)

The quiet reverie of *The Love Call* is an excellent illustration of the calm, introspective side of Remington's psyche, most evident in his last works. Here narrative is subservient to mood; line and detail give way to a delicate flow of pattern and light. The spontaneity and vitality of his technique enabled Remington to complete *The Love Call* in a single setting. The painting brings to mind a statement made in 1909 by Remington's friend, the critic Giles Edgerton. Remington, Edgerton wrote, "has grown to think through his paint so freely and fluently that in some of his more recent work he seems to have used his medium unconsciously, as a great musician does his piano and score." (*The Craftsman,* March 1909)

Photograph courtesy Sid Richardson Collection of Western Art, Fort Worth, TX

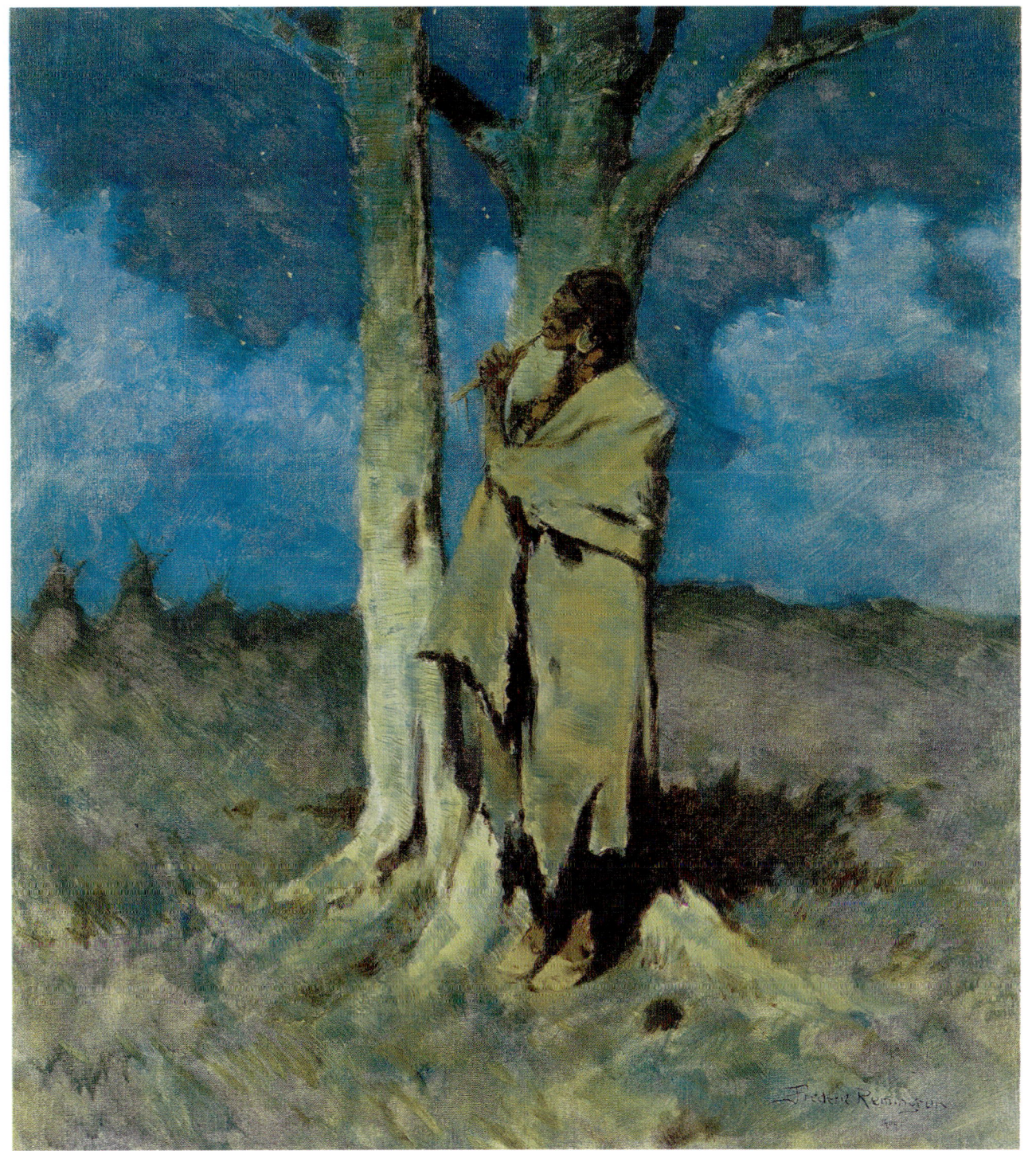

UNTITLED

alternate title: *Around the Campfire*

1909

oil on canvas

27 x 30 inches

signed ll: *Frederic Remington./1909.*

PROVENANCE: Artist's estate; Eva Remington's estate; Frederic Remington Art Museum, Ogdensburg, NY

LITERATURE: Harold McCracken, *The Frederic Remington Book: A Pictorial History of the West* (Garden City, NY: Doubleday & Co., Inc., 1966, p. 283), ill. p. 220; Archie Lee Stobie & Mildred E. Dillenbeck, *The Remington Art Museum: 50th Anniversary*, Ogdensburg, NY (1973); *Frederic Remington: An Exhibition Honoring Harold McCracken*, Buffalo Bill Historical Center, Cody, WY (1974), ill. p. 80, no. 117; Peter Hassrick and Melissa Webster, *Frederic Remington: A Catalogue Raisonné*, Buffalo Bill Historical Center, Cody, WY (1996) ill. p. 836, pl. 2925

EXHIBITIONS: *Frederic Remington: An Exhibition Honoring Harold McCracken*, Buffalo Bill Historical Center, Cody, WY (1974); Rockwell Foundation, Corning, NY (1984)

Photograph courtesy Frederic Remington Art Museum, Ogdensburg, NY

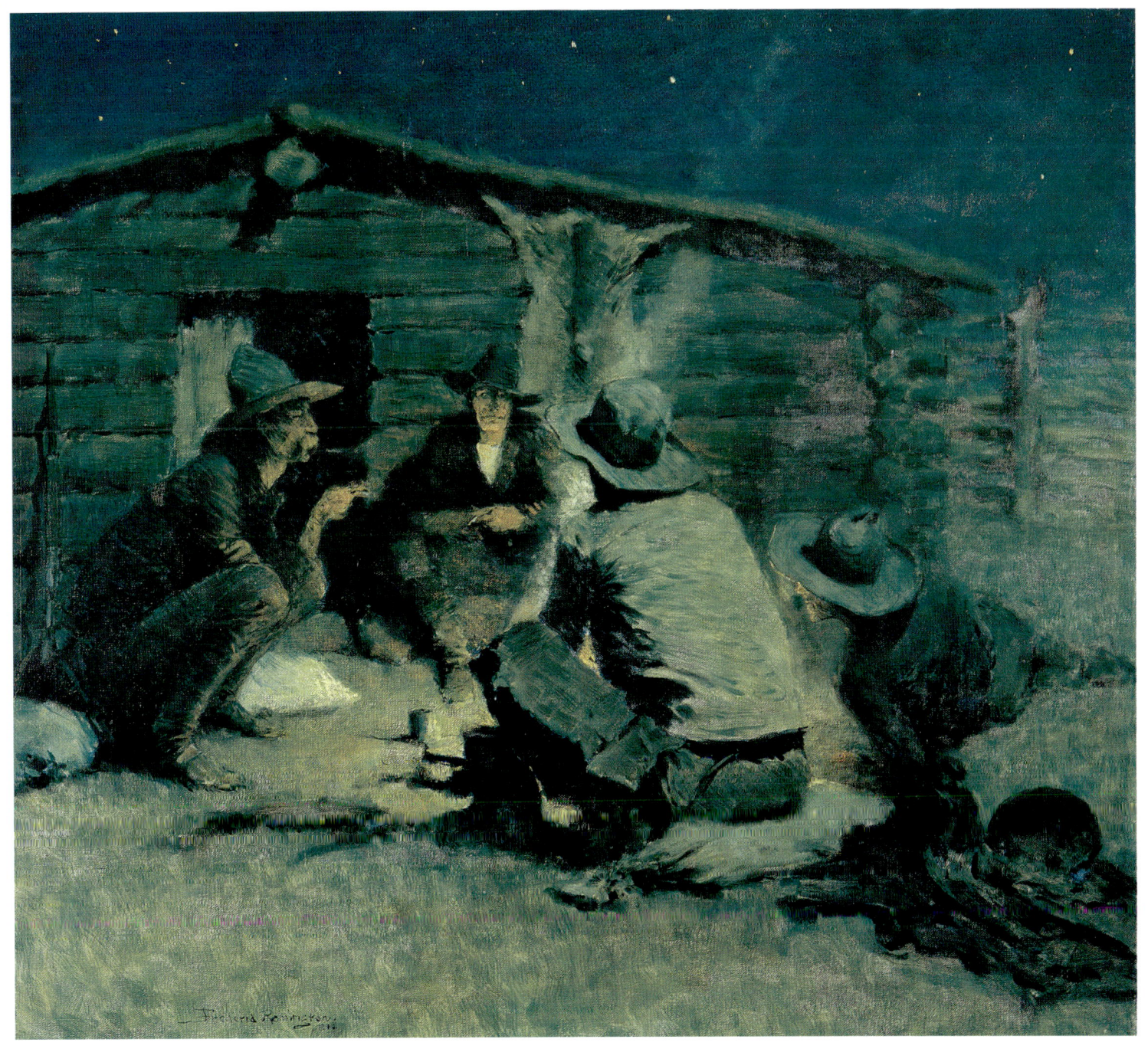

SCULPTURE

PLATES

THE BRONCO BUSTER (large version)

lost-wax bronze, dark brown patina

Roman Bronze Works, cast no. 16

modeled 1909, cast circa 1920

height: 33 ¾ inches

inscribed on base: *Copyright by/Frederic Remington*

Roman Bronze Works N-Y-

stamped under base: *No. 16*

PROVENANCE: Tiffany & Co., New York, NY, circa 1920; H. F. DeVens, New York, NY; [James Graham & Sons, New York, NY]; Amon Carter Museum, Fort Worth, TX, 1951-1996; [Gerald Peters Gallery, Santa Fe, NM, 1996]

LITERATURE: Patricia Broder, *Bronzes of the American West* (New York: Harry N. Abrams, Inc., 1974), pp. 131-133; Michael Shapiro, *Cast and Recast: The Sculpture of Frederic Remington*, Published for the National Museum of American Art by the Smithsonian Institution Press, Washington, D.C. (1981), pp. 42-44, 58; *Frederic Remington: The Masterworks*, The Saint Louis Art Museum in conjunction with the Buffalo Bill Historical Center (New York: Harry Abrams, Inc., 1988), pp. 232-233; Michael Greenbuam, *Icons of the West: Frederic Remington's Sculpture*, Frederic Remington Art Museum, Ogdensburg, NY (1996), pp. 51-64

The Bronco Buster was Remington's first sculpture. Considering that he never received formal training in the medium, it is an extraordinary work. *The Bronco Buster* exhibits all the characteristics that were to typify Remington's subsequent work in the sculptural medium: controlled movement, capturing a fluid sequence of action, concentrated rapport between man and animal, and detailed articulation of costume and anatomy. The composition was derived from Remington's illustration, *A Pitching Bronco*, published in *Harper's Weekly* in April 1882. The preliminary clay sculpture was completed in mid-1895 and copyrighted in October of that year. Judging from the size of the edition, well over 300 casts, *The Bronco Buster* was the most popular of Remington's sculptures.

In 1909, Remington decided that increasing the size of *The Bronco Buster* would allow him to reinterpret his first and most successful sculpture. Remington's diary notes indicate that he continued to work on the large version during November and December of that year with the same intensity that he had applied to the smaller model during the summer of 1895. Excited by his efforts, he wrote to the founder: "Say Bertelli, you ought to see the 1 ½ Bronc Buster—It will make your eyes hang out on your shirt front." The model was completed in December and shipped to the foundry, but Remington died of appendicitis the day after Christmas, 1909— most likely before the first bronze cast of the enlargement had been made.

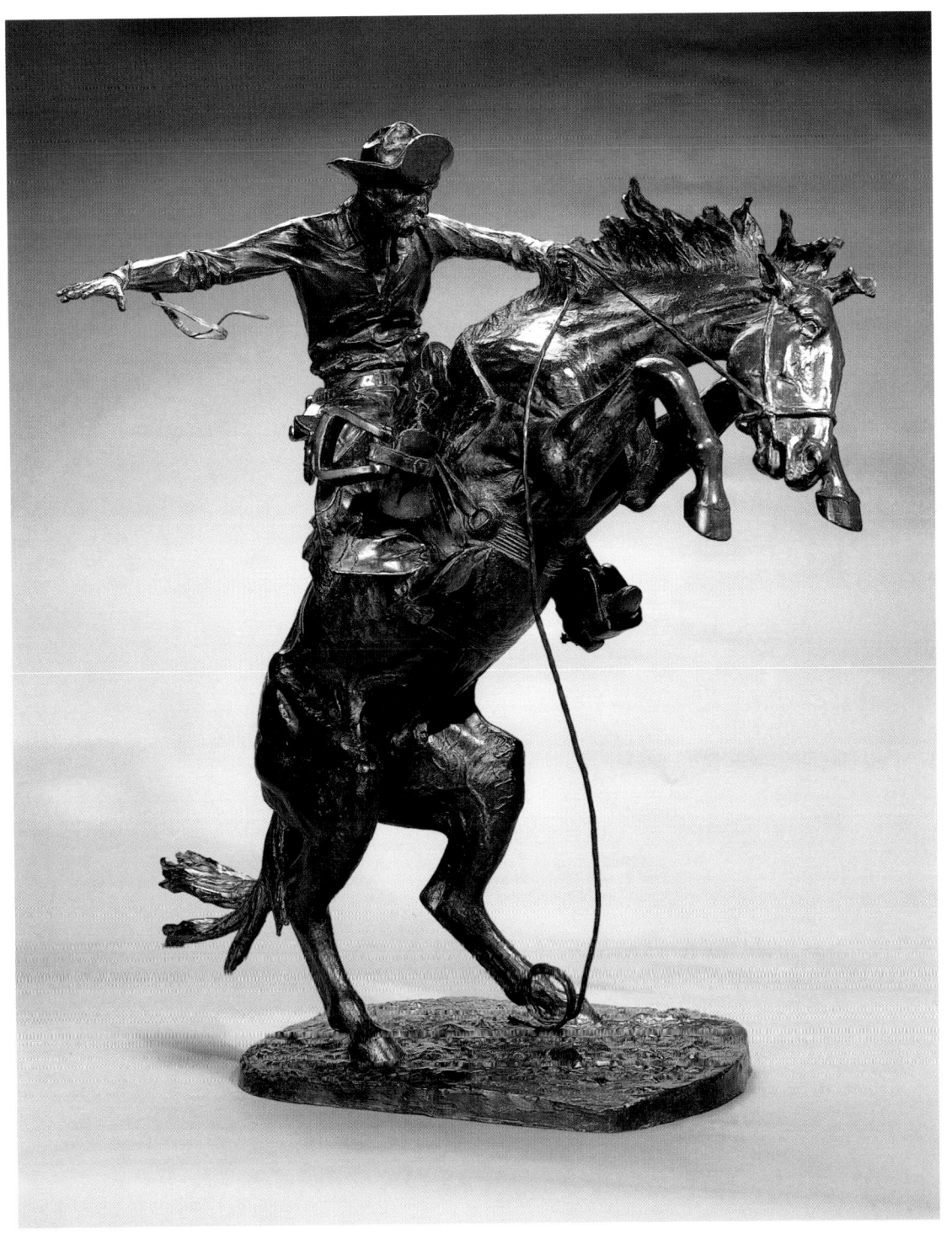

89

WOUNDED BUNKIE

sand cast bronze, brown patina

Henry Bonnard, cast F

modeled & copyrighted 1896

height: 20 ¾ inches

inscribed: *Frederic Remington*

        Copyrighted by Frederic Remington 1896 F

stamped: *CAST BY THE HENRY BONNARD BRONZE CO., N.Y. 1896*

PROVENANCE: (possibly) Tiffany & Co., New York, NY; Mrs. Corbin, New York, NY, c. 1898; Mary K. McAlisster (her grand-daughter); [Parke-Bernet Galleries, Inc., New York, NY, 1971]; Bruce Gottwald, Richmond, VA, 1971; [Kennedy Galleries, Inc., New York, NY, 1971]; Henry W. Bloch, Shawnee, KS, 1972; [Sothebys New York, NY, 1989]; Wendell Cherry, Humana Corporation, Louisville, KY; [Gerald Peters Gallery, Santa Fe, NM]; Private collection

LITERATURE: Harold McCracken, *The Frederic Remington Book*, New York (1966), p. 257; Peter Hassrick, *Frederic Remington: Paintings, Drawings, and Sculpture in the Amon Carter Museum and the Sid Richardson Foundation Collections* (New York: Harry Abrams, Inc., 1973), p. 186; Patricia Broder, *Bronzes of the American West* (New York: Harry N. Abrams, Inc., 1974), pp. 34, 360; Michael Shapiro, *Cast and Recast: The Sculpture of Frederic Remington*, Published for the National Museum of American Art by the Smithsonian Institution Press, Washington, D.C. (1981), p. 43-44; Michael Shapiro, *Bronze Casting and American Sculpture 1850-1900*, Newark (1985), p. 136; *Frederic Remington: The Masterworks*, The Saint Louis Art Museum in conjunction with the Buffalo Bill Historical Center (New York: Harry Abrams, Inc., 1988), pp. 190-2, 195, 199, 206, 210, 215, 219, 221

The Wounded Bunkie was Remington's second sculptural effort, copyrighted less than one year after *The Bronco Buster*. *The Wounded Bunkie* was the only sand cast subject which Remington decided against recreating in lost wax. These sand castings, each measuring approximately twenty and three-quarters inches in height, were all cast by the Henry-Bonnard Bronze Company and are the only edition the artist lettered, rather than numbered, sequentially.

Both technically and thematically, *The Wounded Bunkie* represents an advance for Remington in his sculptural work. He expands beyond a straight-forward depiction of speed and action by incorporating the element of narrative, and the multiple figures interact gracefully and cohesively within the sculpture. Remington heightened the impression of movement by having only two of the horses' hooves touching the ground— the rest seemingly suspended in mid-air.

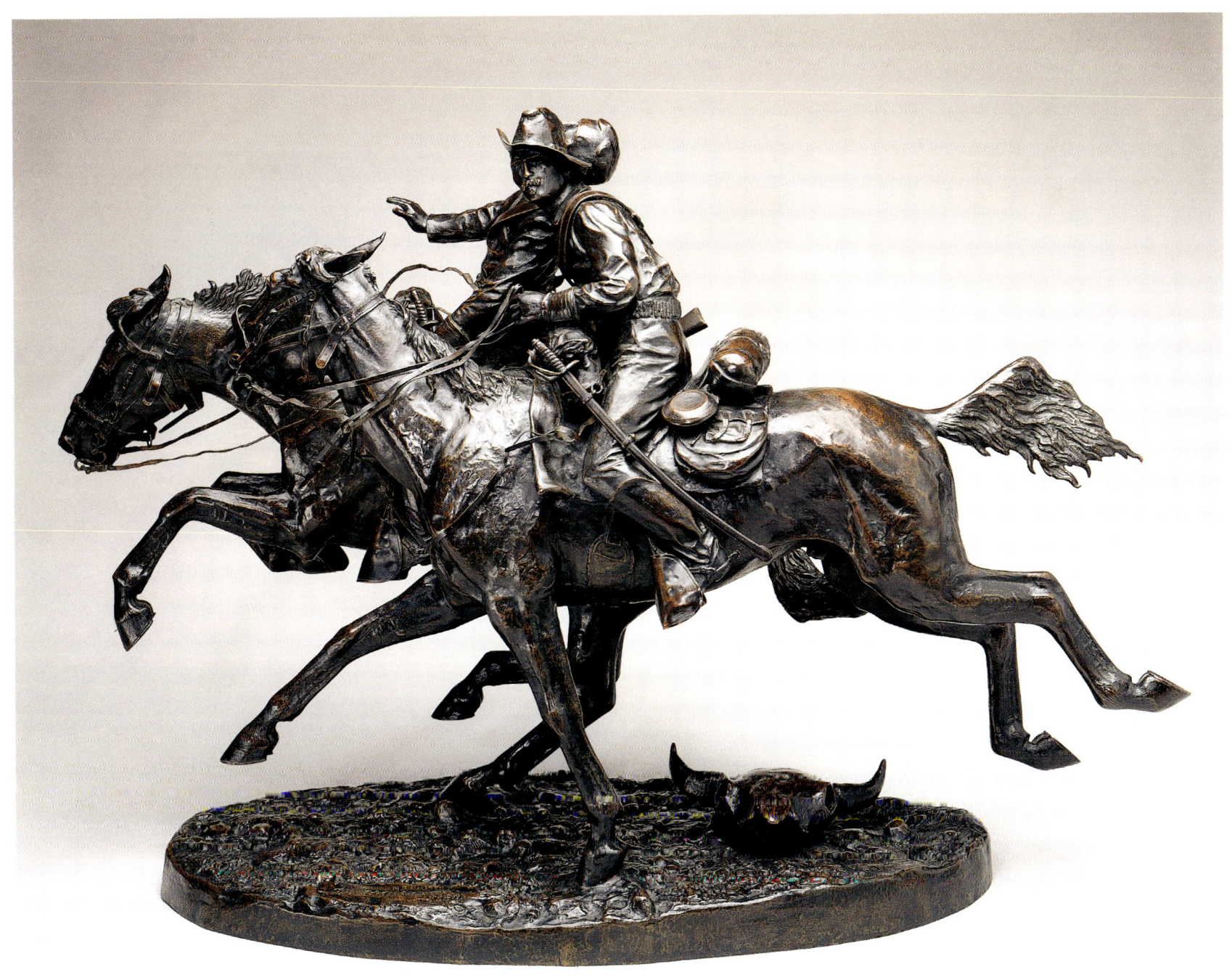

WICKED PONY

sand cast bronze, brown patina

Henry Bonnard, cast #5

modeled 1896-98, cast c. 1898

height: 22 ½ inches, base: 8 ¹¹⁄₁₆ x 18 ⅞ inches

inscribed: *HENRY BONNARD BRONZE CO/FOUNDERS N-Y 1898*

   Copyrighted by/Frederic Remington. 1898

numbered: *5* in the center of the bronze and underneath the base

PROVENANCE: Private collection, Maryland; [Gerald Peters Gallery, Santa Fe, NM]; Private collection

LITERATURE: Peter Hassrick, *Frederic Remington: Paintings, Drawings, and Sculpture in the Amon Carter Museum and Sid Richardson Foundation Collections* (New York: Harry Abrams, Inc., 1973), p. 189; Michael Edward Shapiro, *Cast and Recast: The Sculpture of Frederic Remington*, Published for the National Museum of American Art by The Smithsonian Institution Press, Washington, D.C. (1981), p. 44; *Frederic Remington: The Masterworks*, the Saint Louis Art Museum in conjunction with the Buffalo Bill Historical Center (New York: Harry Abrams, Inc., 1988), pl. 51; *Frederic Remington*, Gerald Peters Gallery in association with Mongerson-Wunderlich, Santa Fe, NM (1991), p. 65; Rick Stewart, *Frederic Remington: Masterpieces from the Amon Carter Museum*, Fort Worth, TX (1992), p. 30; Michael Greenbaum, *Icons of the West, Frederic Remington's Sculpture*, Frederic Remington Art Museum, Ogdensburg, NY (1996)

Remington's copyright described this sculpture as "show(ing) a cowboy who has been thrown. Is lying flat on the ground, holding onto the bronco's left ear with left hand. The horse is lashing out with hind legs." Remington completed the model and commenced casting at Henry Bonnard Bronze Company in 1898. Very few casts of *The Wicked Pony* were made: perhaps only six sand casts by Henry Bonnard, and one lost wax cast by Roman Bronze Works.

Remington conceived *The Wicked Pony* as a companion piece to *The Bronco Buster*, substituting a fallen cowboy endangered by his animal's bucking hind legs for the victorious cowboy on a rearing horse. Together the pair of sculptures describes the poles of in extremis situations— triumph and defeat— to which Remington would turn repeatedly. (*Frederic Remington: The Masterworks* p. 194.)

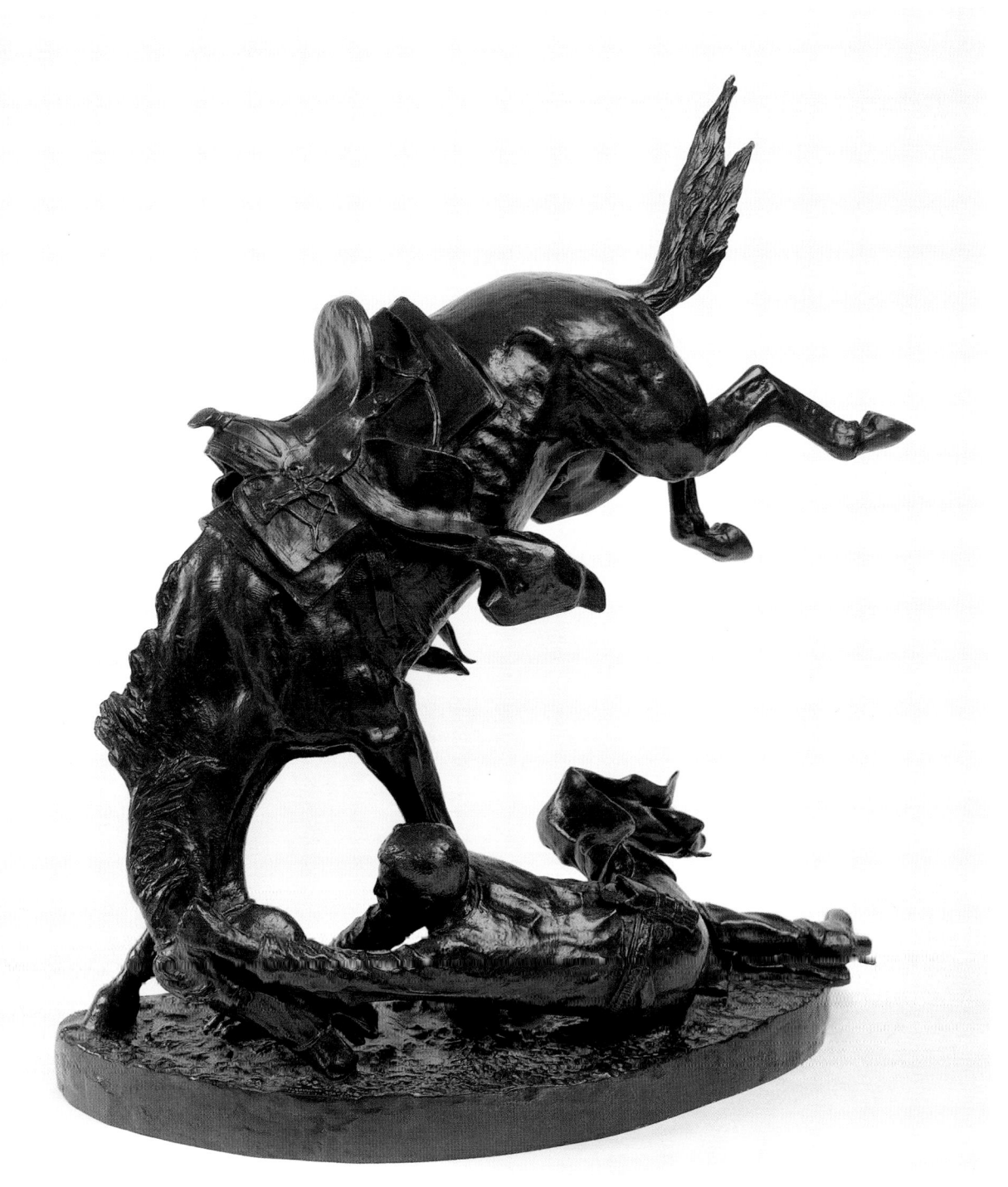

93

THE SCALP

lost-wax bronze, brown patina
Roman Bronze Works, cast no. 11
modeled & copyrighted 1898
height: 24 ⅞ inches, base: 19 ⁵⁄₁₆ x 9 inches
inscribed on base: *COPYRIGHTED BY/Frederic Remington*
                        ROMAN BRONZE WORKS, N.Y.
                        CM/XMAS/1924/GRD
incised under base: *No. 11*

PROVENANCE: [Tiffany & Company, New York, NY, 1918]; General George Dyer, circa 1918; by descent to Charles Madison, circa 1945; Estate of Charles Madison, New York, NY, 1988; [William Doyle Galleries, New York, NY, 1988]; Private Collection; [Gerald Peters Gallery, Santa Fe, NM]; Private Collection

LITERATURE: *Frederic Remington: The Masterworks*, The Saint Louis Art Museum in conjunction with the Buffalo Bill Historical Center, Cody, WY (New York: Harry N. Abrams, Inc., 1988), pp. 185, 199, 206, 210, 227, 231; *Frederic Remington*, Gerald Peters Gallery in association with Mongerson Wunderlich, Santa Fe, NM (1991), p. 84 - 85, ill; Michael Greenbaum, *Icons of the West: Frederic Remington's Sculpture*, Frederic Remington Art Museum, Ogdensburg, NY (1996), pp. 78-83

EXHIBITIONS: Gerald Peters Gallery, Santa Fe, NM; Mongerson-Wunderlich Gallery, Chicago, IL, *Frederic Remington* (May 3 - July 31, 1991)

A Sioux warrior is the subject of Remington's fourth bronze, copyrighted December 8, 1898 as *The Triumph*. Michael Shapiro observes that *The Scalp*, as the bronze was later titled, may be indebted in form to Saint-Gaudens' Logan Monument of the same period. The Henry Bonnard foundry produced ten sand castings of the piece between 1898 and 1899. With *The Scalp*, as with many of his other sculptures, Remington modified and improved his initial composition. The later Roman Bronze Works version displays a textured rocky base that supports the horse in a more dramatic stance. The warrior in the lost-wax version has a bow and quiver; in the earlier sand castings, the Indian carries a rifle and sheath. In addition, the lost-wax method enabled Remington greater freedom to manipulate the surface of each cast. Hence, the horse and rider are extensively textured in the Roman Bronze Works version of the composition.

The appeal of this subject is heightened by the fact that relatively few castings were produced. Eva Remington authorized only seven more casts after Remington's death. The highest number authorized by the artist's estate is number 14, produced in 1920 for the Remington Art Memorial in Ogdensburg, New York.

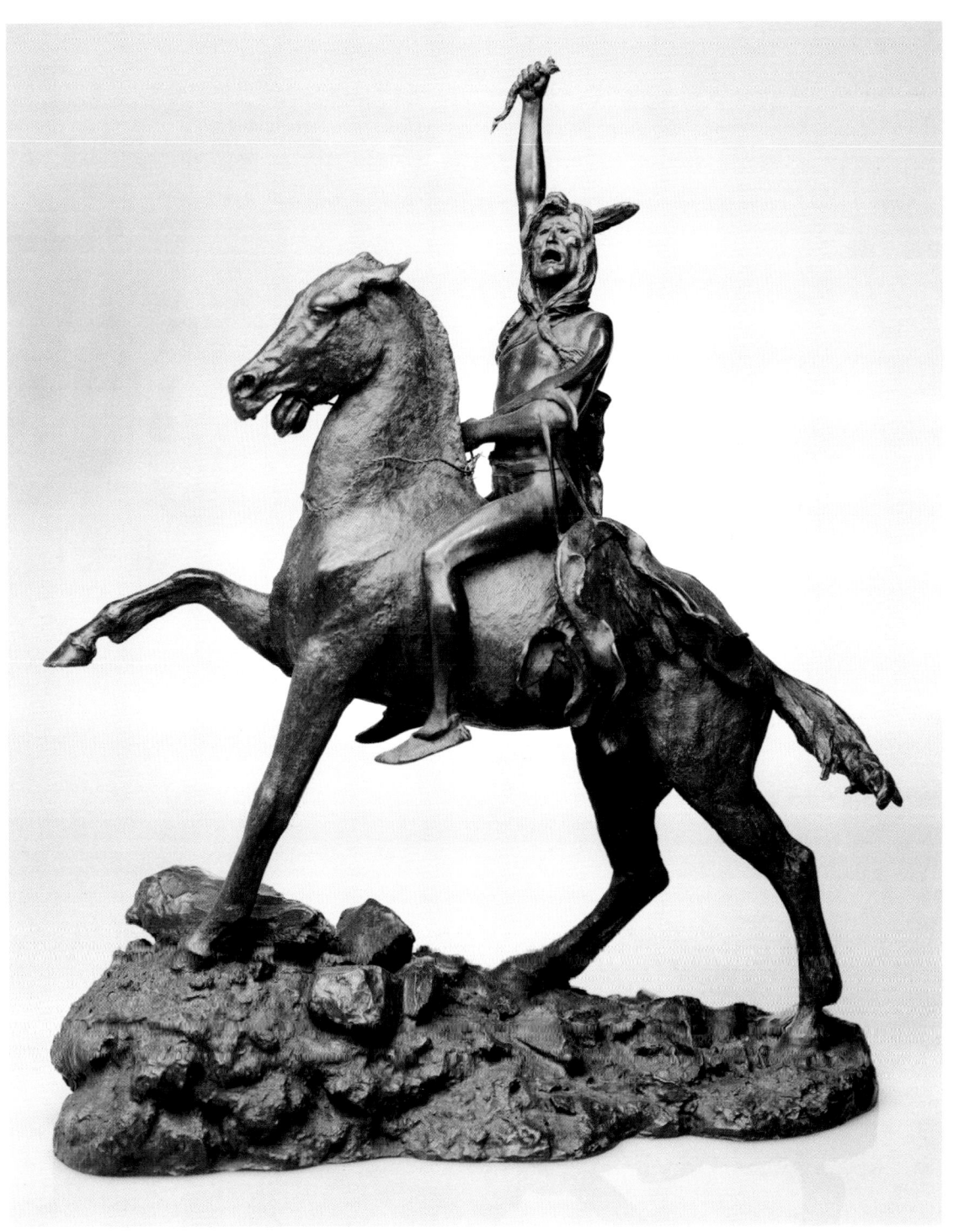

95

THE NORTHER

lost-wax cast, golden brown patina
Roman Bronze Works, unnumbered cast
modeled & copyrighted 1900
height: 21 ½ inches
inscribed: *Frederic Remington*

COPYRIGHTED 1900 BY FREDERIC REMINGTON
CIRE PERDUE CAST/ROMAN BRONZE. WKS. N.Y.

PROVENANCE: The artist; Grant B. and Elizabeth Baker Schley, NY and NJ; Evelyn Schley Behr, NY and NJ; Betty Behr Engelhart Cannon, NJ and Danville, CA (by descent); [Sotheby's, NY 10/22/82]; National Cowboy Hall of Fame, Oklahoma City, OK; [J.N. Bartfield Galleries, NY]; Private collection, NY; [Gerald Peters Gallery, Santa Fe, NM]; Private collection

LITERATURE: *Frederic Remington: The Masterworks*, The Saint Louis Art Museum in conjunction with the Buffalo Bill Historical Center (New York: Harry Abrams Inc., 1988), pl. 54, p 198; Michael Greenbaum, *Icons of the West: Frederic Remington's Sculpture*, Frederic Remington Art Museum, Ogdensburg, NY (1996), pp. 84-87

Copyrighted July 2, 1900, and cast later that year utilzing the lost-wax process, *The Norther* initiated Remington's long and successful collaboration with the Roman Bronze Works. This method allowed the artist the freedom to manipulate the surface of each individual cast to create new effects of light, line, and detail. Remington exploited this process to create the windblown effects on horse and rider, effects which would not have been possible with the sand-cast method.

In *The Norther*, Remington abandons the physical action and bravado that typify his early work for a more contemplative theme. "The almost unnaturally still pose, which stems from the sculptor's efforts to achieve textural effects through the lost-wax process, evokes a powerful mood of isolation and introspection. *The Norther* is a bronze whose inwardness may be seen as analogous to European Symbolist painting and sculpture, like Gauguin's dreaming women or Rodin's *The Thinker*." (*Frederic Remington: The Masterworks*, p. 198)

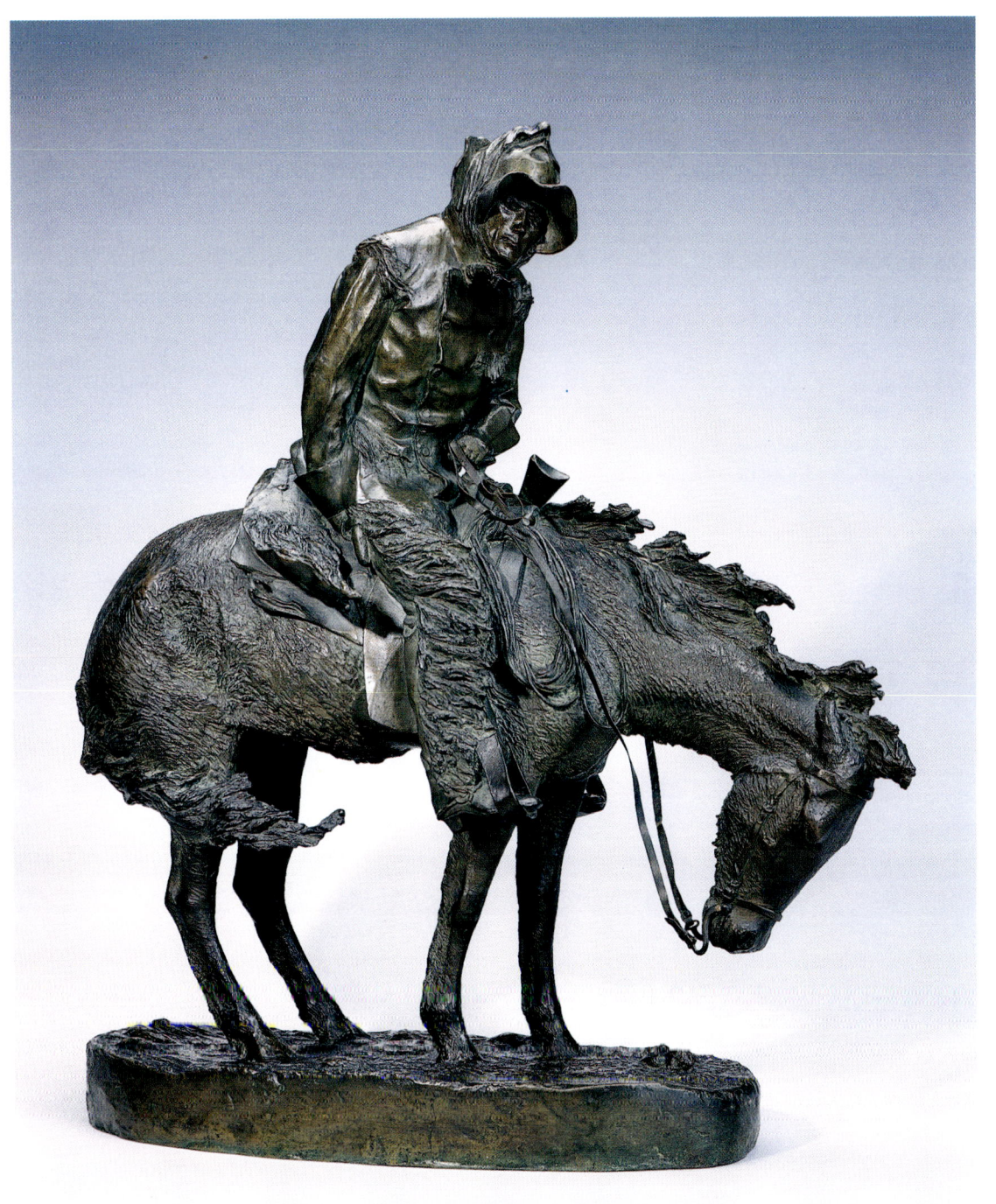

THE CHEYENNE

lost-wax bronze, with golden patina

Roman Bronze Works, cast no. 6

modeled 1901, cast c. 1903

height: 20 ½ inches, base: 7 ⅜ x 14 ¾ inches

inscribed: *Frederic Remington*

        COPYRIGHTED BY/Frederic Remington

        6./CIRE. PERDUE. CAST/ROMAN BRONZE WORKS N.Y.

PROVENANCE : Private collection; Museum of Western Art, Denver, CO; [Gerald Peters Gallery, Santa Fe, NM]; Amon Carter Museum, Fort Worth, TX 1997

LITERATURE : Peter Hassrick, *Frederic Remington: Paintings, Drawings, and Sculpture in the Amon Carter Museum and the Sid Richardson Foundation Collections* (New York: Harry Abrams, Inc., 1973), p. 192; Michael Shapiro, *Cast and Recast: The Sculpture of Frederic Remington*, Published for the National Museum of American Art by The Smithsonian Institution Press, Washington, D.C. (1981), pp. 73-77; *Frederic Remington: The Masterworks*, The Saint Louis Art Museum in conjunction with the Buffalo Bill Historical Center (New York: Harry Abrams, Inc., 1988), pp. 195, 198-99, 210, 214, 227; Michael Greenbaum, *Icons of the West: Frederic Remington's Sculpture*, Frederic Remington Art Museum, Ogdensburg, NY (1996), pp. 89-93

Copyrighted on November 21, 1901, *The Cheyenne* was the second of Remington's bronzes to be cast at the Roman Bronze Works. Remington's portrayal of a horse and rider held aloft by a buffalo robe marked a turning point in the depiction of equine subjects in bronze. Traditionally, horses were represented in static poses, or, if galloping, with outstretched legs. As a diligent student of equine anatomy, Remington was well acquainted with Eadweard Muybridge's stop-action photographs of horses in motion. *The Cheyenne* succeeds in capturing the horse's bullet-like trajectory, which Remington knew well, both as a rider and an observer.

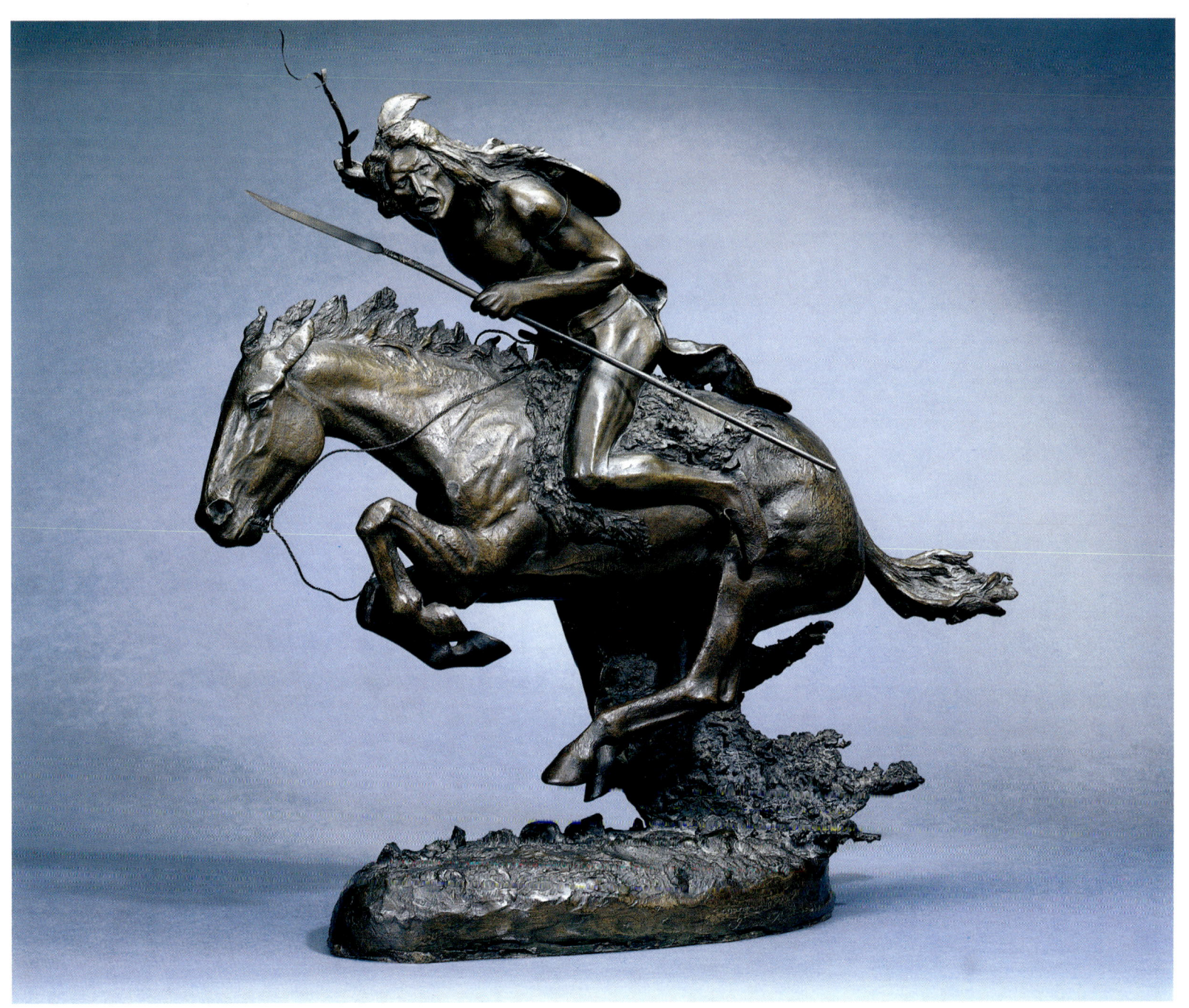

99

THE BUFFALO SIGNAL

lost-wax bronze

Roman Bronze Works, (unnumbered cast)

modeled c. 1902, cast 1902

height: 26 inches

inscribed: *Frederic Remington*
            COPYRIGHT 1902/FRENCH DEVEREUX

PROVENANCE: French Devereux, Cleveland, OH; H. Kelsey Devereux, Delray Beach, FL; National Cowboy Hall of Fame and Western Heritage Center, Oklahoma City, OK, 1980-present

LITERATURE: Michael Shapiro, *Cast and Recast: The Sculpture of Frederic Remington*, Published for the National Museum of American Art by the Smithsonian Institution Press, Washington, D.C. (1981), p. 50; Michael Greenbaum, *Icons of the West: Frederic Remington's Sculpture*, Frederic Remington Art Museum, Ogdensburg, NY (1996), pp. 94-97

EXHIBITIONS: Cummer Gallery of Art, Jacsonville FL (1964)

Copyrighted in 1902, *The Buffalo Signal* was created for French Devereux, a fifteen-year-old boy whose family befriended Remington during a western trip. This unique lost wax casting is a striking portrait of an Indian brave engaged in an act vital to the success of his hunting party. Shortly after the piece was cast, Remington broke the mold and model of *The Buffalo Signal* in front of young Devereux to ensure that the unnumbered bronze would be the only one of its kind.

The sculptural composition was derived from an oil painting by the same title, executed in 1900. Originally conceived as an illustration for Owen Wister's chronicle of the West, *Done in the Open, The Buffalo Signal* is one of Remington's signature images of the vanishing Native American culture of the western plains.

Photograph courtesy of National Cowboy Hall of Fame and Western Heritage Center, Oklahoma City, OK

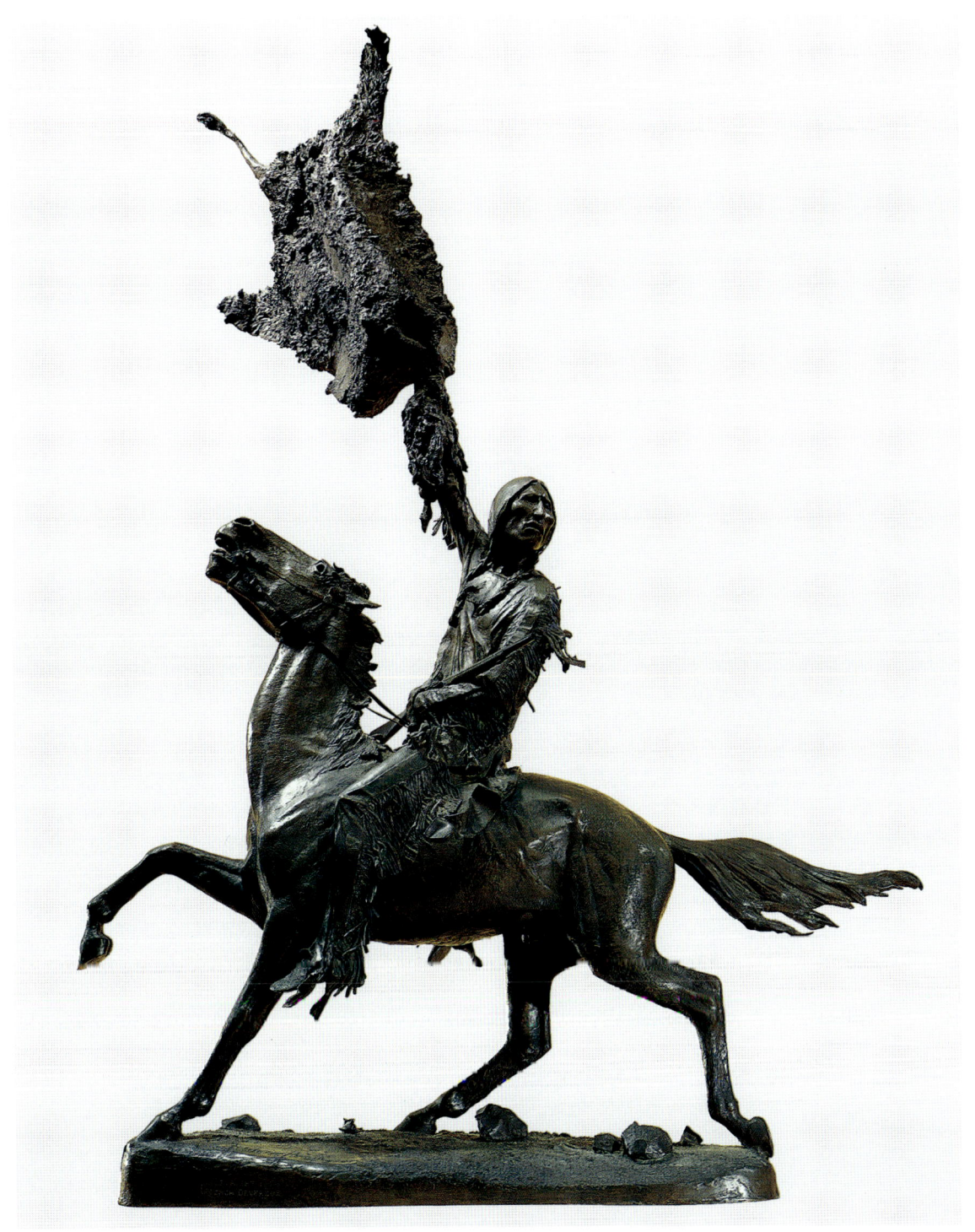

COMING THROUGH THE RYE

lost-wax bronze

Roman Bronze Works, cast no. 3

modeled 1902, cast 1902

height: 30 inches

inscriptions: *FREDERIC REMINGTON*
ROMAN BRONZE WORKS, N.Y. 1905

stamped underneath: *3*

PROVENANCE: [Tiffany & Co., New York, NY]; Franklin Farrel, San Francisco, CA; E.J. McWhiter; Seattle Historical Society, Seattle, WA; [M. Knoedler & Co., Inc., New York, NY]; W.R. Coe Foundation, 1959; Buffalo Bill Historical Center, Cody, WY; [James Maroney, Inc., New York, NY]; private collection; [James Graham & Sons, New York, NY]; private collection

LITERATURE: *Frederic Remington: The Masterworks*, The Saint Louis Art Museum in conjunction with The Buffalo Bill Historical Center (New York: Harry Abrams, Inc., 1988), pp. 207, 210; Michael Greenbaum, *Icons of the West: Frederic Remington's Sculpture*, Frederic Remington Art Museum, Ogdensburg, NY (1996), pp. 98-104

Coming Through the Rye, copyrighted in 1902, represents Remington's most complicated multifigured sculptural creation. The bronze group depicts a group of mounted cowboys, riding abreast four horses at full gallop in a whiskey-induced euphoria. Remington's sophisticated arrangement has only six of the horses' sixteen hooves touching the ground. Although the bronze dates from 1902, the conception for the piece originated with an earlier illustration for *Harper's Weekly* entitled *Cowboys Coming to Town for Christmas*, 1889.

Remington's sculptures were based on his own observations, rather than on the principles of art taught in the academies. His highly innovative format of four separate horsemen riding so closely together that they form a single unit, defied the traditional rules of sculpture. The subsequent success and popularity of *Coming Through the Rye* was evidenced by the fact that the Corcoran Gallery of Art purchased one for their collection in 1905, along with a casting of *The Mountain Man*. These acquisitions took place shortly after Remington's solo exhibit at M. Knoedler & Co., and were the first examples of Remington's work to be purchased by a museum.

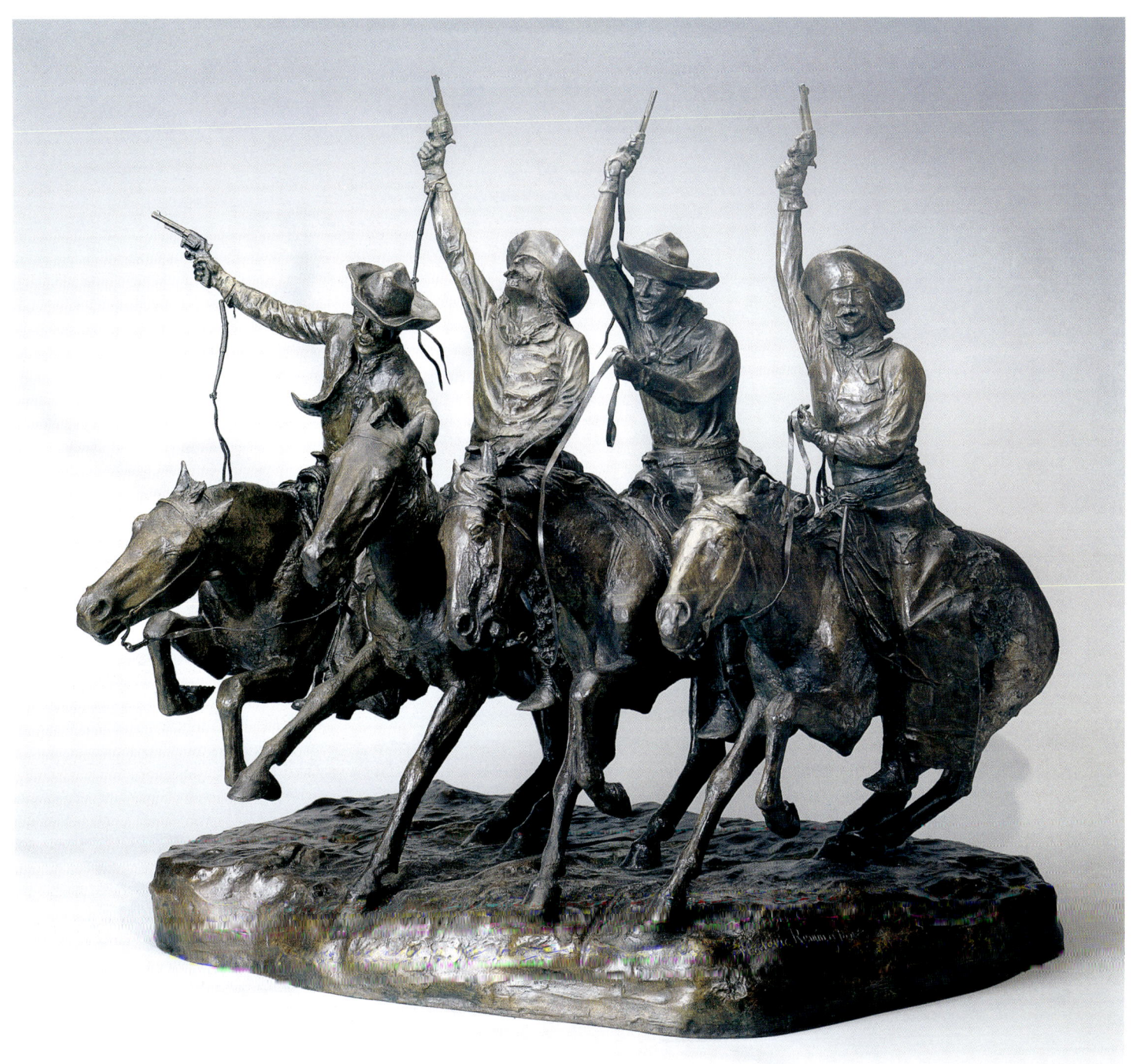

THE MOUNTAIN MAN

lost-wax bronze

Roman Bronze Works, cast no. 16

copyrighted 1903

height: 28 inches, base: 9 ⅝ x 9 ¾ inches

inscribed on base: *Copyright by/Frederic Remington*

stamped on base: *Roman Bronze Works N.Y.*

numbered under base: *No. 16.*

PROVENANCE: The artist; Herman Kasten; Dorothy Kasten Ingersoll (daughter of Herman Kasten), 1923; Kimball Smith (nephew of Dorothy Ingersoll), 1991; [Gerald Peters Gallery, Santa Fe, NM]; Private collection

LITERATURE: Michael Shapiro, *Cast and Recast: The Sculpture of Frederic Remington*, Published for the National Museum of American Art by the Smithsonian Institution Press, Washington, D.C. (1981), pp. 77-81; *Frederic Remington: The Masterworks*, The Saint Louis Art Museum in conjunction with the Buffalo Bill Historical Center, Cody, WY (New York: Harry Abrams, Inc., 1988), pp. 205, 210, 211, 214, 231, 267; Michael Greenbaum, *Icons of the West: Frederic Remington's Sculpture*, Frederic Remington Art Museum, Ogdensburg, NY (1996), pp. 105-112

The sharply inclined base– an unusual form for Remington– is an effective device suggesting the precarious life of the fur trapper, who trusted in only his animal and own skill to survive in a treacherous environment. The detailed costume, accouterments, and perilous descent realistically describe the harsh existence of the frontier mountain man.

The Mountain Man, copyrighted in July, 1903, received critical acclaim from historians and collectors alike. The large size of the edition, consisting of around seventy-five casts, attests to the success and popularity of the subject. Only forty-five casts were authorized by Remington and his widow, Eva. After Eva's death in 1918, Roman Bronze Works continued to produce approximately thirty additional examples of *The Mountain Man* before the models and molds were destroyed in 1920.

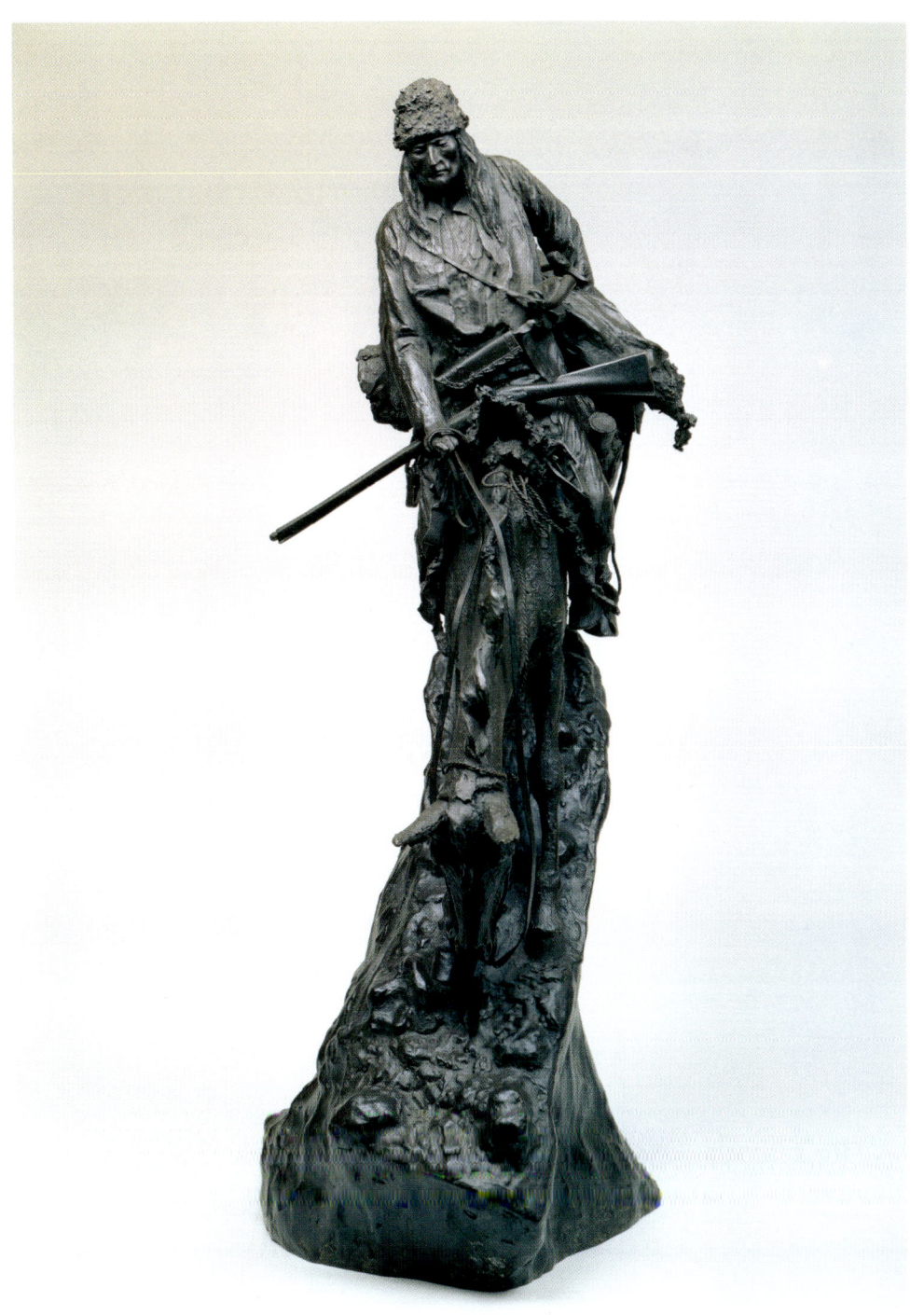

THE SERGEANT

lost-wax bronze, dark green patina with brown highlights

Roman Bronze Works, cast no. 15

modeled 1904, cast c. 1906

height: 10 ⅛ inches

inscribed on base: *Frederic Remington/copyright*

Roman Bronze Works/N.Y.

inscribed under base: *No 15.*

PROVENANCE: Private collection, Washington D.C.; Private collection; [Mongerson Wunderlich Galleries, Chicago, IL]; [Gerald Peters Gallery, Santa Fe, NM]

LITERATURE: Patricia Broder, *Bronzes of the American West* (New York: Harry N. Abrams, Inc., 1974), ill. p. 147; *Frederic Remington: The Masterworks*, The Saint Louis Art Museum in conjunction with The Buffalo Bill Historical Center (New York: Harry N. Abrams, Inc., 1988), pp. 210-11, 224, 267; Michael Greenbaum, *Icons of the West: Frederic Remington's Sculpture*, Frederic Remington Art Museum, Ogdensburg, NY (1996), pp. 113-115

The Sergeant portrays an archetype of the tough American soldier, respectfully described by Remington as "men with the bark on," who rode with Theodore Roosevelt and his Rough Riders in Cuba during the Spanish-American War. The small bust may have been inspired by a suggestion from Riccardo Bertelli, founder of Roman Bronze Works, to create smaller, and thus more affordable statuettes for the buying public. This cast, number fifteen, was one of twenty-five produced in Remington's lifetime.

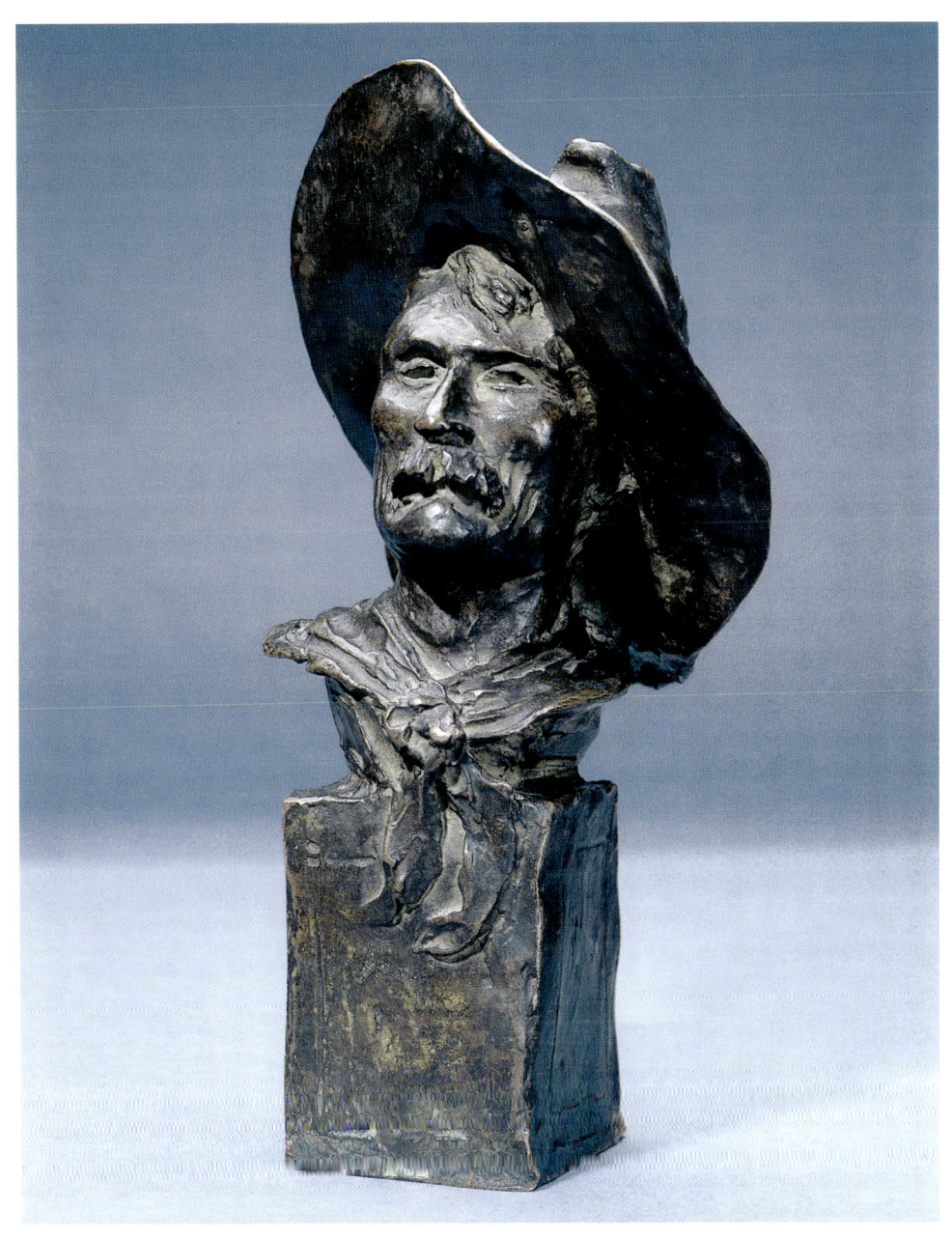

THE SAVAGE
lost-wax bronze, green-brown patina
Roman Bronze Works, cast no. 7
modeled & copyrighted 1908
height: 10 ½ inches
inscriptions: *copyright 1908 Frederic Remington*
                Frederic Remington 1908
                Roman Bronze Works N-Y-
stamped underneath: *No. -7-*

PROVENANCE: Private collection; Mannados Bookshop, New York, NY; Estate of C.C. Moseley, Los Angeles, CA; [Gerald Peters Gallery, Santa Fe, NM]; Private collection

LITERATURE: Peter Hassrick, *Frederic Remington: Paintings, Drawings, and Sculpture in the Amon Carter Museum and Sid Richardson Foundation Collections* (New York: Harry N. Abrams, Inc., 1973), p. 205; *Frederic Remington: The Masterworks*, The Saint Louis Art Museum in conjunction with the Buffalo Bill Historical Center, Cody, WY (New York: Harry N. Abrams Inc.), pp. 210-211, 224; Michael Greenbaum, *Icons of the West: Frederic Remington's Sculpture*, Frederic Remington Art Museum, Ogdensburg, NY (1996), pp. 113-118

The smallest of Remington's bronzes, and one of only two busts in his oeuvre, *The Savage* represents a prototype rather than a portrait of a specific individual. The format may have been derived from a small plaster sculpture by J.S. Hartley, dated 1883 and inscribed "Ye Ancient Mariner." It was in Remington's collection and appears in photographs on the mantel of his studio. Like Remington's sculpture, Hartley's bust rises from a small square plinth decorated with inscribed lines. *The Savage*, number 7, was one of approximately twenty castings in the first authorized edition produced by Roman Bronze Works. (*Frederic Remington: The Masterworks*, p. 211)

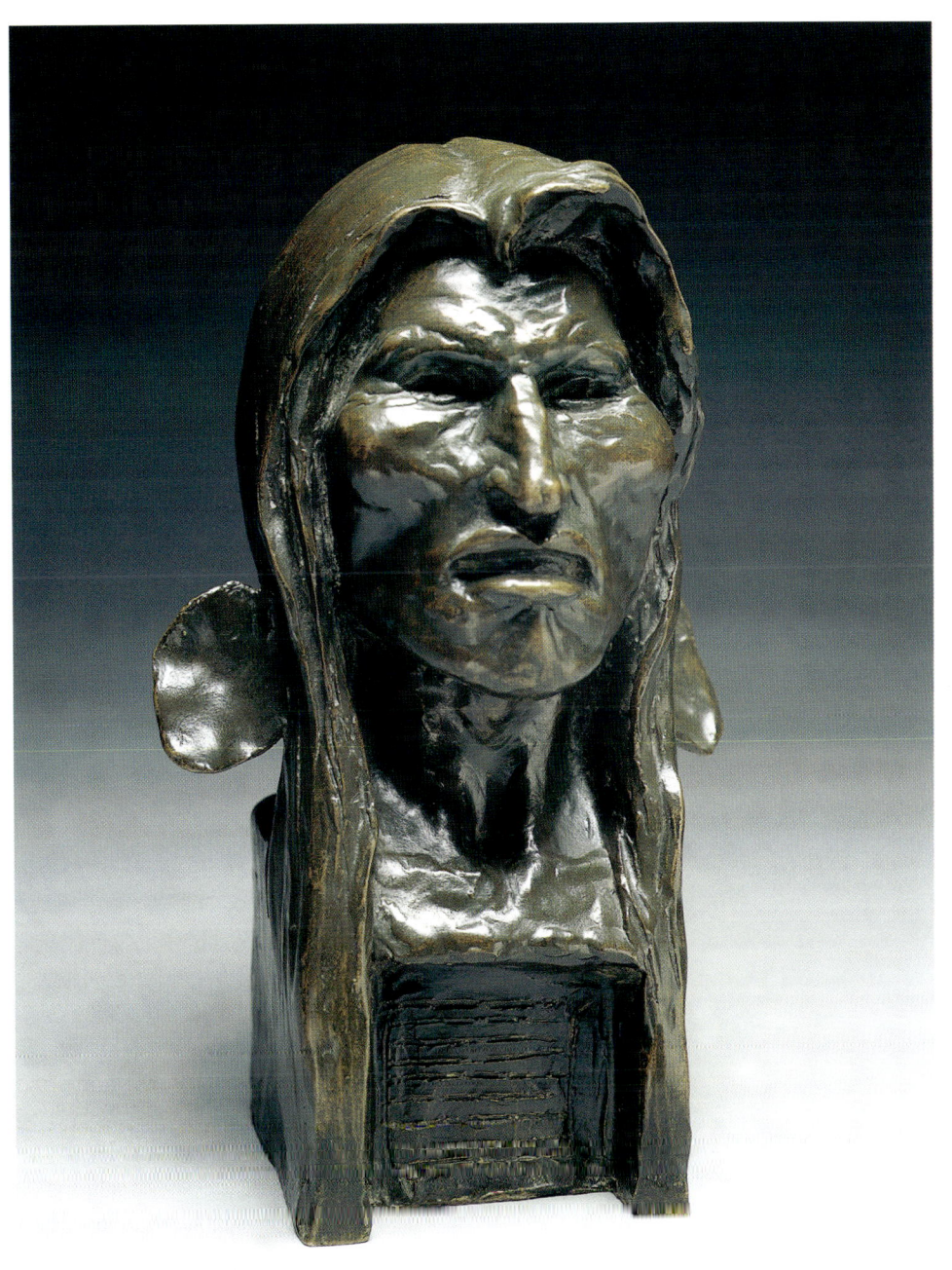

THE RATTLESNAKE

lost-wax bronze, brown patina
Roman Bronze Works, cast #5
copyrighted 1905, cast 1906
height: 21 inches, base: 14 5/16 x 16 inches
inscribed: *Frederic Remington*
            Roman Bronze Works, N.Y.
            No.5.

PROVENANCE: Private collection, Santiago, Chile, c. 1907-1964; Antique Dealer, Santiago, Chile, 1965; Private collection, Chicago, IL, 1965; [Gerald Peters Gallery, Santa Fe, NM]; Private collection

LITERATURE: Michael Shapiro, *Cast and Recast: The Sculpture of Frederic Remington*, National Museum of American Art, Washington, D.C. (1981), p. 53; *Frederic Remington: The Masterworks*, The Saint Louis Art Museum in conjunction with the Buffalo Bill Historical Center (New York: Harry Abrams, Inc., 1988), p. 211, ill. pl. 59 & 60; Michael Greenbaum, *Icons of the West: Frederic Remington's Sculpture*, Frederic Remington Art Museum, Ogdensburg, NY (1996), pp. 123-128

Copyrighted in 1905 and reworked three years later, *The Rattlesnake* was Remington's twelfth bronze. The piece was described by the artist as a "cowboy on bronco...rattlesnake on ground ready to attack horse." The rearing bronc and rider, posed masterfully in a spiraling sweep of motion, became one of Remington's most popular works.

In 1908, after eleven castings of the approximately twenty-one inch tall model had been produced, Remington significantly altered the composition. He worked nearly every day for several weeks to improve the symmetry and movement of the group. The new version, (plate 12) was nearly three inches taller than its predecessor. The cowboy, still dressed in finely textured woolly chaps, lurched forward in a more pronounced curve to accommodate the violent movement of the rearing horse, whose forelegs Remington tucked evenly under its body. As the subject was Remington's second most popular bronze in total production after *The Bronco Buster*, approximately one-hundred Rattlesnake castings were produced before the ordered destruction of the models. (Greenbaum p. 123)

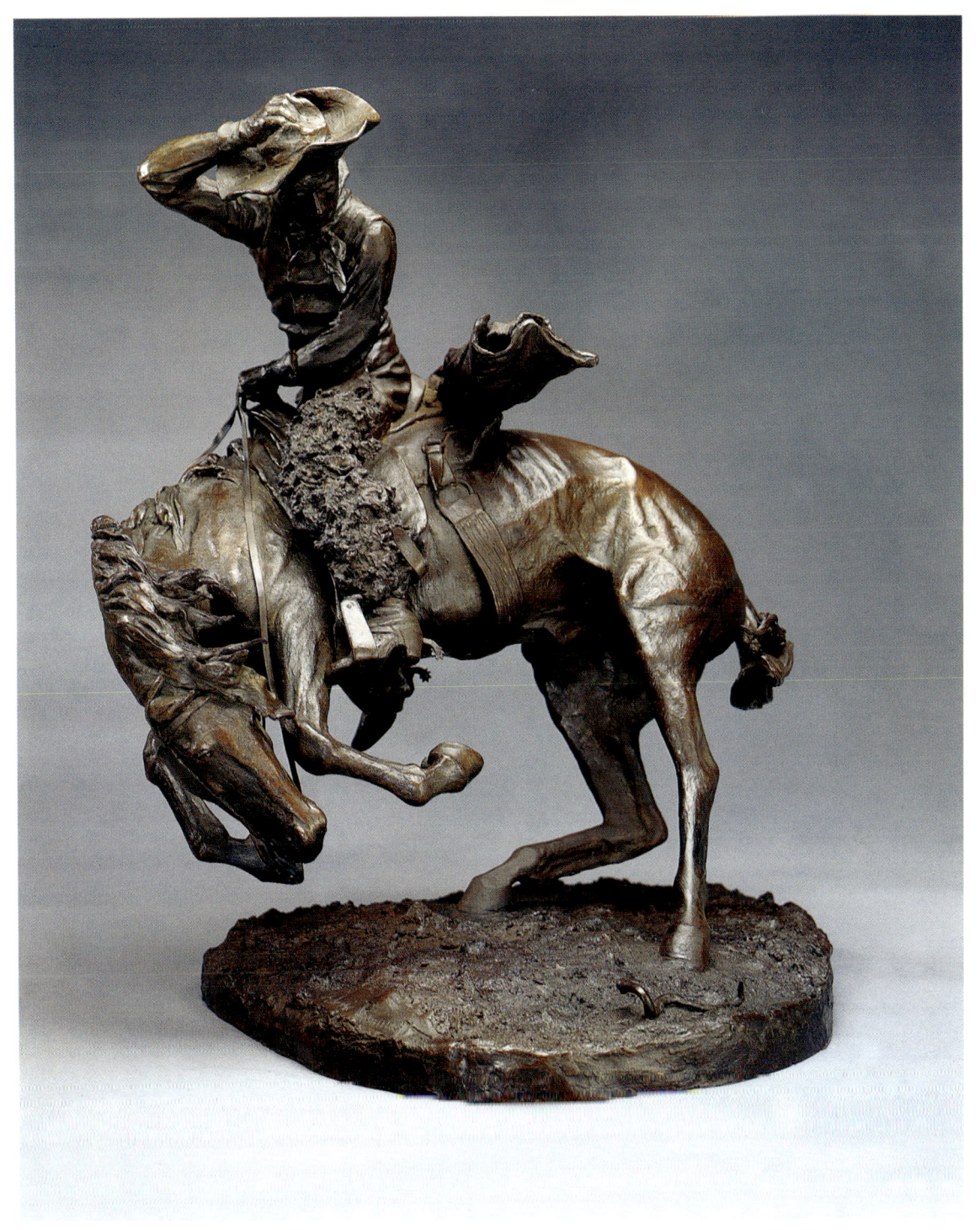

THE RATTLESNAKE
lost-wax cast, brown patina
Roman Bronze Works, cast #19
copyrighted 1905
height: 25 ¼ inches, base: 10 ½ x 16 ½ inches
inscribed: *Copyright by/Frederic Remington*
                 Roman Bronze Works N.Y.
stamped under base: *No 19*

PROVENANCE: Mr. Lehman, c. 1940; A. E. Lehman, New York, NY (gifted by descent); [Gerald Peters Gallery, Santa Fe, NM]; Private collection

LITERATURE: Michael Shapiro, *Cast and Recast: The Sculpture of Frederic Remington*, National Museum of American Art, Washington D.C. (1981), p. 53; *Frederic Remington: The Masterworks*, The Saint Louis Art Museum in conjunction with the Buffalo Bill Historical Center (New York: Harry Abrams, Inc., 1988), p. 211, ill. pl. 59 & 60; Michael Greenbaum, *Icons of the West: Frederic Remington's Sculpture*, Frederic Remington Art Museum, Ogdensburg, NY (1996), pp. 123-128

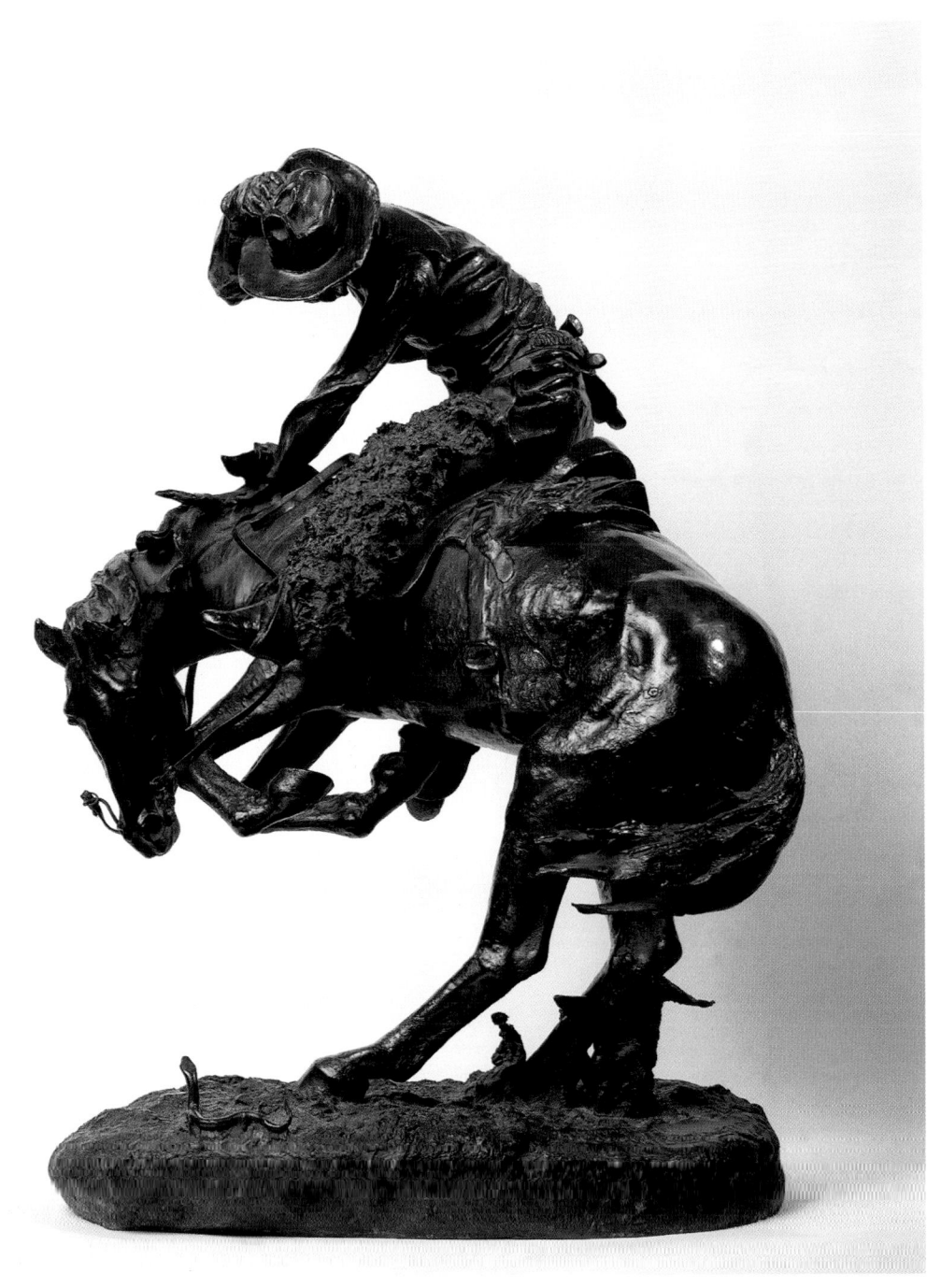

THE OLD DRAGOONS OF 1850
lost-wax bronze
Roman Bronze Works, cast no. 5
copyrighted 1905
height: 25 ⅜ inches
inscriptions: *Copyright by/Frederic Remington*
stamped: *Roman Bronze Works N.Y./No.5*

PROVENANCE: [Tiffany & Co., New York, NY]; Therese Dorrance Groves, Pennsylvania, 1922 - c. 1950; [James Graham & Sons, New York, NY]; Amon G. Carter, Fort Worth, TX, 1951; Amon Carter Museum, Fort Worth, TX, 1961; [Gerald Peters Gallery, Santa Fe, NM]; Private collection

LITERATURE: Peter Hassrick, *Frederic Remington: Paintings, Drawings, and Sculpture in the Amon Carter Museum and the Sid Richardson Foundation Collections* (New York: Harry N. Abrams, Inc., 1973), pl. 86; *Frederic Remington*, Gerald Peters Gallery in association with Mongerson-Wunderlich, Santa Fe, NM (1991), pp. 112-113

Frederic Remington copyrighted *The Old Dragoons of 1850* on December 6, 1905. Because of the size and complexity of the work, very few were cast. Of the six known casts, all but one are in public collections. As with many of the bronzes made by the lost-wax method, details of the figures vary considerably between each version. This cast, number 5, is the first version to bear a cast number, and the ledger date records the date of its production as May 31, 1917.

Unlike the majority of Remington's bronzes which are based on Western prototypes, this work refers to a specific mounted infantry troop. The Dragoons were organized as early as 1834 to aid in the settlement of the Territories west of the Mississippi. Stylistically, *The Old Dragoons of 1850* is perhaps Remington's most complex composition in bronze, with each of the figures engaged in an intricate interplay of action and drama.

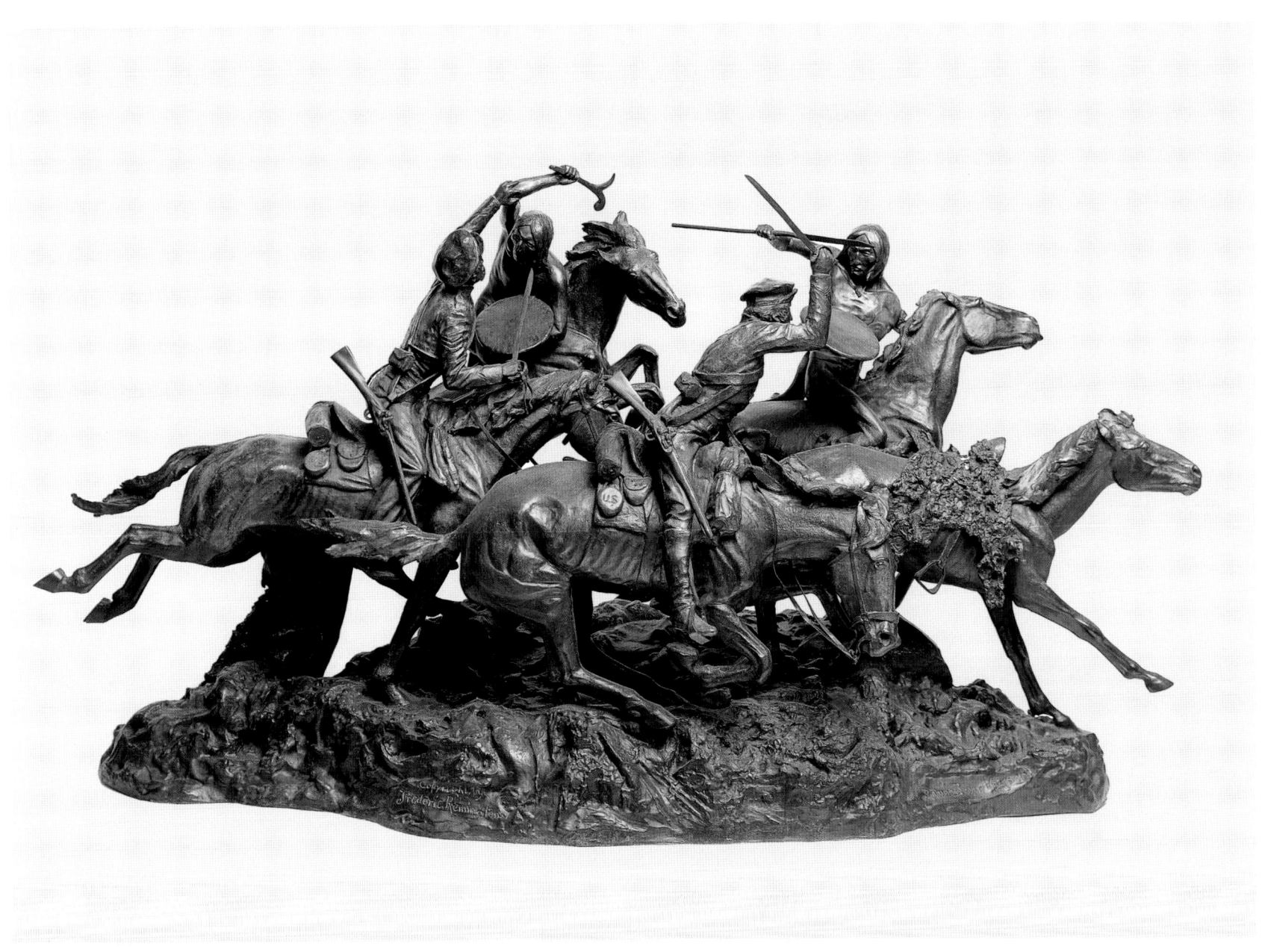

THE OUTLAW

lost-wax bronze with brown patina

Roman Bronze Works, cast no. 18

modeled 1906, cast c. 1909-10

height: 23 ⅜ inches, base: 8 ¼ x 13 ⁵⁄₁₆ inches

inscribed on base: *copyright by/Federic Remington*

ROMAN BRONZE WORKS N.Y.

under base: *No 18-*

PROVENANCE: [Hanzel Galleries, June, 1973]; David Gage Joyce; Estate of Beatrice Kean; Private collection, California; [Gerald Peters Gallery, Santa Fe, NM]; Private collection

LITERATURE: Michael Shapiro, *Cast and Recast: The Sculpture of Frederic Remington*, Smithsonian Institution Press, Washington, D.C. (1981); Michael Greenbaum, *Icons of the West: Frederic Remington's Sculpture*, Frederic Remington Art Museum, Ogdensburg, NY (1996), pp. 133-137

With *The Outlaw* of 1906, Remington explored the structural limits of cast-bronze sculpture, challenging himself to move beyond the traditional means of sculptural support. He worked at making the figures appear free from their bases, while still creating works which were structurally stable. This was a persistent concern in twentieth century sculpture, pursued extensively by Degas, for example, in his series of dancers and race horses.

Possibly in response to this challenge, Remington created some of the most innovative bases in modern sculpture, incorporating their elements into the context of the piece. In *The Outlaw*, the horse's right front hoof balances on a clump of sagebrush, and from this point the entire weight of the horse and rider is balanced.

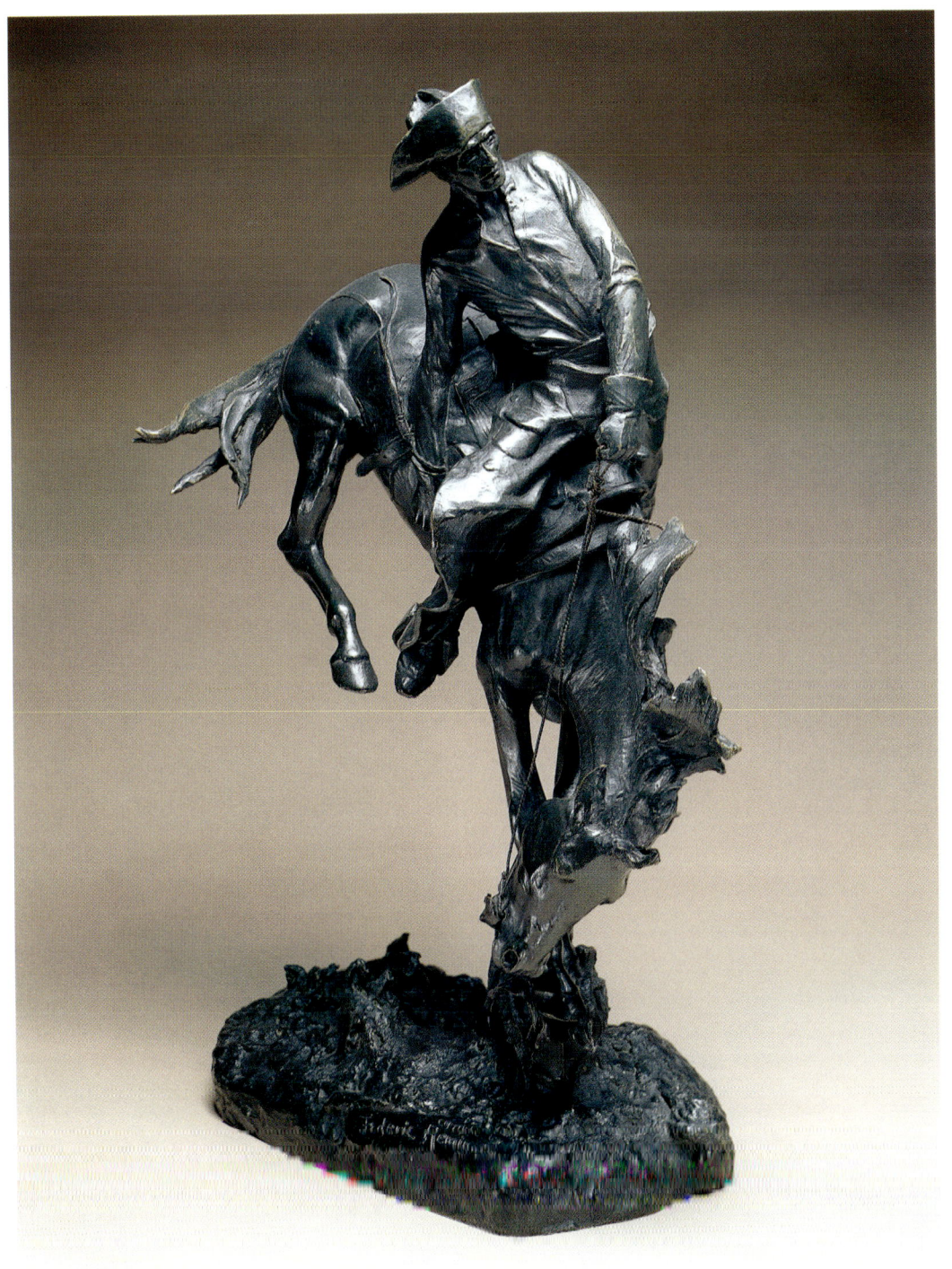

THE HORSE THIEF

lost-wax bronze, variegated golden brown patina
Roman Bronze Works, unnumbered cast
modeled 1907, cast c. 1907-08
height: 25 ¾ inches
inscribed on front of base: *Copyright 1907 by/Frederic Remington*
stamped on back of base: *ROMAN BRONZE WORKS/N.Y.*

PROVENANCE: Private collection; [J.N. Bartfield Galleries, New York, NY]; private collection, on loan to Buffalo Bill Historical Center, Cody, WY

LITERATURE: Patricia Broder, *Bronzes of the American West* (New York: Harry N. Abrams, Inc., 1974), ill. pl. 123; *Frederic Remington: The Masterworks*, The Saint Louis Art Museum in conjunction with the Buffalo Bill Historical Center, Cody, WY (New York: Harry N. Abrams, Inc., 1988), pp. 199, 217, 227, 267; Michael Greenbaum, *Icons of the West: Frederic Remington's Sculpture*, Frederic Remington Art Museum, Ogdensburg, NY (1996), pp. 138-39

Remington's only relief sculpture, *The Horse Thief* is another remarkable testament to the versatility of the artist and Riccardo Bertelli, his collaborator at Roman Bronze Works. Remington's success with his sculpture *The Cheyenne*, encouraged him to continue experimenting with unusual support schemes for his bronzes. *The Cheyenne* is held aloft by a buffalo robe, and a similar trompe l'oeil conception allowed him to support *The Horse Thief* without any of the horse's hooves touching the ground. The Baroque flavor that characterized many of Remington's works indicates that he was eager to explore visual and structural alternatives to the vocabulary of classical sculptural support. This lifetime cast of is one of only three bronzes produced in the edition, all of which are unnumbered.

Photograph courtesy of J.N. Bartfield Galleries, New York, NY

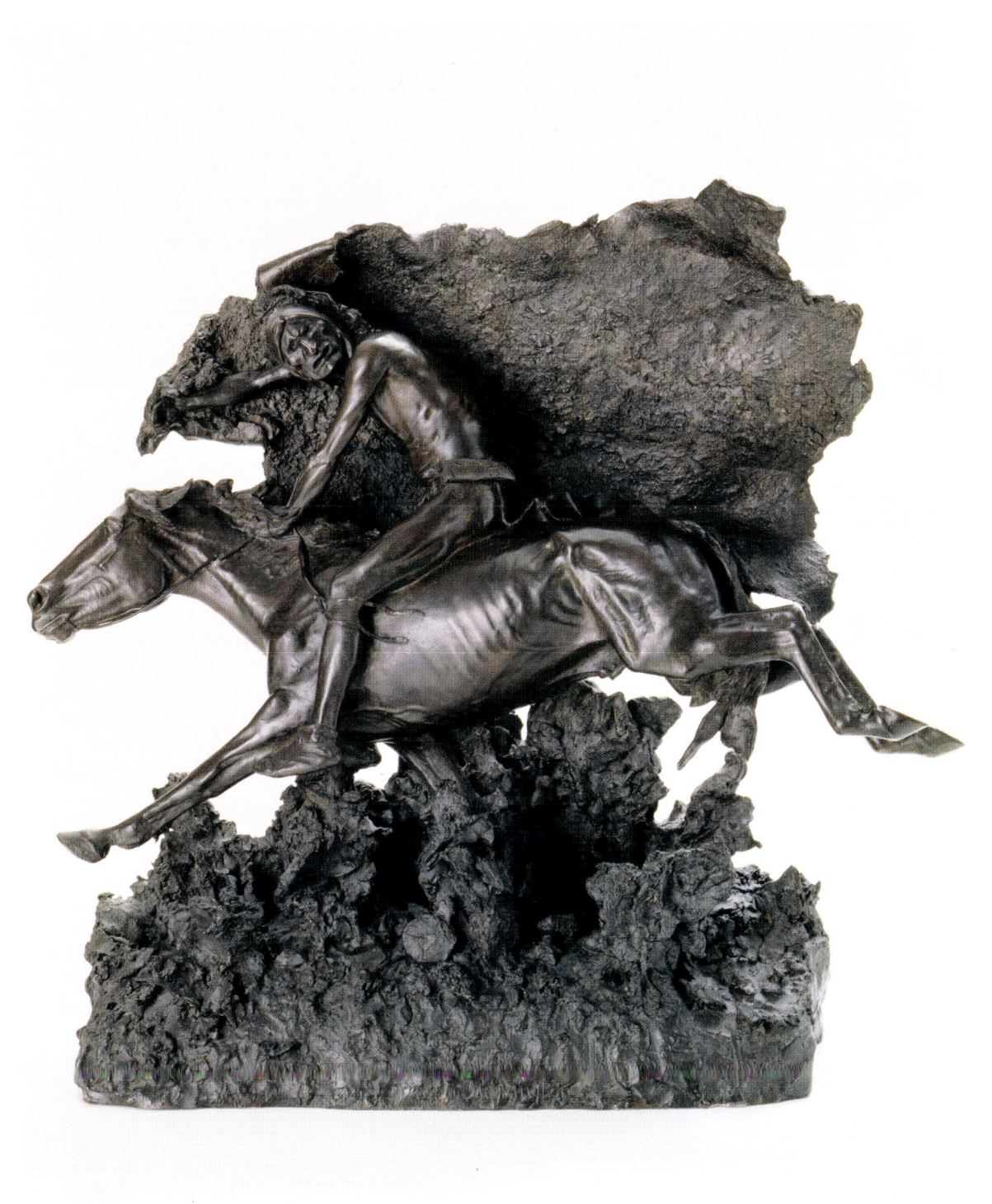

THE BUFFALO HORSE
lost-wax bronze
Roman Bronze Works, (unique cast)
modeled 1907, cast c. 1907
height: 36 inches
inscriptions: *copyright by/Frederic Remington*
Roman Bronze Works N.Y

PROVENANCE: The Artist; Eva Remington; Phillip G. Cole, Tarrytown, NY; Thomas Gilcrease Institute, Tulsa, OK

LITERATURE: Patricia Broder, *Bronzes of the American West* (New York: Harry N. Abrams, Inc., 1974), pp. 143, pl. 141; Peter Hassrick, *Treasures of the Old West: Paintings and Sculpture from the Thomas Gilcrease Institute of American History* (New York: Harry N. Abrams, Inc., 1984), ill. pl. 66; *Frederic Remington: The Masterworks*, The Saint Louis Art Museum in conjunction with The Buffalo Bill Historical Center, Cody, WY (New York: Harry N. Abrams, Inc., 1988), pl. 65, pp. 221, 225, 227; Michael Greenbuam, *Icons of the West: Frederic Remington's Sculpture*, Frederic Remington Art Museum, Ogdensburg, NY (1996), pp. 140-142

EXHIBITIONS: *Treasures of the Old West: Paintings and Sculpture from the Thomas Gilcrease Institute of American History* Thomas Gilcrease Inst., Tulsa, OK (traveling exhibition); Denver Art Museum, Denver, CO; Buffalo Bill Historical Center, Cody, WY (1984)

The Buffalo Horse depicts the dramatic moment when a mounted Indian is thrown from his horse by the impact of a headlong collision with a buffalo. Remington portrays the rider somersaulting over the two animals, and enhances the acrobatic drama of the scene by utilizing the Indian's lance as the sole support for the entire composition. The precarious pose of pony and rider flung above the buffalo inspired a critic to term the work "a daring violation of many of the rules of sculpture."

The liberal correlation between Remington's paintings and his bronzes was more than an exchange of poses. The encrusted surface of *The Buffalo Horse* directly translated into the vigorous brushwork exemplified in a later painting of the same subject, *Episode of the Buffalo Hunt*, 1908. Both the bronze and painting were originally purchased by Phillip Cole and are currently housed at the Gilcrease Museum.

Photograph courtesy of Thomas Gilcrease Institute, Tulsa, OK

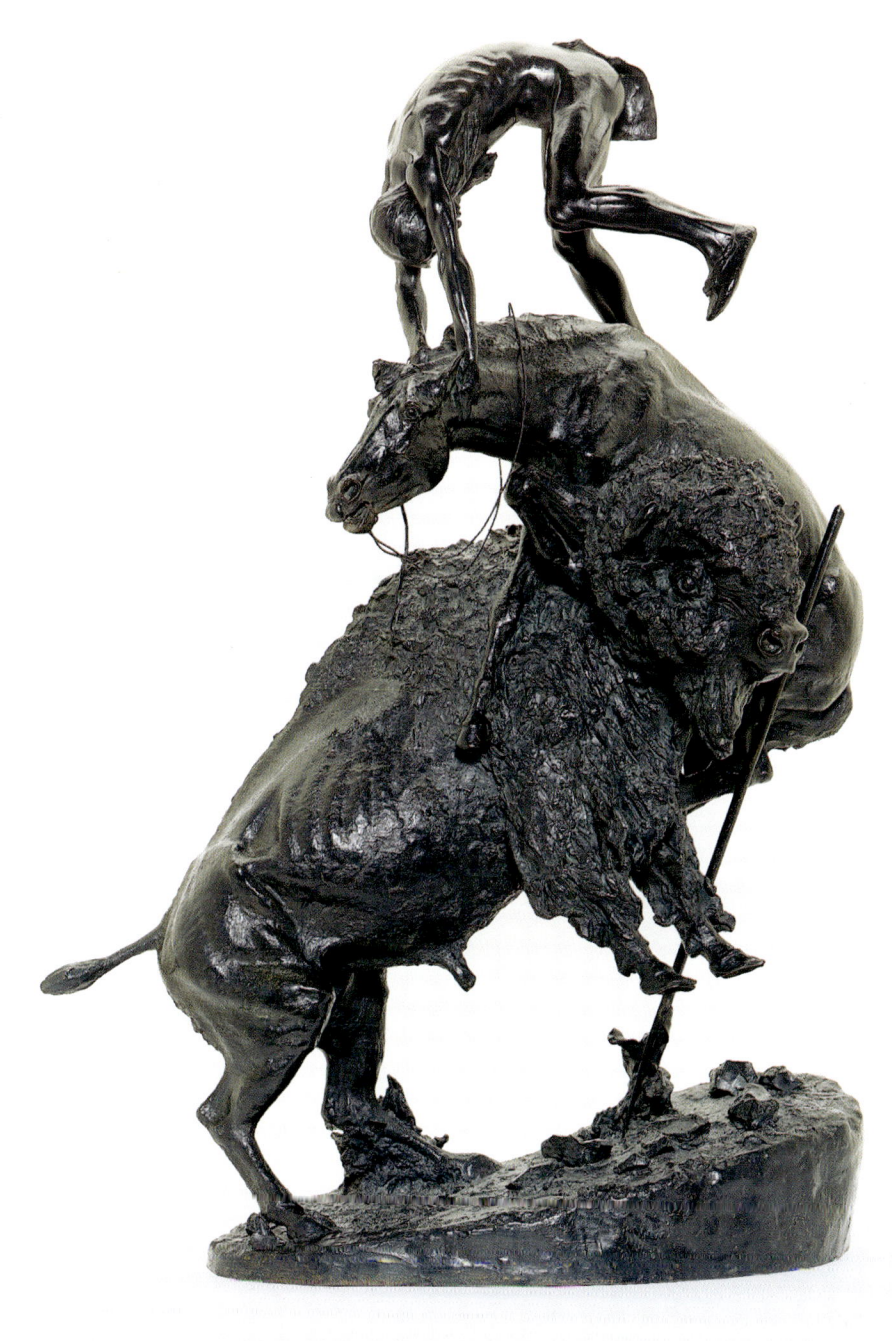

TROOPER OF THE PLAINS

lost-wax bronze

Roman Bronze Works, cast no. 8

modeled 1908, copyrighted 1909

height: 25 ⅜ inches, base: 7 ¾ x 19 ⅝ inches

inscriptions on base: *Copyright by/Frederic Remington*

ROMAN BRONZE WORKS N-Y-

under base: *No.8*

PROVENANCE: M.Q. Petersen, Louisiana, (inherited from his father c. 1945); bequeathed to his wife Mrs. M.Q. Petersen, 1990; [Gerald Peters Gallery, Santa Fe, NM]; Private collection

LITERATURE: Peter Hassrick, *Frederic Remington: Paintings, Drawings, and Sculpture in the Amon Carter Museum and the Sid Richardson Foundation Collections* (New York: Harry N. Abrams, Inc., 1973), pp. 206-07; Patricia Broder, *Bronzes of the American West* (New York: Harry N. Abrams, Inc., 1974), p. 121; *Frederic Remington: The Masterworks*, The Saint Louis Art Museum in conjunction with The Buffalo Bill Historical Center, Cody, WY (New York: Harry N. Abrams, Inc., 1988), pp. 218, 221, 230, 231; Michael Greenbaum, *Icons of the West: Frederic Remington's Sculpture*, Frederic Remington Art Museum, Ogdensburg, NY (1996), pp. 147-151

Defying the traditional means of sculptural support was a consistent theme in Remington's work: He continually sought to devise inventive new methods for anchoring his elaborate compositions of horses and riders. Remington formulated more innovative bases that any other American sculptor of his time, incorporating their elements into the context of the narrative drama. In *Trooper of the Plains* and *The Outlaw*, a clump of sagebrush carries the weight of horse and rider.

As with many of Remington's bronzes, the *Trooper of the Plains* finds its precedent in an earlier oil canvas entitled *Cutting Out the Pony Herds* (Museum of Western Art, Denver). The sculpture, like the painting, shows a horse and rider in full gallop— all of the horse's hooves are off the ground.

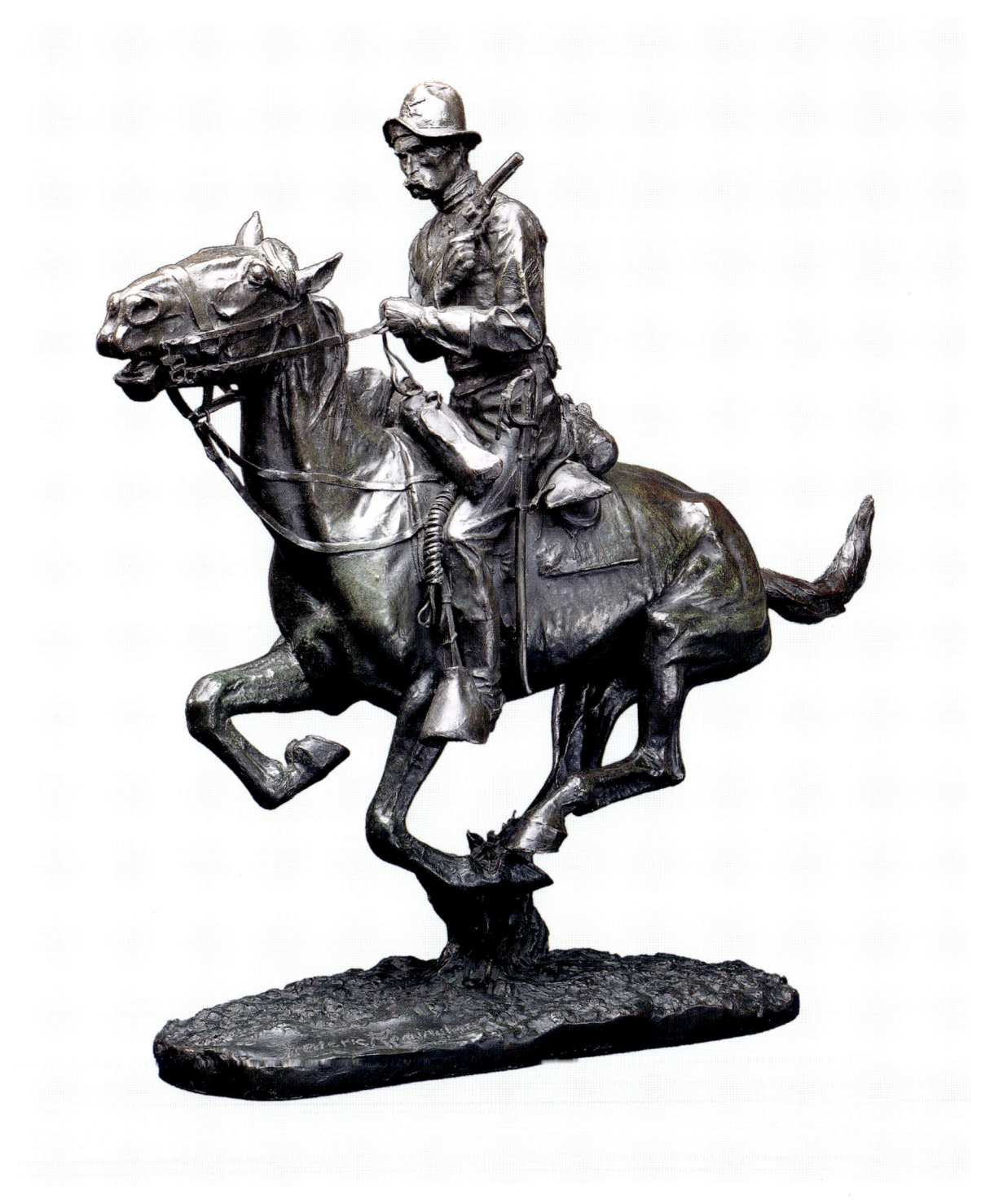

THE STAMPEDE

lost-wax bronze
Roman Bronze Works, cast no. 2
modeled 1909, cast c. 1915-1918
height: 21 ¾ inches, base: 13 ⅞ x 46 inches
inscriptions: *Copyright by/Frederik Remington*
No2 ROMAN BRONZE WORKS N-Y-

PROVENANCE: [Tiffany & Co., New York, NY]; Phillip Cole, Tarrytown, NY; Thomas Gilcrease Inst., Tulsa, OK

LITERATURE: Peter Hassrick, *Treasures of the Old West: Paintings and Sculpture from the Thomas Gilcrease Institute of American History* (New York: Harry N. Abrams, Inc., 1984), ill. pl. 65; *Frederic Remington: The Masterworks*, The Saint Louis Art Museum in conjunction with The Buffalo Bill Historical Center (New York: Harry N. Abrams, 1988), p. 232; Michael Greenbaum, *Icons of the West: Frederic Remington's Sculpture*, Frederic Remington Art Museum, Ogdensburg, NY (1996), pp. 156-159

EXHIBITIONS: *Treasures of the Old West: Paintings and Sculpture from the Thomas Gilcrease Institute of American History* (traveling exhibition) The Thomas Gilcrease Inst., Tulsa, OK; Denver Art Museum, Denver, CO; Buffalo Bill Historical Center, Cody, WY (1984)

The Stampede, Remington's last work, illustrates his expanding development as a sculptor. Measuring forty-six inches in its greatest dimension, the sculpture is the largest format that Remington attempted for an indoor bronze. Michael Shapiro compares its densely packed and onward-moving elements to several of Antoine-Louis Barye's works, as well as to Gutzon Borglum's *Mares of Diomedes*, of 1903. Remington died before he could complete the frieze-like group, but his wife, Eva, commissioned Sally Farnham, a sculptor and family friend, to finish *The Stampede*. Working at Roman Bronze Works in New York, Farham assembled the figures, signed Remington's signature, and copyrighted the work on April 13, 1910.

Photograph courtesy Thomas Gilcrease Institute, Tulsa, OK

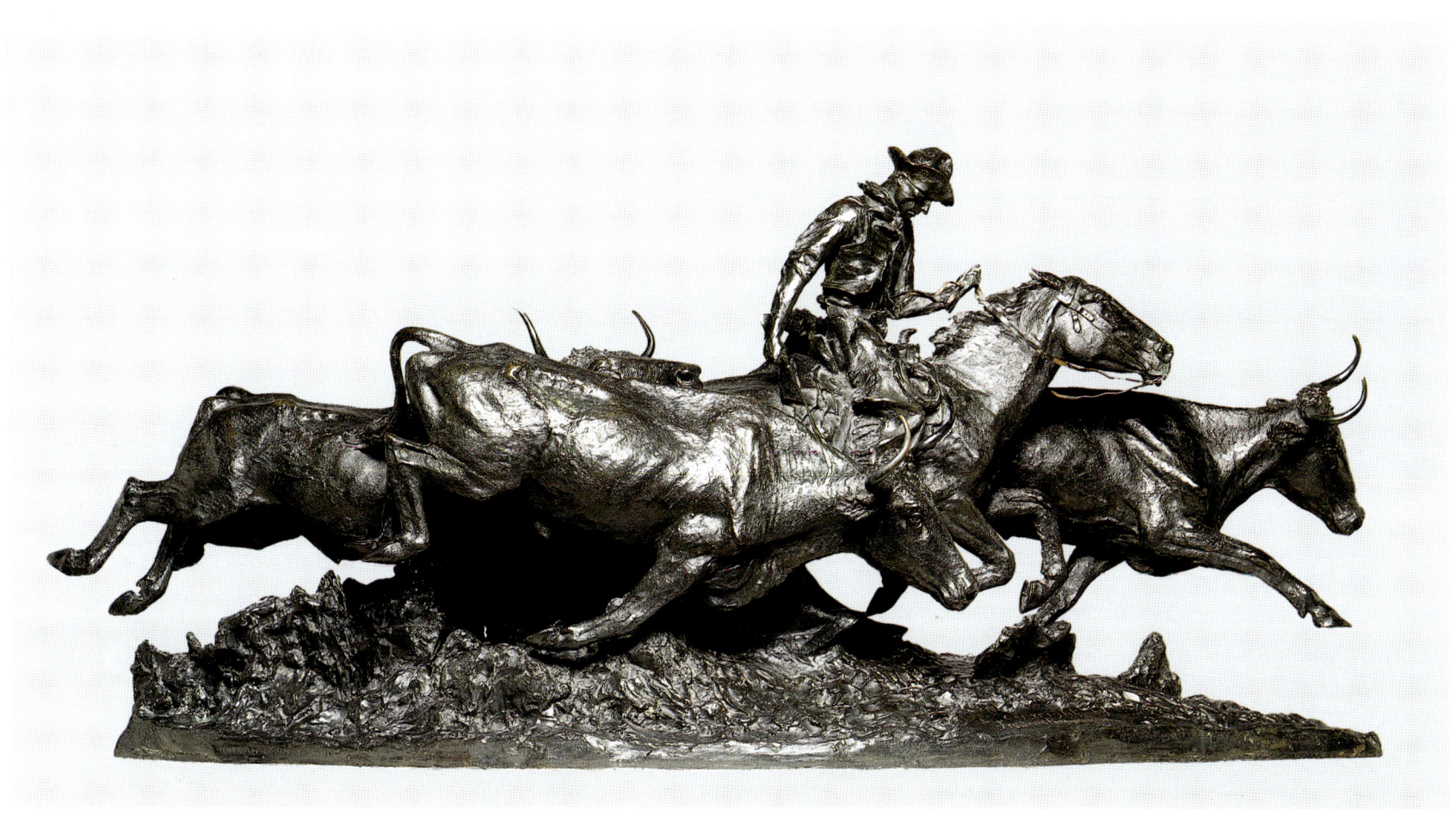

REMINGTON CHRONOLOGY

This chronology, is in part, derived from the time line presented in *Frederic Remington: A Catalogue Raisonné* by Peter Hassrick & Melissa Webster.

1861 On October 4, Frederic Remington is born to Seth Pierre and Clara Sackrider Remington in Canton, New York.

1873 The Remington family moves to Ogdensburg, New York.

1875 Remington attends Vermont Episcopal Institute, Rock Port, Vermont, where he receives his first formal art instruction.

1876 Attends Highland Military Academy, Worcester, Massachusetts

1878 Remington enrolls at Yale College of Art, New Haven, Connecticut, under the tutelage of John H. Niemeyer and John F. Weir.

1880 Meets Eva Caten (his future wife) in Canton, New York.

1881 Travels west to Montana Territory where he works as a cowboy, scout, sheep and mule rancher; records his experiences in sketches and notebooks.

1882 February 15th, *Harper's Weekly* publishes Remington's first illustration entitled *Cowboys of Arizona-Roused by a Scout*.

1884 Remington moves to Kansas City; invests in hardware store, then in a saloon. He marries Eva Caten in Gloversville, New York, and together they return to Kansas City.

1885 Moves to Brooklyn, New York, to pursue an illustration career.

1886 Attends Art Students League in New York City for three months. Travels to Arizona, Mexico, and New Mexico on a sketching tour with Lt. John Bigelow. Remington launches a successful illustration career through his regular contributions to *Harper's Weekly*.

1887 Remington has his first exhibition of drawings and watercolors at the National Academy of Design and the American Water Color Society. Travels to Dakota, Wyoming, Montana Territories and western Canada on *Harper's* commission. Receives additional commissions from *Outing* and *Century Magazine*.

1888 Journeys through Texas, Arizona, and New Mexico on a commission from *Century Magazine*. The commission results in his first illustrated night scene entitled *On Guard at Night* for Theodore Roosevelt's serialized article "Sheriff's Work on a Ranch." Secures Hallgarten & Clarke Awards at National Academy Annual Exhibition for *Return of a Blackfoot War Party*.

1889 Travels to Mexico and Canada. Receives a Silver Medal for *Last Lull in the Fight* at the Paris International Exposition.

1890   Remington buys a spacious home in New Rochelle, New York, where he and his wife reside for 19 years. His first one-man exhibition is presented at the American Art Association in New York. Accompanies General Nelson Miles' expedition to the Dakota Badlands to put down Sioux Uprising. The expedition culminates in the defeat of the Sioux Nation at Wounded Knee.

1891   The National Academy of Design elects Remington an Associate Member. He publishes illustrations for Henry Longfellow's *Song of Hiawatha* and begins work for Francis Parkman's *Oregon Trail*. Escorts General Miles to Mexico and Cuba to sketch Mexican Army.

1892   Journeys to Europe, Russia and North Africa with Poultney Bigelow on a commission from *Harper's*. Also accepts commissions from *Century Magazine*, *The Cosmopolitan*, *Outing*, and *Scribner's Magazine* through 1893.

1893   The American Art Association holds one-man exhibit and sale. Remington exhibits fifteen works at Chicago World's Columbian Exposition.

1894   Travels with Bigelow to Algiers and Oran to sketch French and Algerian soldiers on *Harper's Weekly* commission. Illustrates for *The Cosmopolitan*, *Harper's* and author, Owen Wister.

1895   *Harper's Weekly* publishes a compilation of Remington's Western articles and illustrations entitled *Pony Tracks*. His first bronze sculpture, *The Bronco Buster*, is sand-cast by the Henry-Bonnard Bronze Company. Again exhibits his work at the American Art Association where his illustrations appear more popular than his paintings.

1896   Remington explores new color effects using pastel. *Harper's Monthly* publishes his first color illustration. Illustrates for *The Cosmopolitan*, *Harper's*, and *Metropolitan Magazine*. Copyrights his second sculpture, *The Wounded Bunkie*.

1897   London Royal Academie exhibits *The Wounded Bunkie*. Hart & Watson, Boston, Massachusetts, exhibit forty works. Illustrates for *Century Magazine*, *The Cosmopolitan*, *Harper's*, *New York Journal* and *Advertiser*.

1898   Remington publishes a collection of short stories and illustrations entitled *Crooked Trails*. Travels to Florida, Cuba, and Puerto Rico with Richard Harding Davis to document the Spanish-American War. Copyrights additional subjects in bronze, *The Wicked Pony* and *The Scalp*.

1899   *Harper's*, in financial difficulty, releases Remington from exclusive contract. Travels to Havana, Cuba as war correspondent for *Collier's Weekly*. Exhibits with the National Academy of Design for the last time. First encounters the work of California tonalist painter, Charles Rollo Peters, during an exhibition at the Union League Club, New York. Peters's work inspires Remington's mature nocturnes.

1900   Casts first bronze, *The Norther*, with Roman Bronze Works, New York, using the lost-wax method. Receives honorary Bachelor of Fine Arts degree from Yale. Purchases a summer home at Ingleneuk, an island on the St. Lawrence River.

1901   Remington publishes *A Bunch of Buckskins*, a portfolio of eight color lithographs and *Done in the Open*, a collection of paintings. Authors his first novel, *John Ermine of the Yellowstone*, Macmillan Company, publishers. Copyrights *The Cheyenne* bronze.

1902   Copyrights his eighth bronze group, *Coming Through the Rye*.

1903   Union League Club, New York, exhibits Remington's nocturne entitled *A Reconnaissance*. His novel, *John Ermine of the Yellowstone*, is adapted for the stage and produced on Broadway. He obtains a four-year contract with *Collier's Weekly* which leaves him free to choose his own subjects. The self-governing contract initiates Remington's exploration of impressionist principals and the synthesis of a new artistic style. Copyrights one of his most popular bronzes entitled *The Mountain Man*.

1904   Receives one-man exhibition with Noé Galleries, New York. Detroit Museum of Art exhibits forty black and white illustrations. Copyrights *The Sergeant* bronze. Louisiana Purchase Exposition in St. Louis, Missouri exhibits a monumental plaster version of Remington's bronze, *Coming Through the Rye*.

1905   The Corcoran Gallery of Art, Washington, D.C., acquires *Coming Through the Rye* for its permanent collection. M. Knoedler & Co., New York, holds one-man exhibition of Remington bronzes and signs contract for subsequent annual exhibitions. Receives another one-man exhibition at Noé Galleries. Copyrights *The Old Dragoons of 1850* and *The Rattlesnake* bronze groups. *Collier's Weekly* publishes a compendium of Remington's art and stories about his life and work titled *Remington Number*.

1906   Copyrights *The Outlaw* sculpture. One-man exhibition at Noé Galleries. One-man exhibit of paintings at M. Knoedler & Co. results in critical acclaim for Remington's nocturnes.

1907   The Metropolitan Museum of Art acquires three additional bronzes including *The Old Dragoons of 1850*, *The Mountain Man*, and *The Cheyenne*. Remington copyrights the sculptures *The Horse Thief* and *The Buffalo Horse*. M. Knoedler & Co. holds second one-man exhibition of paintings.

1908   Remington buys property for a new home and studio in Ridgefield, Connecticut. Copyrights *The Savage* bronze. M. Knoedler & Co. exhibit nineteen paintings in a one-man show, of which three-quarters of the large canvases are nocturnes. The Union League Club and The Corcoran Gallery of Art exhibit *Taint in the Wind* and *Fired On* respectively.

1909   Although *Collier's Weekly* terminates Remington's contract, they continue to publish his paintings until 1913. Remington receives a one-man exhibition at Doll & Richards Gallery, Boston. O'Briens Art Gallery, Chicago exhibits *Apache Medicine Song*. Art Institute of Chicago exhibits *Fired On*. William Evans purchases *Fired On* for the National Gallery of Art, Washington, D.C. Exhibition opens at M. Knoedler & Co. to rave reviews. Remington copyrights the bronze, *Trooper of the Plains*. He dies on December 26 of peritonitis following an emergency appendectomy at home in Ridgefield.